Best Beach Vacations

THE CAROLINAS & GEORGIA

By Lan Sluder

A Beachscape Publishing, Inc. production for
MACMILLAN TRAVEL • U.S.A.

Frommer's Best Beach Vacations: The Carolinas & Georgia

Publishers/Editors *Gary Stoller and Bruce Bolger*
Managing Editor *Nicola S. Coddington*
Design Director/Macmillan USA *Michele Laseau*
Art Director *Sun Design/Lauri Marks*
Beach Consultant *Dr. Stephen Leatherman*
Senior Editor *Marita Begley*
Research Editor *Betty Villaume*
Map Designer *John Grimwade*
Cartographer *Joyce Pendola*

Frommer's Best Beach Vacations: The Carolinas & Georgia is produced for Frommer's by Beachscape Publishing, Inc. Please address any comments or corrections to Beachscape at 145 Palisade St., Suite 397, Dobbs Ferry, N.Y. 10522; tel. 914-674-9283, fax 914-674-9285.

Macmillan Travel

A Simon & Schuster Macmillan Company
1633 Broadway, New York, NY 10019-6785
Copyright 1996 by Beachscape Publishing, Inc.

All rights reserved. No part of this book may be reproduced or transmitted in any form or by any means, electronic or mechanical, including photocopying, recording, or by any information storage or retrieval system, without permission in writing from the publisher.

Macmillan is a registered trademark of Macmillan, Inc.

The Library of Congress Cataloging-in-Publication Data is available from the Library of Congress.

ISBN 0-02-860661-2

Manufactured in the United States of America

10 9 8 7 6 5 4 3 2 1

First Edition

Also Available:
Best Beach Vacations: California
Best Beach Vacations: Florida
Best Beach Vacations: Hawaii
Best Beach Vacations: The Mid-Atlantic
Best Beach Vacations: New England

Special Sales

Bulk purchases (10+ copies) of Frommer's Travel Guides are available to corporations at special discounts.

The Special Sales Department can produce custom editions to be used as premiums and/or for sales promotions to suit individual needs. Existing editions can be produced with custom cover imprints such as corporate logos. For more information, write Special Sales, Macmillan Travel, 1633 Broadway, New York, NY 10019-6785.

A word from the author

A heartfelt thank you to: my wife, Sheila M. Lambert, for taking time from her busy law practice to help, and to take care of things in my absence; my son, Brooks Bradley Lambert-Sluder, and my daughter, Rose Emory Lambert-Sluder, for their understanding about my being away so much at the beach and at my Mac; my parents-in-law, Ace and Nita Lambert, for their hospitality in Savannah; the many people who gave advice and information about beaches, restaurants, hotels, and sights, in particular the owners of bed-and-breakfasts and small inns, who know more than most about their locales; Glenn Morris, Henry Leifermann, David Poyer, Daniel Barefoot, Stacy Ritz, and Kap Stann, who are among the many regional travel writers whose work I admire; my editor, Nicola Coddington, whose insightful queries made this a better book; Dr. Stephen Leatherman, for useful background information on beaches; and the people of some of my favorite places along the coasts of North Carolina, South Carolina, and Georgia, who shared their favorite places, including Ocracoke Island, Hatteras Island, Cape Lookout National Seashore, and Beaufort and Down East, North Carolina; Wilmington, Bald Head Island, Georgetown, Charleston, Kiawah Island, Edisto Island, and Beaufort, South Carolina; and Savannah, Sapelo Island, Jekyll Island, Little St. Simons Island, and Cumberland Island, Georgia.

In a book covering such a large area, mistakes and omissions are bound to occur. They are honest errors, however, for in the months of research that went into this guide, I paid (at the same rates any traveler would) for every single hotel room, restaurant meal, tank of gas, and attraction admission. Nothing was subsidized by any destination or tourism operator.

About the author

Lan Sluder is a North Carolina native who has been a fan of the beaches of the Carolinas and Georgia since his childhood. A former newspaper editor in New Orleans, he is a travel and business writer with credits in newspapers and magazines around the world, including the *Bangkok Post, Caribbean Travel and Life, The Chicago Tribune, The New York Times, Country Journal,* and *The Miami Herald.* He was co-author of *SmartTravel: Total Travel Planning by Computer,* published in 1995. A long-time habitué of the Internet and on-line services, he is a volunteer sysop on the Travel Forum on CompuServe (his e-mail address is 74763.2254@compuserve.com). In his spare time, he edits and publishes *Belize First,* a quarterly magazine he founded on travel, life, and retirement in Belize and elsewhere on the Caribbean Coast of Central America. Sluder was educated at Duke University and the University of North Carolina and in the U.S. Army in Vietnam. He lives on a mountain farm near Asheville, North Carolina, with his wife, son, and daughter and is at work on new books on North Carolina and Belize.

Table of Contents

Introduction

Beach Locator Maps

North Carolina

South Carolina

Georgia

The Best Beach Vacations Rating System

Going to the beach is a great American pastime. Whether for a vacation or just a day, Americans flock to the nation's shores in search of the inexplicable pleasure that comes with a stay by the water. That's about all we have in common regarding our love of beaches, since each person has his or her own special tastes. Some come for serenity, others for action, and there are a hundred variations in between. *Best Beach Vacations* is designed to help you find the beach experience that's right for you, be it for a day, a weekend, or an entire vacation.

Best Beach Vacations uses a unique rating system that systematically evaluates each beach area according to the categories that matter most to beach lovers: **Beauty, Swimming, Sand, Hotels/Inns/B&Bs, House Rentals, Restaurants, Nightlife, Attractions, Shopping, Sports,** and **Nature.** A brief review of the ratings will help you quickly narrow your selection. The overview and service information in each chapter provide everything you'll need to start planning your beach experience.

To select the beaches featured in this book, we began with information gathered by professor Stephen Leatherman, sometimes called Dr. Beach, a coastal geologist and director of the University of Maryland's Laboratory for Coastal Research. For years, Leatherman has collected information on water quality, scenic beauty, sand conditions, surf, temperature, and tourist amenities at beaches around the United States, data he uses to determine an overall rating for each beach. Using that data, along with their own knowledge and input from regional and local sources, the authors visited each beach and combed nearby areas to personally evaluate all of the other important elements that go into a beach experience.

The ratings at the beginning of a chapter summarize the entire area. Within each chapter, individual beaches are listed. Each has its own description, with more specific ratings. It's easy to understand the rating system, because it's based on the A through F scale that's used for grade-school report cards; if you see NA (not applicable) in a ratings category, it means that this particular feature does not apply to the beach.

Here are the criteria used to formulate a grade for particular aspects of each beach or beach area. *Beauty:* overall setting, sand, and views offshore.
Swimming: water quality, temperature, and wave conditions.
Sand: texture, color, and cleanliness.
Amenities: rest rooms, food concessions, lifeguards, and sports equipment.

Beauty	A
Swimming	B
Sand	C
Hotels/Inns/B&Bs	B
House rentals	A
Restaurants	B
Nightlife	B
Attractions	B
Shopping	C
Sports	A
Nature	A

The grades for all other categories are based on the quality and quantity of offerings in and around the beach area. The rating for **Attractions**, for example, assesses the quality and quantity of all types of things to do in the area surrounding the beach.

Best Beach Vacations makes every attempt to warn readers of specific safety concerns in each area. However, readers should visit all beaches mindful of the potential dangers posed by water, wave, and sun, and take appropriate precautions.

We hope you have a wonderful beach vacation.

–Gary Stoller and Bruce Bolger

Best Beach Vacations: Overview

The Carolinas And Georgia At A Glance

No matter what kind of beach vacation you want, you can probably find it in the Carolinas and Georgia.

NORTH CAROLINA

North Carolina, and this guidebook, both begin with the Outer Banks, a 100-mile ribbon of windswept barrier islands, at points as close to the Gulf Stream as to the mainland. The Banks offer a yuppie beach paradise at the north end, busy Nags Head in the middle, and great fishing and solitude along the Cape Hatteras National Seashore of Hatteras and Ocracoke islands. The 12-mile beach at Ocracoke is a jewel, ranked No. 1 in the region by "Dr. Beach," Stephen Leatherman, the beach consultant to this series. The water quality off the Outer Banks beaches is generally the highest of any in the region. Cape Lookout National Seashore, to the south of the Outer Banks, is if anything even more wild and pristine, and its isolation and the difficulty of access is likely to keep it that way. To the south, where the brisk barrier island and coastal climate edges toward the semitropical, there's a series of family-oriented beach destinations: Bogue Banks, the beaches around Wilmington, and the Brunswick Isles. Bald Head Island is a private resort of luxury homes, accessible only by boat, where cars are verboten, making it a safe and quiet haven in an internal-combustion world.

SOUTH CAROLINA

The Grand Strand of South Carolina begins at the North Carolina state line and runs exuberantly down the coast for about 60 miles, through North Myrtle Beach, a favorite of college kids and shag dancers, to booming Myrtle Beach, with its Miami-style high-rises and country music theaters, down to the quieter, tonier part of the Strand, at Pawley's Island, Huntington Beach, and Georgetown. After a stretch of little-developed swamp-fox country, you're in Charleston, the sultry lady of the South, full of history and life and ranked high in national polls as a favorite tourist destination, with a choice of not one but three beaches nearby. South of Charleston are a series of less well-known but highly appealing beach areas: Kiawah and Seabrook islands, upscale and private; comfortable-as-an-old-shoe Edisto Island; and Beaufort, Hunting Island, and Fripp Island, each very different but with a lot to offer. Then you're on Hilton Head, an electric combination of good beaches, great golf and tennis, and plenty to eat, buy, and do.

GEORGIA

Savannah, at the northernmost tip of Georgia's coast, is often compared with Charleston, but Savannah is its own city, with a personality as unique as any in America. Nearby Tybee Beach may disappoint some, but others say it's like Key West in the 1960s, and all appreciate its proximity to the restaurants and bright lights of Savannah. The four Golden Isles of Georgia are a wonderful mix of island destinations, although the water here is often full of sediment from the marshes: bustling St. Simons, with its restaurants and retirees; Jekyll, perhaps locked forever in 1974, when development on the state-owned island effectively stopped, but with much natural beauty and the region's best values in golf; Little St. Simons, privately owned, with a beach you can't help but fall in love with; and Sea Island, a subdued enclave of wealth and social cachet. Not far from St. Simons lie exotic Sapelo and other little-visited islands. Finally, almost to Florida, is Cumberland Island, another national seashore—one where no more than 300 visitors a day are allowed to roam its high-duned beaches and moss-draped forests of oak and cypress.

When To Go

With day temperatures in the high 80s and low 90s and lows mostly in the 70s, the hot days of summer are prime beach time in the Carolinas and Georgia—the period stretching longer and longer the farther south you go. On the breezy Outer Banks, early June through late August forms the brief period when hotels, rental houses, and restaurants are full, and the ocean water finally warms to the high 70s. By the time you get to

Hilton Head, Savannah, and the Golden Isles of Georgia, with their true subtropical climate—more like north Florida than North Carolina—spring and fall are very busy. For golfers, tennis buffs, and sightseers, summer here is simply too hot and humid for extended outdoor activities, except directly on the water, where the ocean breezes help cool you down. Swimming can be pleasant from May through October.

Savvy beach travelers know that the off-season means big bargains: 30 to 70 percent discounts on accommodations and rentals. If you go to the beach for shelling, quiet walks, and just to enjoy the ocean, spring and fall are wonderful times to visit. Even winter can be pleasant, especially from southern North Carolina down, where freezing weather is possible but not common.

How To Get There

About 95 percent of travelers to the beaches of the Carolinas and Georgia arrive by car. Once at the beach, with few exceptions, you'll find a car a necessity, since things are spread out and there's little public transportation.

The major north-south route through the region is Interstate 95, one of the country's busiest highways. Interstates 40, 26, and 16 are the main east-west routes for North Carolina, South Carolina, and Georgia, respectively.

The major airports in the region are Raleigh-Durham, Charleston, and Savannah, with Norfolk, Virginia, serving as a possible air destination for travelers to North Carolina's Outer Banks, and Jacksonville, Florida, for visitors to South Georgia. Wilmington and Myrtle Beach also have limited jet service. Several other destinations have commuter air flights. Amtrak serves Jacksonville, Savannah, Charleston, and Raleigh, as well as some smaller towns along the route from Florida to the Northeast.

SERVICE INFORMATION

Here are a few notes about the service information in this book.

Hotels/Inns/B&Bs

Our four price categories are based on double-occupancy, peak-season nightly rates (before gratuities and taxes, which vary by location but range from six to ten percent):

     Very Expensive: More than $180

     Expensive: $111 to $180

     Moderate: $76 to $110

     Inexpensive: $75 or less

Restaurants

Restaurants fall into four price categories, based on the approximate cost of an appetizer, main course, and dessert for one person at dinner (not including wine, drinks, tax, or tip):

     Very Expensive   More than $50

     Expensive $31 to $50

     Moderate $16 to $30

     Inexpensive $15 or less

Safety Tips

Any dangers associated with the beaches of the Carolinas and Georgia can be minimized with care and awareness. Too often, travelers let down their guard, yet a few simple precautions can reduce the chances of trouble.

Sunburn may be the biggest problem for beachgoers. Use plenty of sunblock and tanning lotion. Mosquitoes can sometimes annoy, especially in less-developed areas such as state parks and marsh areas, where there are no mosquito-control programs. The bugs are worst after periods of rain, usually late spring to early fall. In areas with steady winds, such as the Outer Banks, you'll be bothered less than in the steamy, subtropical parts of coastal Georgia and South Carolina. Mosquito repellents containing DEET can be effective. Several kinds of biting flies can appear briefly in the late spring and early summer. No-see-ums, tiny gnats and sandflies, may occasionally be irritating, especially in grassy areas. Avon's Skin So Soft lotion may help some people.

Alligators are common in much of the region, from southern North Carolina southward. Few incidents involving humans and gators occur, but it's wise to give these ancient reptiles a wide berth—despite their awkward appearance, they can outrun you for short distances. Several poisonous snakes, including diamondback rattlers, are indigenous to the region and may snuggle up in a warm spot in a sand dune. Just watch where you step and put your hands—chances are you'll never see a snake. As for sharks, typically a few shark attacks, mostly not serious, are reported along the coast each year. They usually occur in murky waters near rivermouths or inlets, where sharks mistake a swimmer or surfer for another prey. The odds of death or injury from alligators, snakes, and sharks, all combined, are very small.

Especially in the warm-water months, stinging jellyfish, including the Portuguese man-of-war, may occasionally be present in coastal waters. Most jellyfish stings in these waters don't pose any danger, although they can cause burning or swelling. Man-of-war stings are more serious and can cause shortness of breath or fainting: Scrape off the stings with sand and seek help (lifeguards have first-aid equipment).

Though beautiful, the surf along the Atlantic Ocean can be treacherous, because of strong undertows and rip currents. Rip tides can carry even a strong swimmer out to sea quickly. If you get caught in one, swim parallel to the beach until you're out of the current. Most rips are narrow, only a few yards wide. Undertows can happen when waves break on the beach and the water sucks you back out. Again, don't panic, and don't resist. Let the undertow carry you out a short distance and you'll be released.

Because the ocean beaches are dynamic, today's safe area can be tomorrow's danger spot. Many beaches do not have lifeguards, and even those that did in the past may not have them when you arrive (because of government cutbacks). Always check locally. In some areas, red flags fly to warn swimmers to stay out of the water at times of special danger, and yellow flags suggest caution: Pay special attention to young children.

Many of the beaches in this book are at or near small towns, where crime rates are low. Crime, however, is a reality in metropolitan areas and near any town frequented by tourists. Use routine precautions, and don't leave valuables in your car or on the beach. Chances are you'll have no problems.

A special word needs to be said about hurricanes, which are possible from June through November all along the coast of the Carolinas and Georgia. If you happen to be on the coast when a hurricane evacuation is issued, heed it immediately.

Beach Area Rankings

Here are the best beach vacation areas in the Carolinas and Georgia, ranked in order of the author's personal preference:

1. Ocracoke Island, NC (Chapter 4)
2. Hatteras Island, NC (3)
3. Cumberland Island, GA (20)
4. Charleston, SC (12)
5. Jekyll Island, GA (19)
6. St. Simons & Sea Islands, GA (18)
7. Bald Head Island, NC (8)
8. Kiawah & Seabrook Islands, SC (13)
9. Hunting & Fripp Islands, SC (15)
10. Wilmington, NC (7)
11. Cape Lookout & Beaufort, NC (5)
12. Northern Outer Banks, NC (1)
13. Southern Grand Strand, SC (11)
14. Bogue Banks, NC (6)
15. Savannah & Tybee Island, GA (17)
16. Hilton Head Island, SC (16)
17. Edisto Island, SC (14)
18. Brunswick Isles, NC (9)
19. Nags Head, NC (2)
20. Myrtle Beach, SC (10)

Best Beaches For . . .

Hotels/Inns/B&Bs: Charleston, SC (12)
House Rentals: Northern Outer Banks, NC (1)
Restaurants: Charleston, SC (12)
Nightlife: Myrtle Beach, SC (10)
Attractions: Charleston, SC (12)
Shopping: Charleston, SC (12)
Fishing: Hatteras Island, NC (3)
Boating: Savannah, GA (17)
Surfing & Windsurfing: Hatteras Island, NC (3)
Diving: Hatteras Island, NC (3)
Bicycling: Bald Head Island, NC (8)
Shelling: Cape Lookout, NC (5)
Beach walking: Ocracoke Island, NC (4)
Golf: Hilton Head Island, SC (16)
Tennis: Hilton Head Island, SC (16)
Nature: Cumberland Island, GA (20)

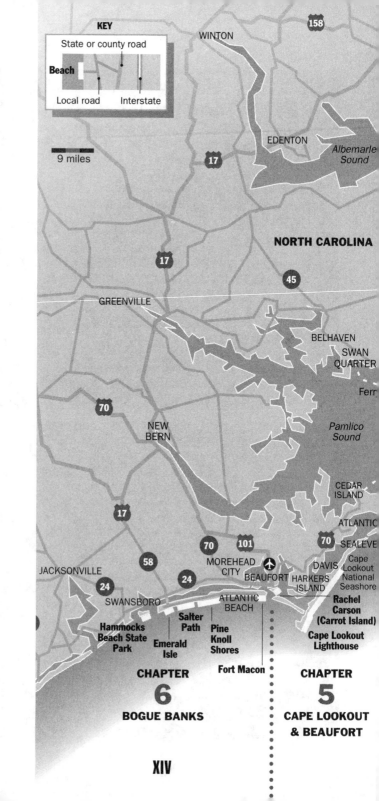

KEY

State or county road

Beach

Local road   Interstate

9 miles

WINTON

158

17

EDENTON

Albemarle Sound

NORTH CAROLINA

45

GREENVILLE

BELHAVEN

SWAN QUARTER

Ferr

70

NEW BERN

Pamlico Sound

CEDAR ISLAND

ATLANTIC

70

17

101

70

SEALEVE

MOREHEAD CITY

DAVIS

Cape Lookout National Seashore

58

JACKSONVILLE

24

24

BEAUFORT HARKERS ISLAND

Rachel Carson (Carrot Island)

SWANSBORO

ATLANTIC BEACH

Cape Lookout Lighthouse

Hammocks Beach State Park

Salter Path

Pine Knoll Shores

Emerald Isle

Fort Macon

CHAPTER

6

BOGUE BANKS

CHAPTER

5

CAPE LOOKOUT & BEAUFORT

XIV

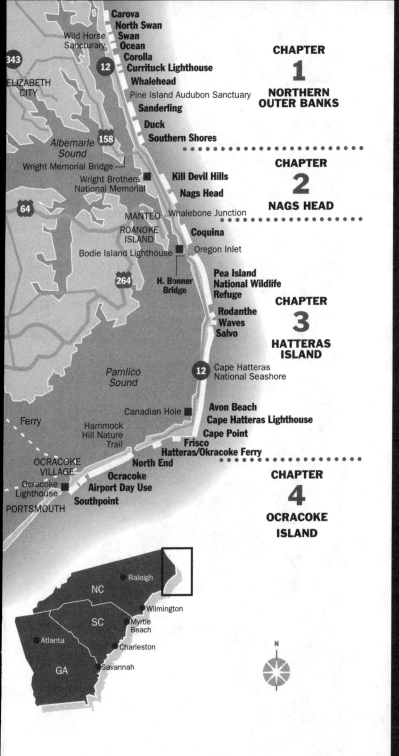

Carova
North Swan
Swan
Ocean
Wild Horse
Sanctuary
Corolla
Currituck Lighthouse
Whalehead
Pine Island Audubon Sanctuary
Sanderling
Duck
Southern Shores

343

12

ELIZABETH
CITY

158

Albemarle Sound

Wright Memorial Bridge
Wright Brothers
National Memorial

64

MANTEO

ROANOKE
ISLAND

264

Bodie Island Lighthouse

H. Bonner
Bridge

Kill Devil Hills

Nags Head

Whalebone Junction

Coquina

Oregon Inlet

Pea Island
National Wildlife
Refuge

Rodanthe
Waves
Salvo

Pamlico Sound

12 Cape Hatteras
National Seashore

Ferry

Canadian Hole

Hammock
Hill Nature
Trail

Avon Beach

Cape Hatteras Lighthouse

Cape Point

Frisco

Hatteras/Okracoke Ferry

OCRACOKE
VILLAGE

North End

Ocracoke
Lighthouse

PORTSMOUTH

Ocracoke
Airport Day Use
Southpoint

CHAPTER

1

NORTHERN
OUTER BANKS

CHAPTER

2

NAGS HEAD

CHAPTER

3

HATTERAS
ISLAND

CHAPTER

4

OCRACOKE
ISLAND

Raleigh

NC

Wilmington

SC

Myrtle
Beach

Atlanta

Charleston

GA

Savannah

N

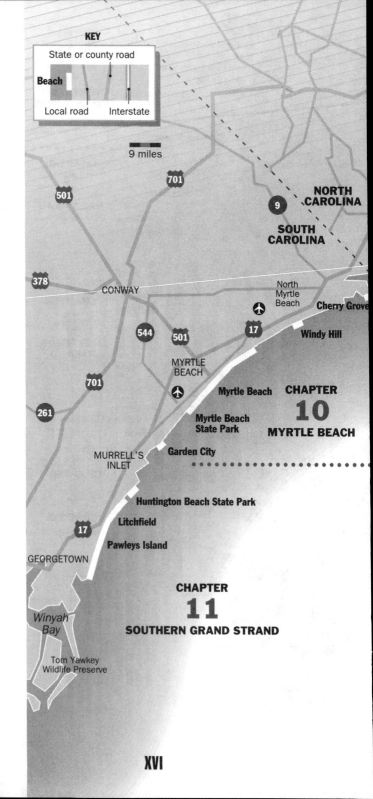

KEY

State or county road

Beach

Local road   Interstate

9 miles

501 **701**

9

NORTH CAROLINA

SOUTH CAROLINA

378

CONWAY

North Myrtle Beach

Cherry Grove

544 **501**

17

Windy Hill

MYRTLE BEACH

701

Myrtle Beach

CHAPTER

10

MYRTLE BEACH

261

Myrtle Beach State Park

MURRELL'S INLET

Garden City

Huntington Beach State Park

Litchfield

17

Pawleys Island

GEORGETOWN

CHAPTER

11

SOUTHERN GRAND STRAND

Winyah Bay

Tom Yawkey Wildlife Preserve

XVI

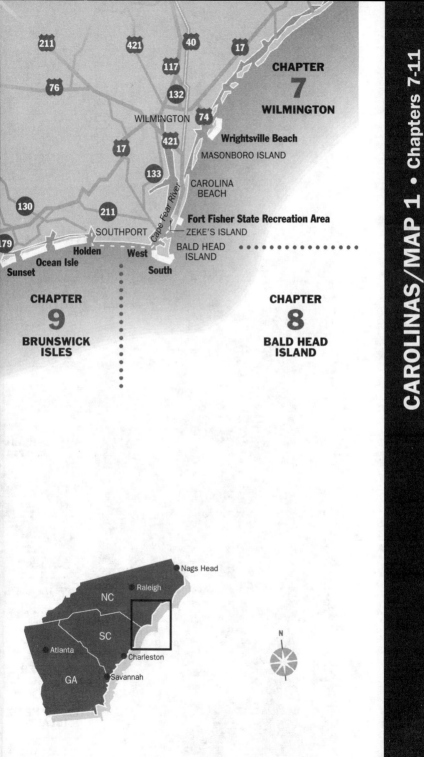

211
421
40
17

117

76

132

74

WILMINGTON

Wrightsville Beach

421

MASONBORO ISLAND

17

133

CAROLINA
BEACH

130

211

Fort Fisher State Recreation Area

179

SOUTHPORT

ZEKE'S ISLAND

BALD HEAD
ISLAND

Holden   **West**

Ocean Isle

Sunset   **South**

Cape Fear River

Nags Head

NC   Raleigh

SC

Atlanta   Charleston

GA   Savannah

N

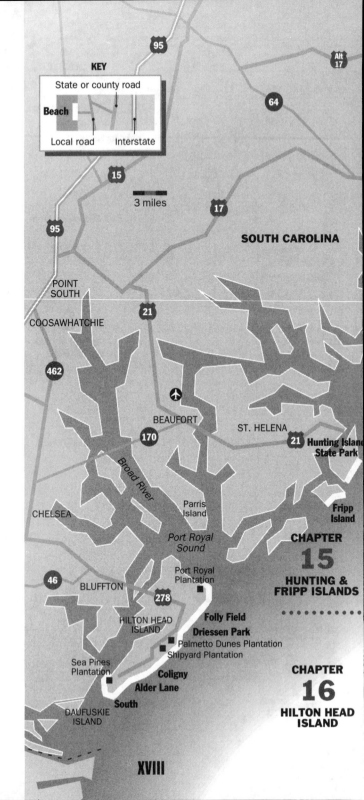

95

Alt
17

KEY

State or county road

Beach

Local road   Interstate

15

64

3 miles

95

17

SOUTH CAROLINA

POINT
SOUTH

21

COOSAWHATCHIE

462

BEAUFORT

ST. HELENA

21 **Hunting Island
State Park**

170

CHELSEA

Parris
Island

*Port Royal
Sound*

Broad River

**Fripp
Island**

**CHAPTER
15**

**HUNTING &
FRIPP ISLANDS**

46

BLUFFTON

278

Port Royal
Plantation

Folly Field

Driessen Park

Palmetto Dunes Plantation

Shipyard Plantation

HILTON HEAD
ISLAND

Sea Pines
Plantation

Coligny

Alder Lane

South

DAUFUSKIE
ISLAND

**CHAPTER
16**

**HILTON HEAD
ISLAND**

XVIII

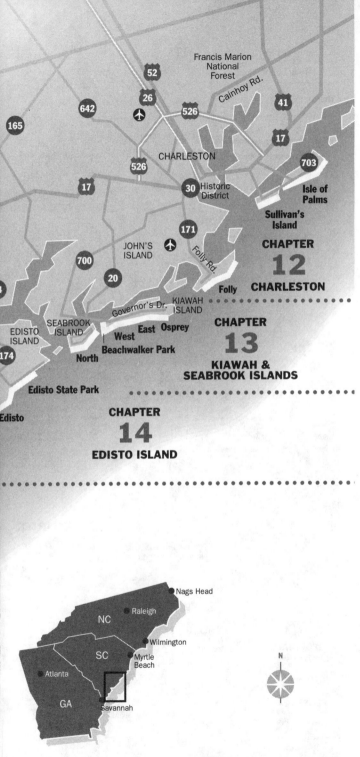

Francis Marion
National
Forest

Cainhoy Rd.

52

26

642

526

41

165

17

CHARLESTON

526

17

30 Historic
District

703

Isle of
Palms

Sullivan's
Island

171

CHAPTER

12

JOHN'S
ISLAND

Folly Rd.

700

CHARLESTON

20

Folly

Governor's Dr. KIAWAH
ISLAND

EDISTO
ISLAND

SEABROOK
ISLAND

West
North

East Osprey

Beachwalker Park

CHAPTER

13

174

Edisto State Park

**KIAWAH &
SEABROOK ISLANDS**

Edisto

CHAPTER

14

EDISTO ISLAND

Nags Head

Raleigh

NC

Wilmington

SC

Myrtle
Beach

Atlanta

N

GA

Savannah

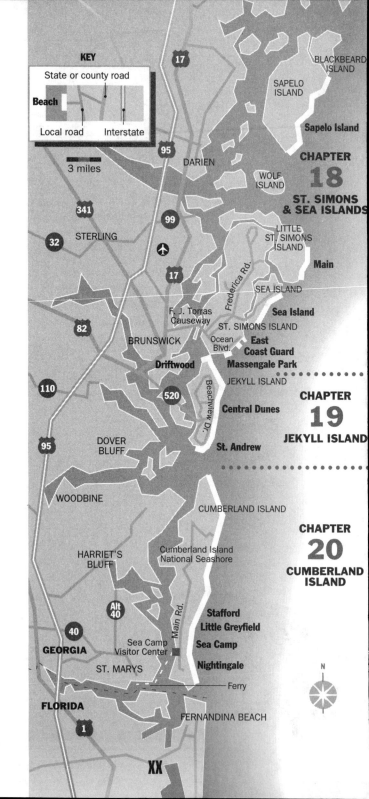

KEY

State or county road

Beach

Local road   Interstate

3 miles

BLACKBEARD
ISLAND

SAPELO
ISLAND

Sapelo Island

CHAPTER
18
ST. SIMONS
& SEA ISLANDS

17

95

DARIEN

WOLF
ISLAND

341

99

STERLING

32

17

LITTLE
ST. SIMONS
ISLAND

Main

Frederica Rd.

SEA ISLAND

82

F. J. Torras
Causeway

Sea Island

ST. SIMONS ISLAND

BRUNSWICK

Ocean
Blvd.

**East
Coast Guard
Massengale Park**

Driftwood

JEKYLL ISLAND

110

520

Beachview Dr.

Central Dunes

CHAPTER
19
JEKYLL ISLAND

95

DOVER
BLUFF

St. Andrew

WOODBINE

CUMBERLAND ISLAND

CHAPTER
20
**CUMBERLAND
ISLAND**

HARRIET'S
BLUFF

Cumberland Island
National Seashore

Alt
40

Main Rd.

Stafford
Little Greyfield

40

Sea Camp
Visitor Center

Sea Camp

GEORGIA

ST. MARYS

Nightingale

Ferry

FLORIDA

1

FERNANDINA BEACH

XX

N

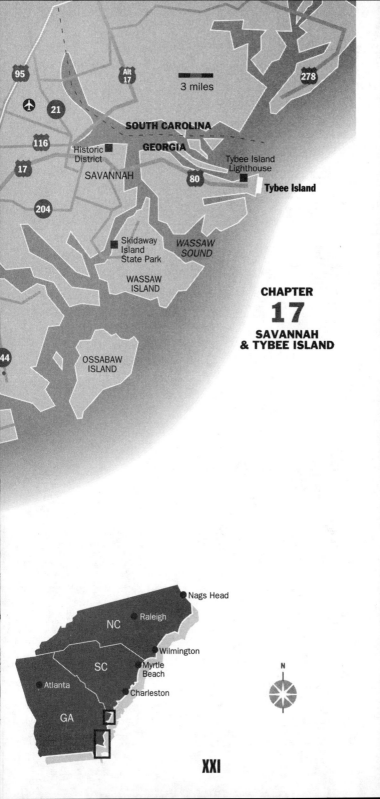

95

Alt
17

278

3 miles

21

SOUTH CAROLINA

GEORGIA

116

Historic
District

Tybee Island
Lighthouse

17

SAVANNAH

80

Tybee Island

204

Skidaway
Island
State Park

WASSAW
SOUND

WASSAW
ISLAND

CHAPTER

17

SAVANNAH
& TYBEE ISLAND

44

OSSABAW
ISLAND

Nags Head

Raleigh

NC

Wilmington

SC

Myrtle
Beach

Atlanta

Charleston

N

GA

CHAPTER 1

Northern Outer Banks

Beauty	B+
Swimming	B+
Sand	B
Hotels/Inns/B&Bs	C+
House rentals	A
Restaurants	B+
Nightlife	C
Attractions	B-
Shopping	B
Sports	B-
Nature	B

The Northern Outer Banks, for the purposes of this book, can be defined as the northern end of the North Carolina Outer Banks, the 100-mile string of narrow barrier islands stretching from the Virginia-North Carolina border in the north to Ocracoke Island in the south. Once isolated and little-developed, the Northern Outer Banks saw explosive growth beginning in the mid-1980s, fueled by the huge mass of yuppie humanity in and around the Washington, D.C./northern Virginia metroplex. On this end of the Banks, you'll see more license plates from Virginia, Maryland, and New Jersey than from North Carolina.

You'll also find more well-fed real estate agents than you will

HOW TO GET THERE

◆ Southern Shores, the entry point to the Northern Banks, is about 2 hr. by car from Norfolk, VA, and about 4 hr. from Raleigh, NC.

◆ From Norfolk and points north, take I-64 to VA Hwy. 168 south. Take that to U.S. Hwy. 158 south to the Wright Memorial Bridge. Then drive north on NC Hwy. 12, the main north-south road on the Outer Banks. (North of Southern Shores but south of Sanderling, Hwy. 12 is called Duck Rd.; north of Sanderling it becomes Ocean Trail. This usage is not consistent; to avoid confusion, most references in this chapter are to Hwy. 12).

◆ From Raleigh and points west, take U.S. 64 east, then go north on U.S. Hwy. 158 Bypass to Hwy. 12.

◆ From points south of Raleigh, take I-95 or U.S. Hwy 17 to U.S. Hwy. 64 east. Take that to U.S. Hwy. 158 Bypass to Hwy. 12.

◆ By air, fly into Raleigh or Norfolk—both have jet and commuter service—and rent a car. There are small general-aviation airstrips on Hatteras and Ocracoke islands, and there's spotty commuter service to Dare County Municipal Airport in Manteo.

the wild horses for which the Northern Banks were once famous. Development generally has been tasteful, however, a kind of Hilton Head without all the golf and big hotels. Wildlife areas like the Pine Island Audubon Sanctuary and the Currituck Banks National Wildlife Refuge offset the highly civilized sections. Unlike year-round communities such as Ocracoke and Frisco farther south, here you'll find mostly seasonal residents and rental homes.

The Atlantic beaches of the Northern Banks are excellent, but public beach access is not nearly as good as it is farther south around Nags Head or on the national seashore sections of Hatteras and Ocracoke islands (*see* those chapters). Visitors renting a house, however, can temporarily be a part of the community. The ambience of the Northern Banks, with its emphasis on family beach activities and backyard barbecues, differs considerably from the beach-town atmosphere of Nags Head, the fishing frenzies on Hatteras, or the English-prof-in-a-Volvo style of Ocracoke.

Approaching the Northern Banks from the south (the only way to reach it by car), you first enter Southern Shores, a quiet residential area. Next comes the village of Duck, a hot commercial area, where new shops and restaurants—some of the best on the Banks—open nearly every week. Beyond it lies Sanderling, a quietly classy residential area.

For most visitors, the Outer Banks end at the Ocean Hill subdivision just north of Corolla (locally pronounced *Ca-RAH-la*, not like the Japanese car), the end of Highway 12, but those on foot or in off-road vehicles can continue up the beach for several more miles. There are even some "four-wheel-drive-only" subdivisions in this area, residential developments as far as 13 miles north of Corolla that have no paved-road access. The basic beach houses of Carova Beach are in a different world from the upmarket homes of Duck or Sanderling.

The high season here is Memorial Day to Labor Day. The biggest crush of visitors to this family-oriented area happens when schools are out, generally early June to late August. The spring shoulder season begins around Easter, and fall too can be fairly busy, usually until late October.

BEACHES

The Atlantic beaches along the 30 miles of the Northern Outer Banks are superb, but access is limited and mostly private. This, and restrictions against parking on many residential streets, limits day-tripping and keeps the beaches quiet even on

Beauty	B+
Swimming	B+
Sand	B
Amenities	C-

peak summer weekends. Seldom are any of the beaches crowded, and, especially north of Corolla, the seagulls far outnumber people. Although the quieter waters of Currituck Sound (pronounced *CURRY-tuck*) on the west side of the Northern Banks offer fishing, boating, and windsurfing, in most places on the sound side there are no real beaches, just marsh and tidal flats. Watch out for off-road vehicles on the beaches north of the Tasman Drive access year-round, and south of that point from October through April.

Swimming: The water is clean, if a bit cool. Water temperatures only get above the high 70s occasionally in July and August. Swimming is excellent at many spots, although caution is advised because of rips and undertows. Lifeguard on duty at only a few areas in summer.

Sand: Most beaches are moderately wide and sandy. Sand colors range from light tan to almost red.

Amenities: Few. Don't expect any changing rooms, bathhouses, or snack bars anywhere along the beaches of the Northern Banks. That's part of their undeveloped charm.

Sports: Fishing, kite flying. Windsurfing in Currituck Sound.

Parking: Other than the public soundside and ocean parking maintained by Currituck County at Currituck Beach Lighthouse in Corolla, at Whalehead Beach south of Corolla, and at the end of the paved road north of Corolla at the Ocean Hill development, public parking is limited, and spaces fill up quickly in the summer. Sanderling and Duck have no public access. Residential subdivisions, legion in this area, attempt with varying success to limit parking to residents only.

Beaches North of Corolla

This 12-mile expanse of wide, sandy beach is one of the least-used stretches of ocean front in the region—although development is increasing, despite the lack of roads. The main access point to Ocean, Swan, North Swan, and Carova beaches (they have different names but essentially are one long stretch of untamed beach) is at the end of the paved road at the Ocean Hill development. Even four-wheel-drive vehicles sometimes get stuck in this sand, so don't even think about attempting it in your family car. If you have the chance, visit this stretch of untamed ocean front. You may even see a wild pony galloping on the beach. *Drive to the end of Hwy. 12 at the Ocean Hill subdivision. Park at the turnaround circle where the pavement ends, although parking spaces are few and at a premium.*

Corolla Beaches

While more developed than the beach front north of Ocean Hill, the Corolla beaches are easier to get to and offer pleasant swimming and a relaxed family atmosphere. The best beach access here is either across Highway 12 from the Currituck Beach lighthouse or at Whalehead Beach. The only rest room facilities are two portable toilets across Highway 12 at the Lighthouse. Guests of the one inn in Corolla (*see* "Hotels/Inns/B&Bs") have ocean and sound access via the Corolla Light development. Lifeguard on duty in season at the lighthouse and near Shad and Bonita streets. *For Whalehead Beach, turn east off Hwy. 12 on Albacore St. just south of Corolla village. There are several parking lots maintained by Currituck County. For the lighthouse beach, park either on Corolla Village Rd. in front of the lighthouse or in the additional 30 spaces on the ocean side across Hwy. 12.*

Duck/Sanderling Beaches

Officially, there are no public access points to the beaches in Duck and Sanderling. Guests at the one inn in Sanderling and the B&B in Duck (*see* "Hotels/Inns/B&Bs") enjoy beach access, as do those renting houses in the area. Intrepid daytrippers sometimes park in residential areas and walk across private boardwalks or paths to the beach. Lifeguard on duty at Ocean Pines, North Snow Geese Drive, Barrier Island, and Plover Drive residential areas.

Southern Shores

This area is almost completely residential. The beaches here are good, but there is no public access to visitors, except those renting cottages here. Renters may, upon payment of a small fee and by arrangement with the realty company, use the parking and beach access provided by a local homeowners groups, the Southern Shores Civic Association. Lifeguard on duty at 13th Street.

HOTELS/INNS/B&BS

You have only a few choices, but those few are first class.

◆ **Inn at Corolla Light** (very expensive). New in mid-1995, this 17-room inn at the Corolla Light development has a wonderful soundside setting. The best rooms are at the back, right on the water, with kitchens, fireplaces, and style. Guests at the inn may use the facilities of Corolla Light, including outdoor and indoor tennis courts, two pools, grass putting golf course, and health club. Ocean access. *1066 Ocean Trail (Hwy. 12), Box 635, Corolla, NC 27927; tel. 919-453-3340, 800-215-0772.*

◆ **Sanderling Inn Resort and Conference Center** (very expensive). On 12 acres fronting both the ocean and the sound, the Sanderling is an attractive option for those who want a resort atmosphere and facilities. There are 87 rooms and suites in three buildings. The Main Inn features Audubon prints and Boehm birds. The South Inn is the newest, having opened in 1994; the corner suites here are the nicest. The North Inn was renovated in 1995. *1461 Duck Rd. (Hwy. 12), Duck, NC 27949; tel. 919-261-4111, 800-701-4111; fax 919-261-1638.*

◆ **Advice 5 Cents** (moderate). This B&B in a new house near "downtown Duck" opened in the spring of 1995. It isn't right on the water, but four bright, attractive rooms and one suite, all with private baths, make up for this. Beach access is available a few blocks away. The owners, Donna Black and Nancy Caviness, transplants from New York, are friendly and helpful. The B&B's slogan: "Life's too short to wear tight shoes." *111 Scarborough Lane, Box 8278, Duck, NC 27949; tel. 919-255-1050, 800-238-4235. Driving south on Hwy. 12, make a right on Scarborough Lane.*

HOUSE RENTALS

Rentals on the Northern Banks are plentiful, and they're among the most luxurious on the North Carolina coast. Some have a swimming pool—a rarity on the Outer Banks. Weekly rentals, from June to Labor Day, range from $1,000 to $3,000 or more. The top end is for a four- or five-bedroom, three-bath home, with every amenity except suntan lotion, suitable for several families together, and on or near a quiet beach. In the spring and fall, rental rates are 40 to 60 percent lower.

◆ **B & B on the Beach.** Despite the name, this is a home rental agency specializing in Corolla. *1023 Ocean Trail (Hwy. 12), Box 564, Corolla, NC 27927; tel. 919-453-3033, 800-962-0201. Open daily.*

◆ **R & R Resort Rental Properties.** Offers some of the most upscale properties. *1184 Duck Rd. (Hwy. 12), Duck, NC 27949; tel. 919-261-1136, 800-433-8805. Open daily.*

◆ **Southern Shores Realty.** Specializing in Southern Shores and Duck rentals. *5 Ocean Blvd., Southern Shores, NC 27949; tel. 919-261-2000, 800-334-1000. Open daily.*

RESTAURANTS

In the Northern Banks, you'll discover some of the best dining anywhere on the 100-mile length of the Outer Banks. Summer people here, used to big-city dining in Washington, D.C., or elsewhere, expect more than fried seafood, and they get it.

◆ **Sanderling Inn Restaurant** (expensive). Located in a restored lifesaving-station building, the Sanderling is one of the most attractive settings for dinner anywhere on the Banks. Here you'll find seafood, local dishes, and traditional Continental fare, including many specials and theme dinners. More formal than most other restaurants on the Banks. *1461 Hwy. 12, Duck, NC 27949; tel. 919-261-3021. Open daily for lunch and dinner.*

◆ **Blue Point Bar and Grill** (moderate). The Blue Point has something of a diner atmosphere, its tables jammed with regulars and visitors alike. The creative, varied menu and a great location directly on Currituck Sound contribute to its being widely considered one of the top dining spots on the Northern Banks. Not surprisingly, it's very busy, and reservations are required. *1240*

Hwy. 12, Duck, NC 27949; tel. 919-261-8090. Open daily for lunch and dinner Apr.-Oct. Closed Thanksgiving-Christmas and Mon. Nov.-Mar. In the Waterfront Shops.

♦ **Elizabeth's Cafe & Winery** (moderate). A small bistro under the oaks in the Scarborough Faire shopping area, it features an exceptional wine list and an eclectic, literate menu: light California dishes, Jamaican jerk, seafood. *Scarborough Faire, Hwy. 12, Duck, NC 27949; tel. 919-261-6145. Open daily for dinner.*

♦ **Nicoletta's Italian Cafe** (moderate). Attractive, small place with a variety of southern Italian and other pasta dishes. *Corolla Light Village Shops, Hwy. 12, Corolla, NC 27927; tel. 919-453-4004. Open daily for dinner.*

♦ **Duck Deli** (inexpensive). Basic sandwiches, subs, and such. *Hwy. 12, Duck, NC 27949; tel. 919-261-3354. Open daily for breakfast, lunch, and dinner Apr.-Oct. In the off-season closed Mon. and hours vary.*

NIGHTLIFE

On the Northern Banks, it's limited. For a wider choice of bars and clubs, drive to Nags Head and environs (*see* Chapter 2).

♦ **Barrier Island Inn.** This spot, one of the first restaurants and bars in Duck, has a lock on most of the evening action. Its picture-postcard setting on Currituck Sound, with a deck on the water and casual dockside atmosphere, is why. Live music most nights in season, pool, video games. *Hwy. 12, Duck, NC 27949; tel. 919-261-3901. Open daily.*

ATTRACTIONS

♦ **Currituck Beach Lighthouse.** First lit in 1875, this 160-foot red brick lighthouse, also called the Corolla Lighthouse, is a delight. It's one of only two lighthouses on the Outer Banks that you can climb (the other is the Cape Hatteras light at Buxton). *Hwy. 12, Box 361, Corolla, NC 27927; tel. 919-453-4939. Open daily 10-6 Easter-Thanksgiving, but it closes at the first hint of lightning. Admission. Turn west on the unpaved road just north of the Whalehead Club grounds. There's parking along the dirt road on the south side of the Currituck Lighthouse, and an additional 30 spaces across Hwy. 12 on the Atlantic side. A couple of* *portable toilets are at the lighthouse.*

◆ **Whalehead Club.** After visiting the lighthouse, walk over to this former hunting and fishing lodge, now owned by Currituck County. The old buildings are in disrepair and aren't open, but the grounds, and especially the marina and docks, are wonderful. The old marina is a good place for kids to fish or crab. *Hwy. 12, Corolla, NC 27927; tel. 919-232-2075. Open daily, no formal hours.*

SHOPPING

You can easily hit your credit card limit shopping on the Northern Banks, home to trendy small boutiques selling unique items at sometimes-heady prices. Although there are many shops along Highway 12 in Duck and Corolla, the shopping centers listed below offer some of the most intriguing stores.

◆ **Scarborough Faire.** The most attractive small shopping complex on the Outer Banks. Good and growing selection of upscale shops, including The Island Bookstore, with a good selection of regional books. *Hwy. 12, Duck, NC 27949. Open daily; individual shop hours vary.*

◆ **Tim Buck II.** A mix of restaurants, gift shops, and one-of-a-kind boutiques. *Hwy. 12, Corolla, NC 27927. Open daily; individual shop hours vary.*

BEST FOOD SHOPS

◆ **Food Lion.** This supermarket is your best bet for basic groceries and supplies. *Monteray Plaza, Hwy. 12, Corolla, NC 27927; tel. 919-426-4009. Open daily. Another branch is south of Duck.*

SANDWICHES: ◆ **Village Wine Shop.** World-class sandwiches as well as deli items and pizza (and yes—wine). *Village Square Shops, Hwy. 12, Duck, NC 27949; tel. 919-261-8646. Open daily.*

BAKERY: ◆ **Duck-In Donuts.** Bagels, muffins, and doughnuts. *Corolla Light Village Shops, Hwy. 12, Corolla, NC 27927; tel. 919-453-4513. Open daily in season; reduced hours off-season.*

ICE CREAM: ◆ **Candy Cone.** *Loblolly Pines Shopping Center, Hwy. 12, Duck, NC 27949; tel. 919-261-8055. Open daily Mar.-Nov.*

BEVERAGES: ◆ **ABC Store.** Liquor and cordials only—no beer, wine, or mixers. *1123 Ocean Trail, Hwy. 12, Corolla, NC 27927; tel. 919-453-2895. Open Mon.-Sat. Apr.-Oct. and Mon., Wed., Fri.-Sat. Nov.-Mar.*

WINE: ◆ **Village Wine Shop.** *Village Square Shops, Hwy. 12, Duck, NC 27949; tel. 919-261-8646. Open daily.*

Sports

The Northern Banks offer most beach and water sports: swimming, bodysurfing, windsurfing on Currituck Sound, sailing, Jet Skiing (north of Corolla only), kite flying in the near-constant breezes, and beach riding in off-road vehicles. In addition, bicycling in this area is excellent. Duck has bike paths along Highway 12, and a series of walking and jogging trails are being developed.
◆ **Kitty Hawk Kites.** This is a branch of what is billed as the "largest kite store on the East Coast." Another location is in Corolla at the Tim Buck II shopping center. Kites of all types, plus kayak rentals. *Wee Winks Square, Hwy. 12, Duck, NC 27949; tel. 919-261-4450. Open daily mid-Feb.-Dec. Closed for 6 weeks beginning the end of Dec.*

FISHING

Fishing on the Northern Banks is not the big deal it is on Hatteras Island or even around Nags Head, but this area does offer good-to-excellent ocean surf and sound fishing, particularly in the fall. Day-trips to the fishing piers around the Kitty Hawk/Kill Devil Hills/Nags Head area (*see* Chapter 2) or to the charter boat marina at Oregon Inlet (*see* Chapter 3) are also practical. The Dare County Tourist Bureau provides a fishing and weather information service (tel. 800-446-6262).
◆ **Whalehead Guides & Outfitters.** Light-tackle fishing. *Corolla, NC 27927; tel. 919-453-3579. Open daily, weather permitting.*

BOATING

◆ **Barrier Island Sailing Center.** Sales and rentals of Jet Skis and windsurfing, kayaking, sailing, parasailing, and other equipment; lessons. *Hwy. 12, Duck, NC 27949; tel. 919-261-7100. Open daily in season.*

TENNIS

◆ **Pine Island Racquet Club.** Three indoor and two outdoor courts open to the public. Guests at the Sanderling Inn, which has its own tennis courts, also have privileges at Pine Island. *Box 133, Corolla, NC 27927; tel. 919-441-5888. Open daily in season. Admission. About 2 1/2 mi. north of Sanderling.*

NATURE

The Northern Banks lack the long stretches of protected national seashore of Hatteras and Ocracoke islands, but several tracts of undeveloped private and public lands provide a welcome glimpse of how this area looked just a couple of decades ago.

◆ **Currituck Banks National Wildlife Refuge.** Three tracts total more than 1,800 acres, with management by the Mackay Wildlife Refuge. *Corolla, NC 27927; tel. 919-429-3100. Visitors center open daily 8-4. Drive to the end of Hwy. 12 and proceed north by foot or off-road vehicle. The first undeveloped area you come to is part of the wildlife preserve, as is another tract about 2 mi. north. The third tract is in Currituck Sound, accessible only by boat.*

◆ **Pine Island Audubon Sanctuary.** Strictly speaking, this private property is posted and off-limits to visitors, except with advance permission, but birders and other nature lovers do routinely hike in the sanctuary. *Hwy. 12, Corolla, NC 27927; tel. 919-453-2838. Open daily; no fixed hours. Pine Island Sanctuary is on both sides of Hwy. 12 just north of the Sanderling Inn, beginning at the Dare/Currituck county line.*

◆ **Wild Horse Sanctuary.** The remaining feral horses of the Northern Banks are presumably descendants of Spanish mustangs left by early explorers. To protect these "Banker ponies," they have been herded into this 15,000-acre preserve. *Hwy. 12, Corolla, NC 27927; tel. 919-453-8152. Open daily; no fixed hours. Drive to the end of Hwy. 12 north of Corolla and proceed by foot or off-road vehicle into the Currituck National Wildlife Refuge and other areas north of Ocean Hill.*

TOURIST INFORMATION

◆ **Dare County Tourist Bureau.** *704 Hwy. 64/264, Box 399, Manteo, NC 27954; tel. 919-473-2138, 800-446-6262. Open Mon.-Fri. 8:30-5 and Sat.-Sun. 9-5. Closed weekends in the off-season.*

◆ **Outer Banks Chamber of Commerce.** *Box 1757, Kill Devil Hills, NC 27948; tel. 919-441-8144. Open Mon.-Fri. 8:45-5.*

CHAPTER 2

Nags Head

Beauty	C+
Swimming	B
Sand	B-
Hotels/Inns/B&Bs	B+
House rentals	A
Restaurants	B+
Nightlife	B+
Attractions	A
Shopping	B
Sports	B+
Nature	C+

66 "Let's go to the beach at Nags Head" is a refrain that's likely been heard millions of times over the years in North Carolina and the surrounding states. Nags Head has been a beach resort since the mid-19th century, and it remains among the best-known vacation destinations in the region, a name familiar to people even if they know nothing else about the Outer Banks (the 100-mile string of barrier islands stretching from

the Virginia-North Carolina line in the north to Ocracoke Island in the south).

In some ways Nags Head is an icon for the beaches of the entire region, a symbol of both the good and the bad. Its fine beaches and raw beauty were bound to attract beach-loving visitors. The development that followed, however, obscured much of Nags Head's powerful charm, and left visitors with less to enjoy—a story that has been repeated over and over along the coast of the Carolinas and Georgia.

Settled in the late 18th century by families from Virginia and

HOW TO GET THERE

◆ Nags Head is about 2 hr. by car south of Norfolk, VA, and about 4 hr. east of Raleigh. For detailed directions, *see* Chapter 1, Northern Outer Banks. From the Wright Memorial Bridge, go south on U.S. Hwy. 158 Bypass (often referred to locally as Rte. 158 or "the Bypass" and also known as Croatan Hwy.) to Kill Devil Hills and Nags Head. For the beaches, from the bridge continue straight to Hwy. 12 (also referred to as Rte. 12; it's known here as both Beach Rd. and Virginia Dare Trail).

◆ Note that in this part of the Outer Banks, milepost signs on Hwy. 158 Bypass and Beach Rd. are used to help identify locations. Milepost numbers increase southward: Milepost 1 is on Hwy. 158 Bypass near the north end of Kitty Hawk, and Milepost 21 is on Old Oregon Inlet Rd. south of Nags Head. Since Rtes. 158 and 12 are more or less parallel for much of the distance, the same milepost numbers apply to both from the Wright Memorial Bridge to U.S. Hwy. 64/264. Milepost references given (e.g., Milepost 3 1/2) are approximate.

eastern North Carolina, the Nags Head area drew only small numbers of travelers until the 1930s. Then, with the opening of the Wright Memorial Bridge, the trickle became a steady stream. Today, the toast-colored sands of Nags Head's beaches are lined with cottages of various vintages and styles, as well as with condos and motels. About two million tourists come to the Outer Banks every year, and most of them stay in Nags Head or close by. Shops and fast-food restaurants line U.S. Highway 158, the busy bypass around old Beach Road.

It was not natural beauty but steady wind that attracted Orville and Wilbur Wright and their flying machines to the Outer Banks—that and soft sand for easier landings. At Kill Devil Hills (then a part of Kitty Hawk), which adjoins Nags Head to the north, Orville made his pioneering flight.

Despite the development, there's much to enjoy in the area. Jockey's Ridge State Park contains immense and fascinating sand dunes, the highest in the East and fun for the whole family to explore. Nearby lie significant historic landmarks: In addition to the Wrights' famous airstrip at Kill Devil Hills, on Roanoke Island you can visit the site of England's first attempt to colonize the New World—an attempt that failed when the colonists mysteriously disappeared, giving rise to the name Lost Colony. Hang gliding and windsurfing draw international attention, and the many wrecks off the coast attract divers. The beaches are as good as they ever were, with some of the cleanest water on the East Coast—although in summer they're wall to wall with warm bodies.

Summer is the prime time here, especially from early June to late August, when the Atlantic waters are warm enough—in the high 70s—for pleasant swimming. Fall and spring attract fishermen and fisherwomen—not to mention savvy beachgoers who know that the Banks weather will be perfect for beach walking and that prices will be as much as 60 percent less than in the peak summer months. Nags Head and its environs, more so than most of the rest of the Outer Banks, stay alive in winter as well, although some motels and quite a few restaurants and shops close from December through February. Because of the moderating influence of the Gulf Stream about 30 miles offshore, winters are relatively mild.

14

BEACHES

The beaches we recommend in this area are Kill Devil Hills and Nags Head. While Kitty Hawk lies on the same long beach that stretches some 21 miles along the Atlantic, it's a bit too weather-beaten to be included in this book.

There are also a few beaches on the Roanoke Sound side. Here, the water is calmer and, with the steady winds, good for windsurfing, but the low water clarity and small amount of sand make these beaches far less appealing than the ocean beaches for swimming. One of the best is at the end of Soundside Road near Milepost 13. This sound beach access point, near Jockey's Ridge State Park, has parking and a small beach.

KILL DEVIL HILLS BEACHES

Kill Devil Hills, famous as the site of the first powered flight (it was then a part of Kitty Hawk), has almost five miles of beach front, much of it occupied by condos and motels, with a few private homes.

Beauty	C+
Swimming	B+
Sand	B
Amenities	A

Kill Devil Hills provides excellent beach access, with more than two dozen access points, clearly marked on Beach Road (look for blue-and-orange signs). There is a regional access point at Ocean Bay Boulevard. Vehicles are permitted on the beach October through April. *From U.S. Hwy. 158 Bypass, take Ocean Bay Blvd. east to the regional beach access point, just south of the Wright Memorial. Many other east-west streets off U.S. Hwy. 158 Bypass lead to beach access points.*

Swimming: Good on calm days in the summer, when the water temperature is in the high 70s. Waves can be large and violent at times. There are lifeguards at about 19 points along the beach from 9:30 to 5:30 Memorial Day through Labor Day (check locally to confirm places and times). Roving lifeguards may also be present.

Sand: Mostly wide, tan-colored beaches with a gentle to moderate slope.

Sports: Swimming, kite flying, surfing, surf and pier fishing.

Amenities: There are showers and rest rooms at several points along the beach, including Ashville Drive, Woodmere Avenue, and Atlantic Street. The regional beach access point at Ocean Bay Boulevard has a bathhouse with showers. Small shops and restaurants line Beach Road.

Parking: Free parking is available (in season, arrive early) at about 20 access points, including Ashville Drive, Woodmere and Sutton avenues, Ocean Bay Boulevard, and 5th, 2nd, 1st, Oregon, Clark, Martin, and Atlantic streets.

NAGS HEAD BEACHES

Nags Head encompasses about 11 miles of beach front. The 6-mile-long section north of Whalebone Junction is largely covered with chain and independent motels, condos, and time-shares. South of Whalebone (where Route 12 runs

Beauty	B-
Swimming	B+
Sand	B
Amenities	A-

into Old Oregon Inlet Road/NC Route 1243), the other 5 miles of beach front is, in contrast, mostly residential—a pleasant mix of older and newer cottages and some condos, with little of the jarring commercial development present north of here.

There are almost three dozen access points along Beach Road and Old Oregon Inlet Road in Nags Head. Regional access points are at Bonnett Street (Milepost 11), Epstein Street (Milepost 15 1/4), and Hargrove Street (Milepost 17 1/2). Look for the blue-and-orange beach access signs along Beach Road. Driving on the beach is allowed, with a permit (fee), from October through March only. *From U.S. Hwy. 158 Bypass north of Whalebone Junction, turn east on most east-west streets: The beach is only about 1 or 2 blocks away. To get to the beach south of Whalebone Junction, follow U.S. Hwy. 64 to Rte. 12 and turn south on Rte. 1243 (which is Old Oregon Inlet Rd. from this point until it reconnects with Rte. 12 below Milepost 21).*

Swimming: Good on calm days in the summer, when the water temperature is in the high 70s. Watch for large and violent waves when the wind is strong. There are lifeguards at about four points along the beach from 9:30 to 5:30 Memorial Day through Labor Day (check locally to confirm places and times). Roving lifeguards may also be present.

Sand: Mostly wide beaches, with gentle to moderate slope. Tan sand.

Sports: Swimming, kite flying, surfing, surf fishing, and pier fishing at Nags Head, Jennette, and Outer Banks piers.

Amenities: You'll find bathhouses, rest rooms, and showers at the regional access points at Bonnett, Epstein, and Hargrove streets, as well as small shops and restaurants along Beach Road.

Parking: Nags Head has about 500 free parking spaces at some two dozen sites. The main paved parking lots are at regional access points at Bonnett, Epstein, and Hargrove streets. In summer, these go early.

HOTELS/INNS/B&BS

Accommodations in the Nags Head area are primarily in motels, most located along Beach Road.

◆ **First Colony Inn** (very expensive). Despite its location on busy, highly developed Highway 158 Bypass, the First Colony can rightfully claim to be the best hotel in Nags Head. It's not directly on the beach, but there's beach access and a gazebo about a block away. The only surviving inn from Nags Head's earlier resort period, it is listed on the National Register of Historic Places (the building, which dates from the early 1930s, was moved from its original site in 1988). Each of the 26 rooms is decorated differently; deluxe rooms 10, 16, 18, 20, 25, and 27 are the choicest. Large heated swimming pool, attractively landscaped grounds. *6720 S. Virginia Dare Trail, Nags Head, NC 27959; tel. 919-441-2343, 800-368-9390; fax 919-441-9234. At Milepost 16.*

◆ **Nags Head Inn** (expensive). This is not an inn but a five-story motel with 100 rooms. However, it's well run and enjoys a location directly on the beach. The best choice among rooms, which are clean and attractively decorated, are the balconied units on the ocean side, on the third floor and above. Refrigerators in all rooms. The beach here is good and has lifeguards. Heated pool. *Hwy. 12, Box 1559, Nags Head, NC 27959; tel. 919-441-0454, 800-327-8881; fax 919-441-0454. On Beach Rd. at Milepost 13 3/4.*

◆ **Blue Heron Motel** (moderate). This pleasant independent motel sits directly on the beach. All 30 rooms (11 of which are efficiencies) face the ocean. Room 16 has a Jacuzzi. Two pools; the indoor one has a small spa. *6811 Virginia Dare Trail, Nags Head, NC 27595; tel. 919-441-7447. At Milepost 15 1/2.*

♦ **Cherokee Inn B&B** (moderate). Originally a fishing and hunting lodge, this B&B is across the road from the ocean. You'll find the wraparound front porch inviting, and the six rooms, with cypress paneling, wicker, and beds with firm new mattresses, homey and pleasant. Continental breakfast. *500 N. Virginia Dare Trail, Kill Devil Hills, NC 27948; tel. 919-441-6127, 800-554-2764. Open Apr.-Oct. On Beach Rd. at Milepost 8.*

♦ **Hampton Inn** (moderate). This 96-room, four-story Hampton Inn is among the nicest and the best maintained of all the chain motels here. Its drawback is that it's across the road from—not directly on—the beach. Heated swimming pool. Continental breakfast. *804 N. Virginia Dare Trail, Box 1349, Kill Devil Hills, NC 27948; tel. 919-441-0411, 800-338-7761. At Milepost 8.*

HOUSE RENTALS

The area offers a huge supply of rental houses. Three- to five-bedroom ocean-front homes in the nicer developments around Nags Head go for $1,500 to $3,000 a week or more in season. The highest rates are usually early June to late August, with rates nearly as high from late May to early June and from late August to Labor Day. Houses not directly on the ocean rent for as much as one-half less than ocean-front homes. Condominiums, even those on the beach, are usually less than $1,000 in high season.

♦ **Resort Realty.** Rents homes in the Nags Head area. *3608 N. Croatan Hwy., Kitty Hawk, NC 27949; tel. 919-261-8383, 800-458-3830. Open daily 8:30-5:30. At Milepost 5.*

♦ **Sun Realty.** Lists about 1,000 homes and condos on the Outer Banks, including the Nags Head and Kill Devil Hills areas. *6385 N. Croatan Hwy., Suite 101, Kitty Hawk, NC 27949; tel. 919-261-3892, 800-334-4745. Open daily 8:30-5:30.*

RESTAURANTS

Most restaurants around Nags Head fall into the fried-seafood genre.

♦ **Colington Cafe** (moderate). Arguably the best restaurant in the Nags Head area, the Colington Cafe is so popular that it's often difficult to get reservations in summer. In an old house nestled amid oak trees, away from the bustle of the Bypass and Beach Road, the Colington serves an eclectic mix of seafood, steaks, and French dishes. Start with the crab bisque or crab dip, then have one of the daily specials—you can't go wrong. *1029 Colington Blvd., Kill Devil Hills, NC 27948; tel. 919-480-1123. Open daily for dinner mid-Mar.-late-Nov. and Thu.-Sun. Dec. and mid-Feb.-mid.-Mar. About 1 mi. west of Hwy. 158 Bypass.*

◆ **Owens' Restaurant** (moderate). Owens' is one of Nag Head's oldest (established in 1946) and best-known restaurants. Try the coconut shrimp (shrimp rolled in coconut and served with Dijon mustard and orange marmalade) or the classic seafood platters, fried or broiled. *Hwy. 12, Nags Head, NC 27959; tel. 919-441-7309. Open daily for dinner mid-Feb.-Dec. At Milepost 16 1/2.*

◆ **Rundown Cafe** (moderate). The atmosphere runs to Jimmy Buffet tropical, and the flavors are Caribbean (Jamaican stew and conch fritters), although there are good ol' American dishes too. Fun place, very popular. *5300 Beach Rd., Kitty Hawk, NC 27949; tel. 919-255-0026. Open daily for lunch and dinner. At Milepost 1.*

◆ **Sam and Omie's** (inexpensive). This classic beach shack has been going strong for 50 years. The atmosphere, with wood booths, pool tables, and sports photos, is so authentic you can cut it with a clam shell. Eat your oysters here, or have a burger. For breakfast, the omelets are the thing. *Beach Rd. at Whalebone Junction, Nags Head, NC 27959; tel. 919-441-7366. Open daily for breakfast, lunch, and dinner. At Milepost 16.*

NIGHTLIFE

◆ **Awful Arthurs.** Occasional live music, but mostly just lots of folks eating oysters by the peck and drinking. *Beach Rd., Kill Devil Hills, NC 27948; tel. 919-441-5955. Open daily. At Milepost 6.*

◆ **Gaslight Saloon, Port 'O Call Restaurant.** Live beach, rock, and other music nightly in summer and on weekends at other times. Nice atmosphere, with paneling, overstuffed chairs, and Victorian decor. *504 Virginia Dare Trail, Kill Devil Hills, NC 27948; tel. 919-441-7487. Open daily mid-Mar.-Dec. Admission. At Milepost 8 1/2.*

ATTRACTIONS

◆ **Elizabethan Gardens.** Patterned after a 16th-century formal English garden, Elizabethan Gardens, with beautiful rose, herb, azalea, and other plantings, is as a memorial to the first English colonists in America. *U.S. Hwy. 64, Box 1150, Manteo, NC 27954; tel. 919-473-3234. Open daily 9-dusk and until 8 p.m. when* The Lost Colony *drama is playing (early Jun.-late Aug.; see listing, below). Admission. On Roanoke Island, about 3 mi. north of Manteo. From Nags Head, take U.S. Hwy. 64 west and watch for signs.*

◆ **Fort Raleigh National Historic Site.** This 144-acre site commemorates the first English colony in America—from which every member of the settlement vanished, a mystery that has never been solved. *U.S. Hwy. 64, Manteo, NC 27954; tel. 919-473-5772. Open Sun.-Fri. 9-8 and Sat. 9-6 mid-Jun.-Labor Day and daily 9-5 the rest of the year. Admission. On Roanoke Island, about 3 mi. north of Manteo.*

◆ **Jockey's Ridge State Park.** Kids of all ages absolutely love this place! Jockey's Ridge, covering 410 acres, claims two of the highest sand dunes in the East. The shifting sands sometimes reach 125 feet or more. You can climb the dunes and, if you don't mind getting sand down your back, roll down. This is also one of the most popular locations on the East Coast for hang gliding (permits required, obtainable on site) and a wonderful place to fly kites. *U.S. Hwy. 158 Bypass, Nags Head, NC 27959; tel. 919-441-7132. Open daily 8 a.m.-9 p.m. Jun.-Aug., 8-8 Apr.- May and Sep., 8-7 Mar., and 8-6 the rest of the year. At Milepost 12.*

◆ **North Carolina Aquarium at Roanoke Island.** Children will enjoy this small aquarium with hands-on exhibits (touch a starfish) and a shark tank. *Airport Rd., Box 967, Manteo, NC 27954; tel. 919-473-3493. Open Mon.-Sat. 9-5 and Sun. 1-5. Admission. From Nags Head, take U.S. Hwy. 64 west. Turn left on Airport Rd.*

◆ *The Lost Colony.* Pulitzer Prize-winning author Paul Green's play tells the story of the 117 settlers who came to Roanoke Island in 1587 and, three years later, disappeared without a trace. *1409 U.S. Hwy. 64, Manteo, NC 27954; tel. 919-473-3414. Performances Sun.-Fri. at 8:30 p.m. early Jun.-late Aug. Admission.*

◆ **Wright Brothers National Memorial.** On December 17, 1903, Orville Wright, in a coat and tie, succeeded in making the first self-propelled, heavier-than-air flight. The memorial includes a visitors center with a replica of the brothers' history-making airplane. If you want to see things the way Orville did, book an air tour: Kitty Hawk AeroTours (tel. 919-441-4460) leaves from an airstrip nearby. *U.S. Hwy. 158 Bypass, Kill Devil Hills, NC 27948; tel. 919-441-7430. Open daily 9-5. Admission. At Milepost 8.*

SHOPPING

◆ **Christmas Shop and Island Gallery.** Thirty-six rooms filled with an amazing collection of Christmas ornaments, crafts, porcelain, art, pottery, soaps, and gifts. *U.S. Hwy. 64, Box 265, Manteo, NC 27954; tel. 919-473-2838. Open daily.*

◆ **Manteo Booksellers.** Includes an extensive collection of Outer Banks and nautical books. *105 Sir Walter Raleigh St., Manteo, NC 27954; tel. 919-437-1221. Open daily. On the Manteo water front. From Nags Head, take U.S. Hwy. 64 east.*

BEST FOOD SHOPS

◆ **Food Lion.** Groceries, baked goods, seafood, produce, wine, beer, soft drinks. *1720 N. Croatan Hwy., Kill Devil Hills, NC 27948; tel. 919-480-1517. Open daily.*

SANDWICHES: ◆ **Dairy Mart.** Burgers, sandwiches, and soft ice cream. *4302 S. Virginia Dare Trail, Nags Head, NC 27959; tel. 919-441-6730. Open Thu.-Tue. May-Oct. At Milepost 13.*

SEAFOOD: The fishing center for this part of the Banks lies in the village of Wanchese on Roanoke Island, where several seafood companies that run their own fishing fleets—including the Wanchese Fish Co. and Quality Seafood—are located.

ICE CREAM: ◆ **Mom's Sweet Shoppe.** *Seagate Mall North, U.S. Hwy. 158 Bypass, Kill Devil Hills, NC 27948; tel. 919-441-8911. Open daily. Closed Jan. At Milepost 5 1/2.*

BEVERAGES: ◆ **ABC Store.** Liquor and cordials. *2104 Croatan Hwy., Nags Head, NC 27959; tel. 919-441-5121. Open Mon.-Sat.*

SPORTS

Surf and pier fishing are popular, with the best fishing March through May and again from September through December. There are five fishing piers on the ocean off Beach Road, including Kitty Hawk Pier (Milepost 3), Avalon Fishing Pier (Milepost 6 3/4), Nags Head Fishing Pier (Milepost 11), Jennette's Pier (Milepost 16 1/2), and Outer Banks Pier (Milepost 18 1/2). For offshore charter and party boats to the Gulf Stream, Oregon Inlet (about ten miles south of Whalebone junction) is the place to go.

◆ **Kitty Hawk Bait & Tackle.** Arranges charters, sells bait and tackle, provides a fishing report. *U.S. Hwy 158 Bypass, Kitty Hawk, NC 27949; tel. 919-261-2955. Open daily Mar.-Dec. At Milepost 4 1/2.*

BOATING

Windsurfing is a major sport on the sounds, although Canadian Hole, south of Avon, is the most popular windsurfing spot in the region (*see* Chapter 3). Most local bookstores and windsurfing shops sell a useful guide, *Windsurfing the Outer Banks.*

◆ **Kitty Hawk Sports Sailing Center.** Rents and sells windsurfing, sailing, and kayaking equipment. Offers instruction. *U.S. Hwy. 158 Bypass, Nags Head, NC 27959; tel. 919-441-2756. Open daily Mar.-Oct.; exact dates vary—if the Sailing Center is closed, contact the Kitty Hawk Sports store in Nags Head at Milepost 13 (tel. 919-441-6800). At Milepost 16.*

SURFING

◆ **Wave Riding Vehicles.** Sells and rents boards and equipment. *U.S. Hwy. 158 Bypass, Kitty Hawk, NC 27949; tel. 919-261-7952. Open daily. For a 24-hr. surf report call 919-261-3332. At Milepost 2.*

DIVING

Despite chilly water and poor visibility, wreck diving is becoming increasingly popular on the Outer Banks, with its hundreds of wrecks, old and new. Several near Nags Head—including freighters, tankers, tugs, and even a German sub—are divable.

◆ **Pro Dive Center.** Wreck dive charters on a 50-foot dive boat (based in Manteo). Rentals and instruction. *Kitty Hawk Connection, U.S. Hwy. 158 Bypass, Nags Head, NC 27959; tel. 919-441-7594. Open daily in season. At Milepost 13 1/2.*

BICYCLING

There is a bike path in South Nags Head along Old Oregon Inlet Road.

◆ **Bike Barn.** Rents and sells bikes. *1312 Wrightsville Blvd., Kill Devil Hills, NC 27948; tel. 919-441-3786. Open daily in season and Mon.-Sat. the rest of the year.*

GOLF

◆ **Nags Head Golf Links.** An 18-hole, par-72, 6,100-yard, Scottish-style course. *U.S. Hwy 158 Bypass, Nags Head, NC 27959; tel. 919-441-8073, 800-851-9404. Open daily. Admission. At Milepost 15.*

◆ **Seascape Golf Club.** This 18-hole, par-72, 6,200-yard course has views of the ocean from some holes. *300 Eckner St., Kitty Hawk, NC 27949; tel. 919-261-2158. Open daily. Admission. At Milepost 2 1/2.*

HANG GLIDING

The Outer Banks are known as a world-class spot for hang gliding, with Jockey's Ridge where it's happening. The area's steady winds also make for good kite flying.

◆ **Kitty Hawk Kites.** Offers hang gliding rides. Rents and sells equipment and kites. *3933 N. Croatan Hwy., Nags Head, NC 27959; tel. 919-441-4124. Open daily. On U.S. Hwy. 158 Bypass, at Milepost 13 near Jockey's Ridge.*

NATURE

One of the most beautiful seashores in the east is next door: the Cape Hatteras National Seashore (*see* Chapters 3 and 4).

◆ **Nags Head Woods Ecological Preserve.** This 1,100-acre preserve, owned by the Nature Conservancy, is a serene island of maritime forest in a sea of human development. Explore nature trails; view exhibits at the visitors center. *701 W. Ocean Acres Dr., Nags Head, NC 27948; tel. 919-441-2525. This private property, staffed by volunteers, is open to the public on a limited basis (at present, Mon.-Fri. 10-3). Check in at the visitors center. Off U.S. Hwy. 158 Bypass, at Milepost 10 near Jockey's Ridge.*

TOURIST INFORMATION

◆ **Aycock Brown Visitors Center.** *U.S. Hwy. 158 Bypass, Box 392, Kitty Hawk, NC 27949; tel. 919-261-4644, 800-446-6262. Open daily 9-5. At the junction with Rte. 12, at Milepost 1.5.*

◆ **Dare County Tourist Bureau.** Helpful and friendly organization. *704 Hwy. 64, Box 399, Manteo, NC 27954; tel. 919-473-2138, 800-446-6262; fax 919-473-5106. Open Mon.-Fri. 8:30-5 and Sat.-Sun. 9-5; closed weekends in the off-season. Recorded information available 24 hr. a day year-round on the 800 number.*

Hatteras Island

Beauty	A
Swimming	B+
Sand	B
Hotels/Inns/B&Bs	C
House rentals	A
Restaurants	B-
Nightlife	C
Attractions	B
Shopping	C+
Sports	A
Nature	A

atteras Island is the heart of the Outer Banks. With adjoining Bodie and Pea islands, Hatteras stretches some 55 miles along the North Carolina coast. At some points the barrier islands are several miles wide; at other points only a few hundred feet separate the wild Atlantic Ocean and quieter Pamlico Sound.

The tenor of this region is set by Cape Hatteras National Seashore, the first national seashore in the

United States. The 30,000-acre park was officially established in 1953, following two decades of planning and land acquisition. Most of the seashore here is protected and undeveloped, with

HOW TO GET THERE

◆ By car, the entrance to Cape Hatteras National Seashore at the north end of Bodie Island is about 2 hr. south of Norfolk, VA, and about 4 hr. east of Raleigh. From Norfolk and points north, take I-64 to VA Hwy. 168 and U.S. Hwy. 158 south to the Wright Memorial Bridge (widened in 1995 to four lanes), then go south on Hwy. 158 Bypass to NC Hwy. 12.

◆ From Washington, DC, or points north, an alternate is to get off I-64 at Hampton, VA, and go south on I-664 through the Monitor-Merrimac Memorial Bridge Tunnel. Then take I-64 toward Norfolk. At Deep Creek, VA, go south on U.S. Hwy. 17 to NC Hwy. 343. Follow Hwy. 343 south to U.S. Hwy. 158, then go south on Hwy. 158 Bypass to NC Hwy. 12.

◆ From Raleigh, take U.S. Hwy. 64 east to NC Hwy. 12, then go south. From points south of Raleigh, take I-95 or U.S. Hwy 17 to U.S. Hwy. 64 east and NC Hwy. 12.

◆ An option is to take the toll car ferry from Cedar Island (if driving from the south) or Swan Quarter (if driving from the west) to Ocracoke, and then another (free) ferry from Ocracoke to Hatteras (*see* Chapter 4).

◆ By air, fly into Raleigh or Norfolk—both have jet and commuter service—and rent a car. Dare County Municipal Airport in Manteo has spotty commuter service.

only a few towns and villages, all low-rise, dotting Hatteras Island. This is the part of the Banks for nature lovers, anglers, surfers, campers, and those who like solitary beaches and comfortable beach houses.

As you enter Cape Hatteras National Seashore just south of Whalebone Junction at Bodie Island (pronounced *BODY*), at the point where U.S. Highway 64/264, Highway 158, and Highway 12 meet, you leave behind the fast-food restaurants and video stores of Nags Head. Remnants of an older, quieter Nags Head remain only in a four-mile strip of homes on the Atlantic side, at the northern tip of the park, grandfathered in when the park was established. Bodie, technically no longer a separate island because drifting sands have tied it to the Northern Banks, is the northernmost part of the national seashore. Driving over the dramatic Bonner Bridge at Oregon Inlet, you enter Pea Island National Wildlife Refuge, a park within a park. From here to the end of Hatteras Island at Hatteras Village, you'll see miles of low dunes on the Atlantic side. These hide the ocean from view on Highway 12. The quieter waters of the sound to the west are visible at many points.

Several small villages, whose tall weathered beach houses loom up in the distance, punctuate the drive south. Coming from the north, the first village is Rodanthe (pronounced *Ro-DAN-thee*). Then, quickly, you're in Waves and Salvo. These towns are oriented to fishing, camping, and casual family vacationing. Here, there are only a few motels and restaurants but an increasing number of beach homes. Next, after a long stretch of undeveloped national seashore, is Avon, which is growing rapidly as the vacation-home center of Hatteras. About six miles south of Avon, at the bend of the island's elbow, is Buxton, home to the Cape Hatteras Lighthouse as well as to considerable numbers of surfers and Windsurfers. Next comes Frisco, then Hatteras Village. These are year-round communities, where fishing is serious business: both commercial fishing by locals and sportfishing for tourists. Near the western end of Hatteras Village is the free ferry to Ocracoke Island.

Hatteras is an active destination from March to November. Mid-June to late August is the high season, when families come for beach vacations. Many, though, prefer the spring or fall—the crowds are smaller, and the weather is cool and invigorating, yet usually nice enough for beach activities other than swimming. March to May and September to November are also prime fishing times. Many restaurants and some retail stores and motels close in late November or December and don't reopen until February or March. If you plan to go in the off-season, always check ahead for opening dates and hours.

Weather on the Banks is notoriously unpredictable. It can be beautiful one day, stormy the next, and then beautiful again. You're lucky if you get more than a few days of "perfect beach weather" in a row. The nearby Gulf Stream keeps temperatures in the moderate range year-round, with few days over 90 degrees in summer or under 32 degrees in winter. The high humidity, however, makes temperatures feel more extreme. Winds blow almost constantly on the Outer Banks, ranging from an average of about 11 miles per hour in September to 15 miles per hour in April—making the Banks ideal for kite-flying and Windsurfing. The rainiest months are July to September.

You need a car to get to the Banks and to enjoy them once you're there. A four-wheel-drive pickup, with surf rod holders and cooler attached to the front bumper, is the choice of many Hatteras regulars, but if you don't want to drive on the beach, any car will do.

BEACHES

Hatteras Island has some of the most unspoiled strands in the United States. On the beaches of Cape Hatteras National Seashore, you can walk for miles, shelling, beachcombing, and seeing the occasional whale, bottle-nosed

Beauty	A
Swimming	B+
Sand	B+
Amenities	C

dolphin, or fishing boat and enjoying the ocean breeze and the sun. Development, though increasing rapidly, is limited to the towns and villages. Even on a busy summer weekend, you can usually find a place to be alone on the miles of national seashore.

Hatteras's brand of beauty is rugged and untamed, and when the sea is rough and the sky is gray, the setting can have an air of gloom. Look out at the surging ocean and you can imagine why this part of the Outer Banks is called the Graveyard of the Atlantic, with hundreds of ships lost when they strayed too close to the treacherous shore. At other times, with the sun sparkling and dolphins playing offshore, Hatteras offers its cheerful face.

On the Atlantic side, Hatteras Island is basically one long beach, typically 50 or more yards wide at high tide, backed by low dunes. On the mainland side of the barrier island, the calmer waters of Pamlico Sound mostly abut marshland or, in wider parts of the island, maritime forest, rather than sandy beaches.

Swimming: The water is very clean, if often chilly. Water temperatures seldom rise above the high 70s, even in the warmest summer weeks. From October to May, the cold Atlantic is only for the hardy. In summer, swimming can be excellent, but extreme caution is advised because of rips and undertows. Wave action is often intense, and that's especially true around Buxton. In most cases, no lifeguard is on duty.

Sand: Most beaches on Hatteras are moderately wide, with light-tan-colored sand.

Amenities: Few, except at Coquina Beach and a few other spots noted below. Most visitors stay in rental houses on or near the beach, so they don't need public rest rooms or snack bars.

Sports: Surf fishing, surfing, Windsurfing, kite flying.

Parking: Beaches listed below have free parking that is adequate at most times, except on some busy summer days.

In many cases, beach access is at or near a ramp that provides a way for off-road vehicles to reach the beach or a boat launch. Ramps are numbered—the numbers get higher as you go south—but you have to watch carefully for the small signs. Beaches are listed here from north to south.

Coquina Beach, Bodie Island

Coquina Beach has traditionally been one of the most popular and pleasant beach areas on the Outer Banks, with wide sandy beaches, tidal pools ideal for young children, attractive picnic shelters, and plenty of parking and rest rooms. However, a series of storms in the early and mid-1990s badly damaged parts of the beach and its facilities, which were being repaired and rebuilt in 1995. In the past, lifeguards have been present here in the summer, but funding cuts at the National Park Service could eliminate them—check locally. You can see the remains of the *Laura Barnes*, shipwrecked in 1921, at the south end of the parking area. *Coquina Beach is the first beach access site south of the national seashore entrance, about 5 1/2 mi. south of Whalebone Junction. Park in the lots at the main beach area.*

Pea Island National Wildlife Refuge

The beaches at Pea Island National Wildlife Refuge, an important wintering area for geese, swans, ducks, and other wildfowl (*see* "Nature"), are beautiful and unpeopled, but the swimming can be dicey because of beach erosion and rip currents. No lifeguard. Ask at the refuge's visitors center for current beach information (tel. 919-987-2394). Amenities are available only in the form of a few portable toilets and the facilities at the visitors center. Camping, campfires, unleashed dogs, and driving on the beach are all prohibited. *Pea Island stretches from the south end of Oregon Inlet to just north of Rodanthe. You'll find 8 separate parking areas in the refuge along Hwy. 12, for both ocean and sound access.*

Rodanthe/Waves/Salvo

Public beach access in and near the towns of Rodanthe, Waves, and Salvo is limited. Most people who visit a beach here have rented a cottage or are staying at a motel or camping in one of the many campgrounds. *On the stretch of national seashore between Salvo and Avon, off-road vehicle ramps also offer pedestrians access to the beach. Look for ramps 20, 23, 27, and 30. The beach at Ramp 23 is especially wide and pleasant, although access by foot requires a long trek on a sandy road. Public parking is also available near the Hatteras Island Fishing Pier in Rodanthe. Look for the sign to Hatteras Island Resort.*

Avon

One of the best beaches on Hatteras Island is just south of the town of Avon. The beach is wide and sandy, and the swimming is very good. While there are no amenities, parking is adequate in a paved lot. Surf fishing is excellent. To the north are rental houses, and to the south you can see the Cape Hatteras

Lighthouse in the distance. No lifeguard. Especially in fall and spring, parents with children should be alert for off-road vehicles on the beach. *Look for the first parking area on the ocean side, south of the Food Lion shopping center in Avon, at Ramp 38.*

Cape Hatteras Lighthouse, Buxton

The Cape Hatteras Lighthouse is a beacon for surfers from all over the east. At the two beaches near the towering 208-foot brick lighthouse, waves of eight feet and more roll in. At Buxton, Hatteras Island makes a sharp turn to the west, and the Atlantic here is toward the south and southeast, with Pamlico Sound to the northwest. Amenities, including spotless bathrooms, are available at the Park Service visitors center next to the lighthouse. In summer, visitors can enter the lighthouse and climb to the top for an aerial view of Cape Hatteras and the legions of intrepid surfers. No lifeguard. *At Buxton, turn south off Hwy. 12 at the sign for the Cape Hatteras Lighthouse. Follow the road a short way to a T intersection. Turn left toward the lighthouse. To get a space during peak summer weekends, arrive early.*

Cape Point Beach

This open, windswept expanse of beach is a favorite for surf fishing. Indeed, this may be the most popular spot on the Outer Banks for the sport, especially for channel bass and bluefish. Amenities are limited to a couple of portable toilets. No lifeguard. *At Buxton, turn south off Hwy. 12 at the sign for the Cape Hatteras Lighthouse. Follow the road a short way to a T intersection. Turn right, away from the lighthouse and toward Cape Point Campground. Beach access is near ramps 43, 44, and 45. Parking is usually adequate in the lot at the end of the main Cape Point road. If you have a four-wheel-drive vehicle, you can drive to several parts of Cape Point.*

Frisco Beach

A short walk, less than a quarter mile, on a path over grass- and shrub-covered dunes brings you to one of the most scenic beaches on Hatteras. The high dunes provide some shelter from the constant wind, and the water here is usually less rough than at Cape Point. The National Park Service Frisco Campground, open

June to September, has a beautiful setting between primary dunes and maritime forest. No amenities. Lifeguard in summer near the campground. *Access to the beach and campground is via a paved road to the east off Hwy. 12, past the Billy Mitchell Airport. Follow signs to Ramp 49. There's adequate parking in lots near the ramp.*

Ocracoke Ferry Beach

Just south of the Hatteras-Ocracoke ferry dock and Hatteras Village is an attractive beach access area. A 100-yard wood ramp leads to a lovely, wide beach. If you have four-wheel-drive or want to walk, you can go about two miles farther south to the South Beach area, which has good surf fishing and a little-used beach. There are no amenities at the beach access area, but bathrooms are available at the ferry dock nearby. No lifeguard. *At the end of Hwy. 12 in Hatteras Village, bear left toward the Hatteras Coast Guard Station. There's parking for about 20 cars near the ramp that leads to the beach.*

HOTELS/INNS/B&Bs

Fishing is still king on Hatteras, and most of the accommodations here are modest motel or efficiency units, designed for anglers and their families.

◆ **Comfort Inn** (moderate). Although a chain motel, this wood-shingled model fits right into the Banks environment. On the Atlantic, with a few beach-view units. Phones in all rooms—a rarity in Hatteras motels. Pool. Light continental breakfast included. *Hwy. 12, Box 1089, Buxton, NC 27920; tel. 919-995-6100, 800-228-1222; fax 919-995-5444.*

◆ **Hatteras Island Resort** (moderate). You wouldn't believe it from the brochure, which makes the place look natty and modern, but this is an old-time Outer Banks fishing resort, with 35 cottages (expensive) and two small motel sections. Popular with families and kids. Clean, well-maintained, but not at all fancy; perhaps a little pricey for what you get. Fishing pier (admission), good restaurant, and pool. Fair swimming on the resort's beach. Best rooms are ocean-view units in the two-story motel section. *Hwy. 12, Box 9, Rodanthe, NC 27968; tel. 919-987-2345, 800-331-6541. Open Apr.-Nov.*

◆ **Outer Banks Motel** (moderate). Well-run, immaculately maintained motel on the beach with a variety of one-, two-, and three-bedroom units, most with ocean views. A fine place to relax; highly recommended. The local owners also rent cottages in the village of Buxton. *Hwy. 12, Box 428, Buxton, NC 27920; tel. 919-995-5601; fax 919-995-5082.*

◆ **Falcon Motel** (inexpensive). Spic-and-span, 35-unit, one-story motel with a pleasant and friendly atmosphere, on the soundside. Small pool. Best units are numbers 24 to 35, closest to the sound. Efficiencies and apartments available. *Hwy. 12, Box 633, Buxton, NC 27920; tel. 919-995-5968, 800-635-6911. Open Mar.-Dec.*

HOUSE RENTALS

No question about it: The best way to go on the Banks is to rent a house. That's really the essence of a true Outer Banks vacation, and one you simply can't experience in a motel. Rates vary depending on the season, the size of the house, and its proximity to the water. In season, small two-bedroom houses not on the water start at about $400 a week. Four-bedroom oceanfront houses rent for $1,200 to $2,000, with more luxurious houses going for much more. Fall and spring rates are about 50 to 60 percent of summer rates.

◆ **Midgett Realty.** Properties in all areas of Hatteras Island. Also has offices in Rodanthe and Avon. *Box 250, Hatteras, NC 27943; tel. 919-986-2841, 800-527-2903. Open daily.*

◆ **Hatteras Realty.** *Box 249, Avon, NC 27915; tel. 919-995-5466, 800-428-8372; fax 919-995-4040. Open daily.*

RESTAURANTS

The fare on Hatteras Island runs toward basic fried and broiled seafood.

◆ **Billy's Fish House** (moderate). The best fried seafood on Hatteras Island. All the food is well prepared and fresh, the prices reasonable, the servings large, and the service friendly. In this casual dockside setting, food is served on plastic plates with plastic tableware (the restaurant says it can't use a dishwashing system because it's too close to the water). *Hwy. 12, Box 265, Buxton, NC 27920; tel. 919-995-5151. Open daily for lunch and dinner Easter-mid-Nov.*

◆ **Great Salt Marsh** (moderate). This California-influenced restaurant attempts to do the unusual (for Hatteras) and frequently succeeds. The soft-shell crab, sautéed and served on a bed of garlicky spinach, is popular. The pan-sautéed crab cakes are full of rich crabmeat, not filler. *Hwy. 12, Buxton, NC 27920; tel. 919-995-6200. Open Mon.-Sat. for lunch and dinner in season, dinner only in spring and fall. Closed late Nov.-early Feb.*

◆ **Quarterdeck** (moderate). This unpretentious spot, featuring all varieties of local seafood plus such landlubber choices as chicken and beef, is the favorite of many locals, although portions are smaller and prices a bit higher than at Billy's. *Hwy. 12, Box 277, Frisco, NC 27936; tel. 919-986-2425. Open daily for lunch and dinner mid-Mar.-late Nov.*

◆ **Tides** (moderate). Well-run and popular, with good service and well-prepared food, it has a homey, family atmosphere. Besides basic seafood, there's chicken, ham, and other dishes. It's also a popular breakfast spot, with pecan pancakes and other goodies. *Hwy. 12, Box 945, Buxton, NC 27920; tel. 919-995-5988. Open daily for breakfast, lunch, and dinner Easter-late Nov.*

◆ **Down Under** (inexpensive). Some of the best fried shrimp on Hatteras. Ocean views in a very casual setting. *Rodanthe Pier at Cape Hatteras Resort, Hwy. 12, Rodanthe, NC 27968; tel. 919-987-2277. Open daily for breakfast, lunch, and dinner Apr.-Nov.*

NIGHTLIFE

After a hard day in the surf or on a charter boat, who has the energy for stepping out? Maybe that's why there are so few places on Hatteras Island for boozing, schmoozing, and cruising.

◆ **Froggy Dog.** Beer, pool, and, most nights in season, live music. *Hwy. 12, Avon, NC 27915; tel. 919-995-4106. Open daily Easter-Labor Day. Closed Jan., and Tue. in the off-season.*

ATTRACTIONS

◆ **Bodie Island Lighthouse.** Shorter than the Cape Hatteras Lighthouse, this is perhaps the least interesting of the four main lighthouses on the Banks. You can't climb it, but it's still worth seeing. Small visitors center. *Hwy. 12, Bodie Island, NC; tel. 919-441-5711. Open daily 9-5 Apr.-Labor Day.*

◆ **Cape Hatteras Lighthouse.** This is the admiral of all U.S. light-houses: 208 feet tall, built with one and a quarter million bricks, the highest brick lighthouse in America, painted like a black-and-white barber pole. During limited hours, and weather per-mitting, you can climb the 268 spiraling steps to the top. From there, the view of Hatteras Island is unmatched, as is the wind. There's a visitors center (tel. 919-995-4474) and a book and gift shop in the former caretaker's quarters. *Lighthouse Rd., Buxton, NC 27920. Open daily 9-5. Hours during which you can climb to the top are 10-2 Easter-Memorial Day and Labor Day-Columbus Day and 9:30-4 Memorial Day-Labor Day. Off Hwy. 12, turn on Lighthouse Rd., not Old Lighthouse Rd.*

◆ **Chicamacomico Lifesaving Station.** The beautiful wood buildings at this Lifesaving Station are being restored and made into a museum honoring the crews who saved thousands of shipwrecked sailors. *Hwy. 12, c/o Chicamacomico Historical Assoc., Box 5, Rodanthe, NC 27968; tel 919-987-1552. Open Tue., Thu., and Sat. 11-5 May-Oct.*

◆ **Herbert C. Bonner Bridge.** One of the best views of this dra-matic bridge is from the parking lot at the southeast side of Oregon Inlet.

◆ **Shipwrecks.** Hundreds of ships have been lost on these wild shores. A popular memento is a map to the wrecks of the Outer Banks, available at most tourist shops. Most of the ships are still here, buried under the sand. After a big storm is the best time to find one newly exposed. The only wreck you are always sure to be able to see is that of the *Laura A. Barnes* at Coquina Beach.

SHOPPING

With a few exceptions, shopping on Hatteras places function before form. It's mostly groceries, bait and tackle, beach sup-plies, and some gifts.

◆ **Browning Artworks.** High-quality crafts: pottery, glass, wood, jewelry, photography, paintings. *Hwy. 12, Frisco, NC 27936; tel. 919-995-5538. Open Mon.-Sat.*

◆ **Buxton Village Books.** Intelligent selection, including books of regional interest. *Hwy. 12, Box 829, Buxton, NC 27920; tel. 919-995-4240. Open daily Easter-Dec. Closed Sun. Jan.-Easter.*

◆ **Kitty Hawk Kites.** Hey, if you come to the Banks, you've got to fly a kite, and this branch of the Nags Head minichain has them all, from cheap to wow. *Hwy. 12, Avon, NC 27915; tel. 919-995-6060. Open daily Mar.-Nov. Reduced days and hours in winter; check locally.*

BEST FOOD SHOPS

◆ **Food Lion.** This chain supermarket has the best selection of grocery items on Hatteras, including wine, beer, and mixers. Accepts out-of-town checks. *Food Lion Shopping Center, Hwy. 12, Avon, NC 27915; tel. 919-995-4488. Open daily.*

SANDWICHES: ◆ **Frisco Sandwich Shop.** *Hwy. 12, Frisco, NC 27936; tel. 919-995-5535. Open daily in summer and Mon.-Sat. the rest of the year.*

SEAFOOD: ◆ **Buxton Seafood.** *Hwy. 12, Buxton, NC 27920; tel. 919-995-5085. Open Mon.-Sat. in season. Under the Buxton water tower.*

BAKERY: ◆ **Beach Bites Deli & Bakery.** *Food Lion Shopping Center, Hwy. 12, Avon, NC 27915; tel. 919-995-6683. Open daily in season.*

ICE CREAM: ◆ **Cool Wave Ice Cream Shoppe.** *Hwy. 12, Buxton, NC 27920; tel. 919-995-6366. Open Mon.-Sat. Easter-mid-Oct.*

BEVERAGES: ◆ **ABC Store.** The only place on Hatteras to buy liquor. No wine, beer, or mixers. *Osprey Shopping Center, Hwy. 12, Buxton, NC 27910; tel. 919-995-5532. Open Mon.-Sat.*

SPORTS

Fishing and surfing, surfing and fishing. That's Hatteras, with a little Windsurfing on the side. Bicycling? Forget it, or go to Ocracoke. Wreck-diving and kayaking are growing sports here. Golfers and tennis buffs are out of luck. And yes, Henrietta, you can gallop a horse down a deserted beach.

FISHING

Hatteras is heaven for the avid angler. The best fishing for red drum (channel bass), mackerel, bluefish, and trout is usually between Labor Day and November and again from March to May. Pier fishing on one of three piers on Hatteras Island (at Rodanthe, Avon, and Frisco) follows roughly the same seasons. Crabbing is also good off the piers. Charter boat fishing is big for those after marlin and other billfish in the Gulf Stream. For an updated recorded weather and fishing report, call 800-446-6262.

◆ **Oregon Inlet Fishing Center.** Home to 25 to 30 charter and headboats. *Box 533, Manteo, NC 27954; tel. 919-441-6301, 800-272-5199. Open Easter-Thanksgiving. Hwy. 12 at Oregon Inlet.*

◆ **The Fishin' Hole.** Classic tackle-and-bait shop with the slogan "If they swallow it, we got it." *Hwy. 12, Box 25, Salvo, NC 27972; tel. 919-987-2351. Open daily. "Not around too much" Jan.-Feb.*

BOATING

Pamlico Sound is the ideal environment for skating around the water on a Windsurfer. Canadian Hole, between Avon and Buxton, is *the* spot. Consistent winds make it one of the best in the country. *On Hwy. 12 just south of Ramp 38 and 1/2 mi. north of Buxton. Large parking lot on sound side fills up quickly during the summer.*

◆ **Teach's Lair Marina.** Charter boats, headboats, bait and tackle. *Hwy. 12, Hatteras Village, NC 27943; tel. 919-986-2460. Open daily.*

SURFING

The water off Cape Hatteras Lighthouse at Buxton draws surfers from all over the East Coast. The best action here is June through November.

◆ **Natural Art Surf Shop.** Sales and rentals. *Hwy. 12, Buxton, NC 27920. For a 24-hr. surf report, call Natural Art's surf line, 919-995-4646. Open daily. Closed Jan.-Feb.*

DIVING

For those serious and tough enough to take poor visibility and cold water, wreck diving can be fascinating.

◆ **Hatteras Divers.** *Box 213, Hatteras, NC 27943; tel. 919-986-2557. Open daily in season.*

HORSEBACK RIDING

◆ **Buxton Stables.** Trail rides in Buxton Woods and on the beach. *Hwy. 12, Box 545, Buxton, NC 27920; tel. 919-995-4659. Open daily in season.*

NATURE

Nearly 400 bird species have been sighted within Cape Hatteras National Seashore, with Pea Island National Wildlife Refuge—

the park within the park—being the aviary hot spot. To see migratory shorebirds in the fall and spring, the best areas are Pea and Bodie islands and Cape Hatteras Point. Most resident land birds are to be found at Buxton Woods, with migrating land birds best seen in southern Hatteras and at Pea Island.

◆ **Pea Island National Wildlife Refuge.** The refuge's nearly 6,000 acres provide a stop on the Atlantic flyway. Altogether, more than 270 species of birds have been spotted. There are several nature trails, including the popular North Pond Trail. A visitors center is staffed with helpful volunteers and has new displays on the area. *U.S. Fish and Wildlife Service, Box 1969, Manteo, NC 27954; tel. 919-987-2394. Visitors center open daily 9-4 Easter-Thanksgiving; reduced days and hours at other times.*

◆ **National Park Service Campgrounds.** Three campgrounds close to the ocean. All operate on a first-come, first-served basis; reservations cannot be made by phone or mail. *For information, contact the National Park Service (tel. 919-473-2111). Campgrounds are only open seasonally, usually May-Sep., but the schedule changes yearly.*

TOURIST INFORMATION

◆ **Cape Hatteras National Seashore.** The National Park Service provides information about educational programs in the national seashore, as well as information on the three campgrounds. *Box 675, Manteo, NC 27954; tel. 919-473-2111. Open Mon.-Fri. 8-5. Recorded information 24 hr. daily. Park visitors center at Cape Hatteras Lighthouse (tel. 919-995-4474) open daily 9-5. Park visitors center at Bodie Island Lighthouse (tel. 919-441-5711) open daily 9-5 Easter-Columbus Day.*

◆ **Dare County Tourist Bureau.** *704 U.S. Hwy. 64/264, Box 399, Manteo, NC 27954; tel. 919-473-2138, 800-446-6262. Open Mon.-Fri. 8:30-5 and Sat.-Sun. 9-5. Closed weekends in the off-season. Recorded information 24 hr. daily year-round at the 800 number. Also operates a welcome center at the entrance to Cape Hatteras National Seashore at Whalebone Junction; open daily 9-5 in summer and Thu.-Sun 9-3 in spring and fall; closed late Oct.-Easter.*

CHAPTER 4

Ocracoke Island

Beauty	A+
Swimming	B+
Sand	B+
Hotels/Inns/B&Bs	B
House rentals	B
Restaurants	B
Nightlife	C
Attractions	B-
Shopping	C-
Sports	B
Nature	A

Ocracoke is still stubbornly its own place—eccentric, tuned to the ancient music of sea and sky. It's not a bit like one of those resort islands created by real-estate developers, with golf courses, gift shops, and gated communities—and thank heavens for that. If you're a collector of genuine islands, Ocracoke will likely occupy a special place in your collection. Its beaches, stretching for 16 miles along the Atlantic,

HOW TO GET THERE

◆ Access to Ocracoke is by ferry only. Travel time to Ocracoke is about 4 hr. from Norfolk and about 6 1/2 hr. from Raleigh, including ferry crossing times—not counting waits and delays. If coming from the mainland, you have a choice of two ferries, one leaving from Swan Quarter and one from Cedar Island.

◆ The 28-vehicle Swan Quarter ferry (tel. 919-926-1111 or 800-773-1094 in Swanquarter; 919-928-3841 in Ocra-coke) runs twice a day year-round, departing for Ocra-coke at 9:30 a.m. and 4 p.m. It takes 2 1/2 hr. to cross Pamlico Sound. To get to the ferry landing, from Raleigh take U.S. Hwy. 64 to Zebulon, then U.S. Hwy. 264 through Greenville and Washington to Swan Quarter, a total distance of about 160 mi. One way, the ferry is $10 for a car or truck and $20 to $30 for RVs and cars with trailers, depending on length.

◆ The 50-vehicle Cedar Island ferry (tel. 919-225-3551, 800-856-0343) has 8 crossings daily from 7 a.m. to 8:30 p.m. May-Oct., with 4 to 6 crossings at other times of the year. Crossing time is about 2 1/2 hr. To get to the ferry landing from Raleigh take U.S. Hwy. 70 to Cedar Island, a distance of about 175 mi. (U.S. Hwy. 70 becomes NC Hwy. 12 at Cedar Island). Cost for a car or truck is $10 one way. RVs and cars with trailers are $20 to $30.

◆ If you're already on the Outer Banks, you can reach Ocracoke via a 30-vehicle free ferry (tel. 919-928-3841, 800-345-1665) that departs Hatteras Village at the southern end of Hatteras Island (*see* Chapter 3 for directions to Hatteras) at least every half hour from 7 a.m. to 7 p.m. and at 5 a.m., 6 a.m., and hourly from 8 p.m. to midnight May-Oct. From Nov.-Apr., the ferry leaves Hatteras hourly from 5 a.m. to 10 p.m. Crossing time is 40 min. You arrive at the north end of Ocracoke Island; Ocracoke village is about 12 mi. south on NC Hwy. 12. Actual ferry schedules may, and often do, vary from these published schedules. Although additional ferries may be added, during peak summer weekends several hundred cars may be waiting to board.

◆ Reservations are not available for the Hatteras-Ocracoke ferry, which operates on a first-come, first-served basis; reservations for the other ferries can be made up to 30 days in advance and are a must during the summer, advisable at other times. For recorded information on all North Carolina ferries, call 800-BY-FERRY (800-293-3779).

◆ By air, Raleigh and Norfolk are the closest airports with jet service by major carriers. There is a small general-aviation airstrip just north of Ocracoke village, and the Manteo Airport, about 2 1/2 hr. north, has limited commuter service.

are among the most-pristine in all of eastern America. More than 85 percent of the island, as part of the Cape Hatteras National Seashore, is protected from development. Even on the busiest day of summer, you can find a spot where your only companions will be pelicans and ospreys, not humans. The shelling, fishing, and swimming are excellent.

The island's only settlement, the village of Ocracoke, sits by the edge of a sheltered harbor called Silver Lake ("The Creek" to many locals). It's the right size for a bicycle or walking tour. You can't miss the Ocracoke Lighthouse, the second-oldest operating lighthouse in the country. With its white picket fence and village setting, it's a favorite of photographers.

The village is just imperfect enough to avoid being quaint. A four-story brick motel and an overblown condo building break the line of weathered wooden houses and live oaks lining the harbor, jarring the eye. Here and there a gimcrack souvenir shop reminds you that—in season, at least—tourism is the island's number one industry, or a rusting mobile home suggests that it's not easy to make a living here. Some of the village's streets are still unpaved. There are no fast-food restaurants, no movie theaters, no Wal-Marts—and, sometimes, no water or power, because water shortages and electrical outages are common.

An island's absorbing interest, of course, derives from its people. Whereas many other islands have been overrun by snowbirds and second-homers, about one-half of the 800 resident Ocracokers are descendants of the original 18th-century settlers. Even the language of native Ocracokers is distinctive, because of the traditional isolation of the island. Some of the speech patterns—such as adding an *a* to verbs, as in "the wind's ablowing"—can be traced back to Elizabethan England.

While proud of their unique community, Ocracoke residents are generally friendly and welcoming to outsiders and visitors. This is in marked contrast to Ocracoke's most famous short-term resident, Edward Teach, better known as Blackbeard, a murderous rascal now claimed proudly by dozens of villages and resorts along the coast in this region. The pirate used Ocracoke as his base in 1718, and it was at what is now called Teach's Hole, not far from Ocracoke Village, that he was killed in a battle with two British warships.

The island is a popular visitor destination from around Easter to October, with the busiest season lasting from Memorial Day to Labor Day, when couples and families pour into "the Nantucket of the South." As more and more people discover its charm, Ocracoke is becoming increasingly busy, and advance reservations, especially on weekends and anytime in the summer, are strongly advised.

Ocracoke remains special, however, and most visitors pray it doesn't change. As you board the ferry to leave the island, you may be one of those thinking, "I hope I'm the last one to discover Ocracoke."

BEACHES

From the Hatteras ferry landing at the northeast tip of the island, down to the edge of Ocracoke Village and then to Southpoint, southwest of the town, ranges one of the finest ocean beaches in the East. It's about 16 miles long, all

Beauty	A
Swimming	B+
Sand	B+
Amenities	D

undeveloped and unspoiled, part of the Cape Hatteras National Seashore. The water quality is among the highest of any beach in the country. You won't believe how beautiful it is.

The national seashore here is essentially one long beach with a series of different access points, all on Highway 12. Off-road vehicle access is available at ramps (from north to south) 59, 67, 68, 70, and 72. The easiest access points on foot are Ramp 59, near the Hatteras ferry terminal at the north end of the island; across from the Pony Pen; near the National Park Service Ocracoke Campground at Ramp 68; and at the Ocracoke Day Use Area near Ramp 70. The major beach access points below are listed from north to south. There are no beaches on the sound side.

Swimming: The water is very clean, if cool. Water temperatures get above the high 70s only occasionally in July and August. From late September to May, for most people the ocean is too cool for comfort. In summer, swimming is excellent at many spots, although extreme caution is advised because of rips and undertows. As with all barrier islands, the ocean beaches of Ocracoke are unstable, constantly moving and changing shape with the winds and tidal surges. No lifeguard in most areas.

Sand: Most beaches here are wide, with light tan sand.

Sports: The long and lightly peopled beaches of Ocracoke are wonderful for all the usual beach sports—swimming, bodysurfing, kite flying. Surf fishing is good to excellent, especially in spring and fall. Shelling is best at the north end of the island.

Amenities: Very limited.

Parking: Parking is adequate in free paved lots at most beach access points. But don't damage the fragile ecology by parking on the road and walking across the dunes.

Ocracoke North End

The beaches on the northeast tip of the island are the widest on Ocracoke, with the backshore at times several hundred yards inland. This is also a prime shelling beach. No lifeguard. *Look for the first parking area on the ocean side south of the Hatteras ferry terminal, near Ramp 59.*

Airport Day-Use Area

This is the most popular, and safest, swimming area on Ocracoke. A 500-foot boardwalk leads over the dunes. Portable toilets are available. In the past, the Park Service has provided lifeguards here during the summer, either on a permanent or a roving basis, but budget constraints make the future of the lifeguards uncertain; check locally. The wave action is more gentle here than on some other parts of the Banks, and the beach is wide and sandy. *About 3 mi. north of Ocracoke Village; look for the airstrip and the large parking lot on the Atlantic side near Ramp 70. The 90-vehicle paved lot is close to the beach.*

Southpoint Beach

Southpoint is backcountry Ocracoke. The shelling and fishing are excellent, the picnicking terrific, and the people few. The difficulty is access. You can navigate the three miles of Southpoint Road only by four-wheel-drive or on foot. Don't try it with your family sedan or you'll owe a hefty towing fee. This is a primitive area with no changing areas or bathrooms. No lifeguard. *Leaving Ocracoke Village on Hwy. 12, look for the first sandy road to the right beyond the sheriff's office. Park anywhere you won't get stuck.*

HOTELS/INNS/B&Bs

Ocracoke has a nice, if small, cross-section of places to stay: lodges, B&Bs, old inns, and modern motels. All are in or near the village of Ocracoke. None is on a beach, since the island's beaches are all national seashore, but most are close to Silver Lake Harbor, on the sound. Ocracoke hotels have character rather than pretension. They are heavily booked in the summer, so reserve well ahead. Write to the post office box numbers given below—Ocracoke does not have street mail delivery, and some businesses and houses do not have formal street addresses. Even those accommodations that usually stay open year-round may suddenly decide to close if business is dead in January or February—always call ahead to be sure.

◆ **Berkeley Center Country Inn** (moderate). Rustic accommodations in cedar- or juniper-paneled rooms in a former hunting lodge, some with shared baths. On more than three acres of grounds. *Water Plant Rd. (Box 220), Ocracoke, NC 27960; tel. 919-928-5911. Open Apr.-Nov.*

◆ **Boyette House** (moderate). A locally owned motel, meticulously clean and maintained, with friendly, on-site management. Not directly on the water, but within walking distance of the harbor and village shops and restaurants. The original motel building has 12 pleasant rooms. A new building, opened in mid-1995, features 10 attractive rooms and two suites, some with steam baths, whirlpools, and private porches. Suite 25 is the jewel, bright and sunny and with a view of the harbor in the distance. *Hwy. 12 (Box 39), Ocracoke, NC 27960; tel. 919-928-4261. Closed for a short period in winter—call for exact dates.*

◆ **Crews Inn Bed & Breakfast** (moderate). This comfortable B&B in a rambling 1908 home is set in a shady grove of cedars, pines, and live oaks, about 100 yards from the harbor. It is owned by Ocracoke native Alton Ballance, author of *Ocracokers*, a well-regarded history of the island. The best room in the house is the Captain's Quarters, on the third floor, the only room with air-conditioning (other rooms have fans). No children under ten. *Back Rd. (Box 460), Ocracoke, NC 27960; tel. 919-928-7011.*

◆ **Island Inn** (moderate). This old favorite retains its atmospheric charms, but it's getting a bit scruffy in spots and needs refurbishing. The original inn building, rather than a newer motel section, is the place to be, especially in one of the rooms with king-size beds. Good location, within a short walk of the village center and the Ocracoke Lighthouse. Heated pool. No children in some sections.

$ 160 +89/nt   R~ 101+102   *June 2024*
hot tub

Hwy. 12 (Box 9), Ocracoke, NC 27960; tel. 919-928-4351.

◆ **Silver Lake Motel** (moderate). If you want village convenience *suite +* and harbor views, it's a good choice. There are two buildings: a *from room* rustic 20-room motel built in 1983, with casual, none-too-fancy *couch* rooms, and a newer building with 12 suites, nicely done in red- *+* wood paneling and wicker (suites are expensive). Prime choices *bedroom* are the hot tub suites on the second and third floors of the new section, especially rooms 301 and 201, featuring unbeatable views of Silver Lake from the hammocks on the suites' porches. *Hwy. 12 (Box 303), Ocracoke, NC, 27960; tel. 919-928-5721.*

◆ **Sand Dollar** (inexpensive). Clean, comfortable, unpretentious accommodations; now owned by Ocracoke native Roger Garrish. Located in a quiet, residential area of the village. The new pool is a plus. *Circle Dr. (Box 461), Ocracoke, NC 27960; tel. 919-928-5571.*

HOUSE RENTALS

Renting a cottage is the ideal way to enjoy the casual, laid-back atmosphere of Ocracoke. And the good news is that rentals here are generally less expensive than in other areas of the Outer Banks. Summer rates range from $400 a week for a small cottage on a village side street to $1,200 or more for a four-bedroom upmarket beach home with a view of Pamlico Sound. The bad news is that, unlike rentals in most of the rest of the Banks, few here are on the water or the beach, since most of the island's ocean and sound frontage is national seashore. Note that the tap water in some rental homes is from ground wells and unpotable.

◆ **Ocracoke Island Realty.** *Box 238-A, Ocracoke, NC 27960; tel. 919-928-6261. Open daily.*

◆ **Sharon Miller Realty.** *Box 264, Ocracoke, NC 27960; tel. 919-928-5711; fax 919-928-1065. Open Mon.-Sat.*

RESTAURANTS

For an island with seasonal tourism and a small resident base, Ocracoke has a surprising number of good restaurants. One local specialty, served at most restaurants, is Outer Banks-style clam chowder. Something of an acquired taste, it features clams in their own broth, rather than with milk or tomatoes, plus potatoes, celery, and onions. You can't buy a rum and OcraCoke on the island—

restaurants can serve only beer and wine. However, the village has a state liquor store, and a few restaurants permit "brown-bagging" (bringing your own bottle). Most restaurants close in winter or during slow periods. Check locally for exact dates and hours.

◆ **Back Porch** (moderate). A long-time island favorite consistently enjoyable for fresh seafood in sophisticated combinations. Crab beignets, smoked local fish, and crab cakes with pepper sauce are among the specialties. Eat on the screened porch or in the juniper-paneled dining room. *Back Rd., Ocracoke, NC 27960; tel. 919-928-6401. Open daily for dinner Mar.-Oct.*

◆ **Cafe Atlantic** (moderate). This stylish spot gives the Back Porch a run for its money in the best-on-the-island category. It specializes in grilled and sautéed local seafood. Casual, attractive two-level setting, with a light contemporary feel and plenty of air-conditioning. *Hwy. 12, Ocracoke, NC 27960; tel. 919-928-4861. Open daily for lunch and dinner late Mar.-late Oct.*

◆ **Creekside** (inexpensive). New in spring 1995, the Creekside opened to positive reviews, offering sandwiches, soups, burgers (including an oyster burger), and seafood at very reasonable prices. For something a little different, try the shrimp salad pita or the blackened chicken sandwich. The restaurant has a second-floor location near Silver Lake Harbor. *Hwy. 12, Ocracoke, NC 27960; tel. 919-928-3606. Open daily for lunch and dinner mid-Apr.-late Oct.*

◆ **Howard's Pub & Raw Bar** (inexpensive). This popular spot serves some of the Outer Banks' best burgers, sandwiches, basic seafood, and beer in a friendly, casual setting. *Hwy. 12, Ocracoke, NC 27960; tel. 919-928-4441. Open daily for lunch, dinner, and late-night snacks.*

◆ **Pony Island Motel Restaurant** (inexpensive). Basic fried local seafood. The restaurant will even cook the fish you catch, but clean it before you bring it in. This is also where the locals go for breakfast, with Pony potatoes (hash browns with salsa and cheese) a favorite. *Hwy. 12, Ocracoke, NC 27960; tel. 919-928-5701. Open daily for breakfast, lunch, and dinner in summer; reduced hours other periods. Closed Nov.-Mar.*

NIGHTLIFE

It's limited on Ocracoke, consisting mostly of a beer or soft drink, conversation about fishing or the weather, and maybe some semipro music by a local group. An alternative is to join a beach party. You don't need an invitation—just look for the light from a fire. Usually, public beach parties are held near Ramp 70 by the Ocracoke airstrip. BYOB.

◆ **Howard's Pub & Raw Bar.** Big-screen TV, lots of beer, and, on weekends, live music starting around 10 p.m. Howard's serves food later than any other spot on Ocracoke—usually until around 2 a.m. *Hwy. 12, Ocracoke, NC 27960; tel. 919-928-4441. Open daily.*

◆ **Jolly Roger.** Across the street from the Silver Lake Motel, the Jolly Roger is right on the water. Beer and wine, light menu, live music at sunset some nights. *Hwy. 12, Ocracoke, NC 27960; tel. 919-928-3703. Open mid-Apr.-Nov.*

ATTRACTIONS

◆ **Ocracoke Lighthouse.** If any lighthouse can be called charming, it's this one. Nestled behind a white picket fence in a residential area on the south side of Silver Lake, it's just 76 feet tall. A beacon to sailors since 1823, it's the second-oldest operating lighthouse in the States. *Point Rd., Ocracoke, NC 27960; for information, contact Ocracoke Island Visitors Center, tel. 919-928-4531. Lighthouse and keeper's quarters are not currently open to the public, but you can view and photograph them daily from the grounds. No formal hours. 1/4 mi. from Hwy. 12; turn at the Island Inn.*

◆ **Wild Pony Pens.** Wild ponies, descendants of Spanish mustangs likely freed during shipwrecks, have been on Ocracoke since at least the 17th century. At one time the herd numbered in the hundreds. Today, there are about 25 ponies in a fenced, 170-acre enclosure. Most days, you can see them from a platform beside the pen. Picnic tables here and across the highway. *Hwy. 12, Ocracoke, NC 27960; contact Ocracoke Island Visitors Center, tel. 919-928-4531. Open daily, no fixed hours. About 7 mi. north of Ocracoke Village.*

SHOPPING

You don't come to Ocracoke for the shopping. Locals take the ferry to Hatteras to shop for groceries at the Food Lion in Avon or for household goods at the Wal-Mart in Kitty Hawk. However, the village and environs have a number of unusual shops of interest to visitors. Most are clustered in the village center at Silver Lake and on Highway 12 as you enter the village.

◆ **Community Store.** A general store with groceries, videos, and what-have-you. This old-fashioned place has been a center of community life on Ocracoke since 1918. Stop by and pet Ollie the cat. *Hwy. 12 (Box 432), Ocracoke, NC 27960; tel. 919-928-3321. Open Mon.-Sat.*

◆ **Community Square Shops.** For T-shirts, fudge, gifts, and other tourist necessities, this group of shops is a good bet. *Hwy. 12 (Box 432), Ocracoke, NC 27960; tel. 919-928-3321. Open daily in season.*

◆ **Village Craftsmen.** Craftsperson Philip Howard offers a selection of his own and other local crafts, pottery, and musical instruments including handmade dulcimers. *248 Howard St., Ocracoke Village; tel. 919-928-5541, 800-648-9743. Open Mon.-Sat. except Jan. (if you're there in Jan.: "Just knock and we'll let you in because we're probably straightening up the shop").*

BEST FOOD SHOPS

ICE CREAM: ◆ **The Slushy Stand.** *Hwy. 12, Ocracoke, NC 27960; tel. 919-928-1878. Open daily Apr.-Nov.*

BEVERAGES: ◆ **ABC Store.** This state-run store is the only place to buy liquor on the island. No beer, wine, or mixers. *Hwy. 12, Ocracoke, NC 27960; tel. 919-928-3281. Open Mon.-Sat. Next to the Ocracoke Variety Store.*

SPORTS
FISHING

Surf fishing on Ocracoke is excellent at many spots along the miles of national seashore beach. No license is needed. The best fishing for red drum (channel bass), mackerel, bluefish, and trout is usually between Labor Day and November and from March to May. You can also charter a boat for a half or full day of fishing in Pamlico Sound, Ocracoke Inlet, or the Gulf Stream in the Atlantic. Clamming and crabbing are also popular.

◆ **Tradewinds Bait & Tackle.** Bait, rod rentals, fishing supplies. *Hwy. 12, Ocracoke, NC 27960; tel. 919-928-5491. Open daily Apr.-Nov. Near the Sheriff's Office.*

◆ ***Miss Kathleen.*** Traditional wooden boat captained by Ronnie

O'Neal, a native Ocracoker. Half- or full-day charters. *Ocracoke, NC 27960; tel. 919-928-4841. Operates daily during fishing seasons, weather permitting.*

BOATING

Silver Lake is a picture-book harbor. The marina here is operated by the National Park Service. There are no slips, just tie-up facilities, and you can't make reservations—it's first-come, first-served. Kayaking is a growing eco-sport here.

◆ **Ride the Wind Surf Shop.** Sales and rentals of kayaks; guided kayak nature tours. Also sales and rentals of surfing equipment. *Hwy. 12, Ocracoke, NC 27960; tel. 919-928-6311. Open daily early spring-late Nov.; reduced days and hours in winter.*

◆ **Westwind and Barpoint.** Randy Austin is one of the National Park Service-licensed operators offering boat trips to Portsmouth Island, with its now-deserted village, on Cape Lookout National Seashore (*see* Chapter 5). Scheduled trips in summer cost $15 per person round-trip; on-demand trips off-season are $40 for one or two people, $15 for each additional passenger. *Ocracoke, NC 27960; tel. 919-928-4361. Scheduled trips operate daily Jun.-Aug.; other times, call to arrange a trip.*

SURFING

Surfing is just okay on Ocracoke—not as good as around Buxton on Hatteras (for equipment rentals, *see* "Boating").

DIVING

There are more than 600 wrecks off the Outer Banks, and storms and shifting ocean currents uncover new ones regularly. If you dive, be prepared for possible poor visibility and cold water.

◆ **Ocracoke Divers & Marina Supplies.** PADI-certified divers. *Oyster Creek Marina, Ocracoke, NC 27960; tel. 919-928-1471. Open daily.*

BICYCLING

Ocracoke is one of the best places on the North Carolina coast for biking. The village streets are quiet and safe, and although there are no bike trails on the 12-mile stretch of Route 12 along the beaches, the relatively light traffic makes it safer than biking on Hatteras.

◆ **Beach Outfitters.** Rentals. *At Ocracoke Island Realty, Hwy. 12 (Box 238-A), Ocracoke, NC 27960; tel. 919-928-6261. Open daily.*

NATURE

Of the 5,500 acres of Ocracoke Island, all but 775 are part of the Cape Hatteras National Seashore. Ocracoke's appeal, like that of the island of St. John in the U.S. Virgin Islands, is that it remains mostly in a natural state. The beaches are wild, the landscape beautiful in its windswept spareness, with stunted junipers and pines. Ocracoke is on the Atlantic flyway for migrating birds, and scores of species can be seen in fall and spring. In early summer, pelagic turtles lay their eggs at the back of beaches. Atlantic bottle-nosed dolphins and whales can be spotted in the ocean off Ocracoke's shores.

Beachcombing and shelling are best right after a storm, especially in winter. If you tire of sandy beaches, try Hammock Hills Nature Trail, a three-quarter-mile path near the National Park Service campground (*see* below). It winds through several ecosystems, including dunes, salt marsh, and low maritime forest.

◆ **National Park Service Ocracoke Campground.** It has 136 campsites on level, sandy ground, about three miles from Ocracoke Village on the ocean side. It's a beautiful area, but there's little shade from the sun or protection from the strong winds that often sweep across the area. This is the only Park Service campground on the Outer Banks that accepts reservations. *Hwy. 12, Ocracoke, NC 27960; tel. 919-928-6671. Open late May-early Sep.*

TOURIST INFORMATION

◆ **Ocracoke Island Visitors Center.** Information about Ocracoke and the Cape Hatteras National Seashore. In summer, there are interpretative programs at the center and the small adjoining outdoor theater. *Hwy. 12, Ocracoke, NC 27960; tel. 919-928-4531. Open daily 9-5 Easter-Oct.; usually closes for 1 hr. at lunch. Located next to the toll ferry dock at the edge of Ocracoke Village.*

CHAPTER 5

Cape Lookout & Beaufort

Beauty	A
Swimming	C
Sand	B
Hotels/Inns/B&Bs	B
House rentals	D
Restaurants	B
Nightlife	C-
Attractions	B
Shopping	C+
Sports	B
Nature	A

This destination offers two very different vacation experiences: solitary time on the pristine but not easily accessible barrier islands of the Cape Lookout National Seashore and comfortable enjoyment of the charming seaside village of Beaufort.

Beaufort (pronounced *BO-ford*) is a comfortable home base for exploring the decidedly untouristy "Downeast" area—a squiggly peninsula that juts

HOW TO GET THERE

◆ Beaufort, gateway to Downeast and Cape Lookout, is about 3 hr. by car southeast of Raleigh and about 2 hr. northeast of Wilmington. From Raleigh, take U.S. Hwy. 70 east about 145 mi. From Wilmington, take U.S. Hwy. 17 north to Jacksonville, NC, then NC Hwy. 24 east to U.S. Hwy. 70 east to Beaufort—a total distance of 105 mi. An alternate route from Wilmington is U.S. Hwy. 17 north to NC Hwy. 172 across Camp Lejeune Marine Base, connecting with NC Hwy. 24 east and then U.S. Hwy. 70 east to Beaufort.

◆ From the Outer Banks, take the Ocracoke-Cedar Island ferry from Ocracoke Village. Crossing time is about 2 1/2 hr. Reservations are a must in summer and advised year-round (tel. 919-225-3551, 800-856-0343; for recorded information on all North Carolina ferries, call 800-293-3779). From the ferry landing at Cedar Island, drive about 35 mi. southwest on NC Hwy. 12 and then take U.S. Hwy. 70 west to Beaufort.

◆ Access to Cape Lookout National Seashore is by boat only. Private ferries, sanctioned by the National Park Service, operate from Harkers Island and the towns of Atlantic and Davis, with rates starting at $12 per person round-trip (call the Visitors Center at 919-728-2250). Private boats are available from Beaufort.

◆ By air, there is very limited commuter service at the Morehead City/Beaufort airport; Raleigh-Durham is the closest major airport.

into Pamlico Sound some 30 miles northeast of mainland North Carolina—and for day-trips via car and ferry to the wild beaches of Cape Lookout, the chain of barrier islands stretching 55 miles along the North Carolina coast just south of the Outer Banks, from Ocracoke Inlet to Beaufort Inlet.

Beaufort itself has no beaches, but its harbor offers boat access to the Cape Lookout National Seashore and to protected soundside beaches on the Rachel Carson Component of the North Carolina National Estuarine Research Reserve, a big name for a small group of islands where you can spot more than 150 species of birds and a number of wild horses. Another nearby beach is Fort Macon on Bogue Banks (*see* Chapter 6).

Cape Lookout today is much the way it was before Europeans came to America. There are no bridges to the islands, no improved roads once you get there, only a few off-road vehicles brought over by ferry, no place to stay except in a few rustic fishing cabins, no restaurants, no shops, and only the stars and mosquitoes for nighttime companionship. What you will find aplenty is terrific fishing, beaches where you can often walk for miles and never see another person, beautiful windswept Atlantic vistas, and some of the best shelling on the East Coast. Exploring Cape Lookout takes some energy, grit, time, and money, but it's worth the effort.

The Cape Lookout National Seashore includes, from north to south, Portsmouth Island, North Core Banks, South Core Banks, and Shackleford Banks. Portsmouth Island, with its abandoned seaside village now undergoing restoration, and the Core Banks are windswept, mostly flat islands with low dunes and relatively little vegetation. Shackleford Banks, which, unlike the other Cape Lookout islands lies east to west rather than north to south, forms the last major link in the chain and, because of its different orientation to the prevailing winds, has large dunes and maritime forest.

A former fishing village, Beaufort now successfully walks the fine line between charming and touristy. It is the natural habitat of B&Bs and yachts. The third-oldest town in North Carolina and the county seat of Carteret County, Beaufort has a well-preserved historic district and one of the best maritime museums in America—with free admission to boot. The town's waterfront—on a narrow channel, Taylor Creek—has been developed with shops and restaurants. Front Street, the main street along the harbor, buzzes with visitors in summer and on spring and fall weekends. The 20-block historic district that adjoins the harbor is perfect for walking or biking. Outside the historic area, however, Beaufort quickly becomes much like any other small town, with convenience stores and gas stations.

Next door to Beaufort is Morehead City, a working seaport with modern motels and hotels (less expensive than Beaufort's inns), seafood restaurants, and suburban shopping. The town, the largest in Carteret County, has plenty of water-front ambience but, like Beaufort, no beaches to speak of.

If you drive to Downeast—confusingly located *northeast* of Beaufort—to catch a ferry to the Cape Lookout National Seashore, you'll soon be in an area where fishing is still serious business and the main shopping is for duck decoys. The names of the towns here on the Downeast peninsula may give you an idea of the kind of rough-hewn, New Englandish place this is: Sea Level, Atlantic, Bettie, Otway (named for a pirate), Harkers Island, and Gloucester.

BEACHES
CAPE LOOKOUT LIGHTHOUSE BEACH

The Cape Lookout National Seashore has mile after mile of wild, desolate beach frontage on the Atlantic side, and few shores on the East Coast can compare in raw natural beauty. If you're looking for solitude, this is a great destination.

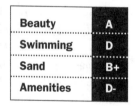

Beauty	A
Swimming	D
Sand	B+
Amenities	D-

Other than a few Park Service volunteers, no one lives here. Even on the busiest day in summer, if you take a short hike along the seashore you will soon find yourself alone.

Caution is advised for anyone visiting the seashore, because nature rules here. Winds can be strong, and since there is little shade, the sun can burn you quickly. During tropical storms in summer and fall or the nor'easters that blow in during fall and winter, waves from the Atlantic can rush over parts of narrow islands, right to the sound.

The main day beach destination from Beaufort is Cape Lookout Lighthouse. This has private ferry service, either scheduled on larger boats or on smaller boats on a walk-in, on-demand basis, from Harkers Island. Because Cape Lookout has no paved roads and few other services, only those doing primitive camping or serious fishing are likely to visit areas other than the Cape Lookout Lighthouse and Portsmouth Village (for information on Portsmouth, *see* "Attractions," below). *Most day visitors to Cape Lookout take a National Park concession ferry from Harkers Island to Cape Lookout Lighthouse. Cost for the ferry is $12 per person round-trip, and there usually is a parking fee of about $4 per car to park at the ferry landing. The boats dock on the sound side, where a boardwalk leads across the island to the Atlantic beaches and the lighthouse. Private companies also offer both four-wheel-drive tours of the area and drop-off/pick-up service to the Cape Lookout point. Private ferries and boats also run from the town of Davis to South Core Banks south of Drum Inlet, from Atlantic to North Core Banks, and from Ocracoke Island to Portsmouth Village. Some ferries from Davis and Atlantic can carry four-wheel-drive vehicles. Access is also possible via boat from Beaufort. Ferry operators change frequently; for current information, call the Cape Lookout National Seashore Visitors Center at Harkers Island (tel. 919-728-2250).*

Swimming: We don't recommend it here. The nearly constant winds and shifting sand bottoms create rip currents and undertows, and signs warn that you swim at your own risk. Keep in mind that on this isolated seashore, there will very likely be no one nearby to help or hear the cries of a swimmer in trouble. No lifeguard.

Sand: The light brown to gold sand on the wide beaches of the Cape Lookout National Seashore is often littered, not with trash but with seashells, including many large conch shells.

Amenities: Except at the lighthouse-keeper's quarters at Cape Lookout Lighthouse and at Portsmouth Village, where there are rest rooms and picnic areas, Cape Lookout offers no amenities. Visitors should bring their own drinking water, foodstuffs, and other supplies, including plenty of mosquito repellent and sunscreen.

Sports: Saltwater fishing (no permit required) is excellent in the surf, particularly in the fall and spring. Surfing is also popular, especially when tropical storms in the Atlantic send in the big waves.

Parking: Since there are few vehicles and no improved roads on the national seashore, if you have an all-terrain or four-wheel-drive vehicle you can park anywhere you won't get stuck.

RACHEL CARSON BEACHES

The Rachel Carson Component of the North Carolina National Estuarine Research Reserve offers a quiet and unspoiled place close to Beaufort for nature walks, bird-watching, and swimming. Carrot Island, Bird Shoal, and

Beauty	B
Swimming	C
Sand	C
Amenities	NA

other lands make up the 2,600-acre Rachel Carson reserve. Access is by boat only, across the narrow Taylor Creek from the Beaufort water front. Tidal flats, filled areas from the dredging of Taylor Creek, and marsh on the island can make for rough walking in places, and, as elsewhere in the region, bugs are hardly unknown. *Take a Carrot Island concessionaire boat from the Beaufort harbor. Walk across the tidal flats to beaches on the sound side.*

Swimming: Swimming is fair. The water is gentle and good for kids, but the sound water is usually discolored from river and marsh sediment. No lifeguard.

Sand: Narrow brownish sand beaches are the rule.

Amenities: You need to pack in your water, food, and other supplies. There are no rest rooms on the islands.

Sports: The main sport here is bird-watching. The North Carolina Maritime Museum (*see* "Attractions") offers birding trips.

Parking: Cars are not permitted in the nature reserve. Leave yours at the Beaufort harbor front, but note that spaces fill up quickly during the summer and on weekends much of the year.

HOTELS/INNS/B&BS

Lodging in Beaufort is primarily in small inns and B&Bs with lots of personality and, in Morehead City, in modern motels. The pickings are slim for accommodations Downeast: The few motels are basic, having been set up for anglers, but you can't beat the low prices. On the Cape Lookout National Seashore, the only accommodations are fishing cabins at the north end of South Core Banks and at the south end of North Core Banks.

◆ **The Cedars Inn** (expensive). Fifteen rooms and deluxe suites, several with working fireplaces, in two old homes—one dating from 1768—directly across Front Street from the water front and the yacht marinas in historic Beaufort. The Bristol Room and the Cottage, both part of the main house, are among the best choices here. Guests are served a full breakfast. *305 Front St., Beaufort, NC 28516; tel. 919-728-7036, 800-732-7036.*

◆ **Captains' Quarters Bed & Biscuit** (moderate). You might think you're staying at your grandparents' home in this pleasant B&B run by Dick Collins—a retired airline pilot—and his wife, Ruby. There are three rooms in the restored turn-of-the-century home, within a short walk of the Beaufort water front. Highlights include a wraparound veranda for catching the sea breezes, a parlor with a fireplace, and rooms full of handmade furniture and antiques. It's called a Bed and Biscuit in tribute to the yeast-raised biscuits created from a secret recipe by "Miz Ruby," as she's known in Beaufort. *315 Ann St., Beaufort, NC 28516; tel. 919-728-7711, 800-659-7111.*

◆ **Pecan Tree Inn** (moderate). When you see the effort that went into the herb and flower garden—5,500 square feet of color and butterflies under a spreading pecan tree in the side yard of this small inn—you'll have no doubt that the owners, expats from New Jersey, also lavish attention on their guests. Everything is fresh, clean, and bright here. Of the seven attractive rooms, the pick is the bridal suite with Jacuzzi. An expansive continental breakfast, a lending library, and free soft drinks are among the added touches at this B&B in the heart of the Beaufort historic district. *116 Queen St., Beaufort, NC 28516; tel. 919-728-6733.*

◆ **Hampton Inn** (inexpensive). An attractive chain motel on Bogue Sound in Morehead City. About half the rooms have water views. Continental breakfast, outdoor pool overlooking the sound, exercise room. *4035 Arendell St., U.S. Hwy. 70, Morehead City, NC 28557; tel. 919-240-2300, 800-538-6338; fax 919-240-2311.*

◆ **Sea Level Inn** (inexpensive). An unpretentious Downeast motel on Nelson's Bay, Core Sound, it has regular rooms, efficiencies, and one-bedroom apartments. The best of the bunch is a water-front suite with a fireplace. *U.S. Hwy. 70, Sea Level, NC 28577; tel. 919-225-3651.*

HOUSE RENTALS

Beaufort and Morehead City offer few vacation rentals. The only houses available on Cape Lookout are basic fishing cabins grandfathered in when the Core Banks was made a national seashore.

◆ **Alger G. Willis Fishing Camps.** For something really different, consider one of the 25 fishing cabins on South Core Banks. These are truly no-frills cottages. Units have gas hot-water showers but no electricity (some are wired for those who bring their own generators), no amenities, and lots of mosquitoes. But the opportunity to be one of a few on miles of pristine seashore is worth roughing it. The cabins, which rent for as little as $250 a week, or under $50 a day, are often booked far in advance by anglers. Bring everything you'll need, including food, drinking water, towels, and linens. *Box 234, Davis, NC 28524; tel. 919-729-2791. The cabins are accessible by ferry only. The ferry dock is about 18 mi. from Beaufort. Take U.S. Hwy. 70 toward the Cedar Island ferry. Look for signs to the South Core Banks ferry. It's a right turn on Community Rd. to Davis. The Willis office is in a mobile home at the ferry landing.*

RESTAURANTS

Beaufort dining caters to the yachting and B&B crowd. Restaurants in Morehead City tend to be either chains or traditional seafood spots oriented to the tourist trade. The few restaurants Downeast are simple spots serving basic seafood and blue plate specials.

◆ **Beaufort Grocery Co.** (moderate). Try the seared duck breast, turkey steak, or grouper with crab and asparagus. Despite its name, and the fact that it has a deli and a large take-out business, this is one of the most sophisticated restaurants in the area. *115-117 Queen St., Beaufort, NC 28516; tel. 919-728-3899. Open daily for lunch and dinner in season. Closed Tue. in the off-season; closed Jan.*

◆ **Clawson's 1905 Restaurant** (moderate). Deservedly popular, Clawson's offers perky service, an appealing menu of seafood, pasta, salads, and other dishes, and a general store atmosphere, with brick walls and bric-a-brac. Try the shrimp and grits, a Dirigible (a stuffed oversize potato), or baby back ribs. Plenty of microbrewery beers and a full bar. *429 Front St., Beaufort, NC 28516; tel. 919-728-2133. Open Mon.-Sat. for lunch and dinner.*

◆ **Front Street Grill** (moderate). This small bistro brings an eclectic menu of grilled seafood, pasta, soups, and Southwest-inspired dishes to the Beaufort water front. The pepper-fried calamari is delicious and different. Good selection of microbrewery beers. *419 Front St., Beaufort, NC 28516; tel. 919-728-3118. Open Tue.-Sun. for lunch and dinner. Closed for about 2 months starting in Dec.*

◆ **Sanitary Fish Market and Restaurant** (moderate). This landmark seafood eatery on the Morehead City water front is touristy, but with a name like Sanitary and a reputation for very fresh seafood in large portions, it's irresistible. The Deluxe Shore Dinner, for hearty appetites only, includes a first course of salad and five kinds of cold seafood, then a seafood platter with fried shrimp, oysters, scallops, fish, and soft-shell crab. "The Sanitary has been here more than 50 years, and it'll probably be here another 50," said a local. No alcohol. *501 Evans St., Morehead City, NC 28557; tel. 919-247-3111. Open daily for lunch and dinner early Feb.-late Nov.*

◆ **Captain's Choice** (inexpensive). Family- and angler-oriented restaurant with nothing on the menu over $12.95 (steak and shrimp). Good fried chicken, calves' liver, and shrimp. No alcohol. *977 Island Rd., Harkers Island, NC 28531; tel. 919-728-7122. Open Tue.-Sun. for lunch and dinner. Closed mid-Dec.-May.*

NIGHTLIFE

Nightlife on Cape Lookout National Seashore? It's watching the stars flicker in the sky. Nightlife in Beaufort is a bit livelier, but it still won't knock your dancing socks off. Just relax and go with the rather slow flow.

◆ **Back Street Pub.** Located behind Clawson's restaurant, this popular bar is quieter upstairs, where there's a swap library. Live entertainment most nights. *113 Middle Lane, Beaufort, NC 28516; tel. 919-728-7108. Open daily.*

ATTRACTIONS

◆ **Beaufort Historic District.** Tour a group of authentically restored and furnished homes, shops, and offices dating from as early as 1767. Four homes, as well as the 1796 courthouse, the 1829 county jail, and the Old Burying Ground cemetery, are open for guided tours. About 100 other houses and buildings in the historic district may be viewed from the outside on walking or vintage English double-decker bus tours. *Beaufort Historical Assoc.,*

138 Turner St., Box 1709, Beaufort, NC 28516; tel. 919-728-5225. Tour schedules vary—call before you visit. Admission. Historical Assoc. office open Mon.-Sat. 8:30-4:30.

◆ **Cape Lookout Lighthouse and Keeper's Quarters.** You cannot climb the lighthouse, but you can visit the keeper's quarters, now a small museum staffed by Park Service volunteers who live on the Cape Lookout National Seashore. Boardwalks lead from the ferry landing to the lighthouse and the wide sandy beach on the Atlantic side. *131 Charles St., Harkers Island, NC 28531; tel. 919-728-2250. Lighthouse grounds open daily. Keeper's quarters and museum closed Nov.-Mar. Access to Cape Lookout Lighthouse area is by concessionaire ferry from either Harkers Island or Beaufort; call the above number for information. The address given above is for the visitors center; the lighthouse is located near the southern tip of South Core Banks.*

◆ **Core Sound Waterfowl Museum.** A treasure for those interested in duck decoys and decoy carving, the museum is currently housed in a temporary location but plans are under way for a permanent home in a new building near the Cape Lookout National Seashore Visitors Center. *Harkers Island Rd., Harkers Island, NC 28531; tel. 919-728-1500; fax 919-728-1742. Open Mon.-Sat. 10-5 and Sun. 2-5 in season. Winter hours vary.*

◆ **North Carolina Maritime Museum.** An absolutely wonderful museum devoted to coastal plant and animal life and to maritime history. The Watson shell collection—5,000 specimens from 100 countries—is on permanent display. In a water-front annex to the museum, you can watch the restoration and construction of wooden boats. The museum also offers bird-watching trips. *315 Front St., Beaufort, NC 28516; tel. 919-728-7317. Open Mon.-Fri. 9-5, Sat. 10-5, and Sun. 1-5.*

◆ **Portsmouth Village.** This is one of the most fascinating places on the barrier islands of North Carolina. Once one of the largest villages in the region, today Portsmouth has no permanent residents and is a part of the Cape Lookout National Seashore. Some of the old buildings are occupied by National Park personnel or private leaseholders. The village looks much as it did at the turn of the century. Take a self-guided walking tour of the old houses, church, school, and general store, some of which are under restoration. *Cape Lookout National Seashore,*

131 Charles St., Harkers Island, NC 28531; tel. 919-728-2250. Open daily, weather permitting. Access to Portsmouth is by boat only. Concessionaire ferry services operate from the town of Atlantic. One such operator is Morris, which transports people and vehicles (tel. 919-225-4261). Boat transportation may also be arranged from Ocracoke (see Chapter 4). Bring your own food and drinking water.

SHOPPING

For gift shops and boutiques, the water front in Beaufort is your best bet in this area. You'll have to go to Morehead City for groceries and other needs. Shopping in Downeast is limited to routine things, such as groceries and fishing supplies, with one exception: waterfowl decoys. Downeast is one of America's centers of decoy carving, with scores, if not hundreds, of talented carvers. Get a free list of decoy makers from the Core Sound Waterfowl Museum in Harkers Island (*see* "Attractions").

◆ **Rocking Chair Bookstore.** *Somerset Square, 400 Front St., Beaufort, NC 28516; tel. 919-728-2671. Open Mon.-Sat. and Sun. "by whim."*

BEST FOOD SHOPS

◆ **Beaufort Grocery Co.** This popular restaurant also has a deli and prepares picnics for those boating to area beaches. *115-117 Queen St., Beaufort, NC 28516; tel. 919-728-3899. Open daily for lunch and dinner in season. Closed Tue. in the off-season; closed Jan.*

◆ **Taste Makers.** A gourmet food shop that also sells wine and beer. *513 A. Arendell St., U.S. Hwy. 70, Morehead City, NC 28557; tel. 919-247-5095. Open Tue.-Sat. Closed Jan.*

Seafood: ◆ **Sanitary Fish Market.** *501 Evans St., Morehead City, NC 28557; tel. 919-247-3111. Open daily early Feb.-late Nov.*

Bakery: ◆ **Bountiful Bagel.** *4050 Arendell St., U.S. Hwy. 70, Morehead City, NC 28557; tel. 919-726-5434. Open Mon.-Sat. 7-3 and Sun. 9-2.*

Ice Cream: ◆ **The General Store.** *Front St., Beaufort, NC 28516; tel. 919-728-7707. Open Mon.-Sat.*

Beverages: ◆ **ABC Store.** State-run ABC stores sell only liquor, not wine and beer, which can be bought at grocery and convenience stores. *U.S. Hwy. 70, Morehead City, NC 28557; tel. 919-*

726-2160. Open Mon.-Sat.

Wine: ◆ **Gourmet Galley.** *4050 Arendell St., U.S. Hwy. 70, Morehead City, NC 28557; tel. 919-726-9303. Open Mon.-Sat.*

SPORTS
FISHING

Fishing is serious business Downeast, although large-scale commercial fishing is limited by the lack of ocean access other than through New Drum Inlet between North and South Core Banks. You can hire charter boats in Atlantic, Harkers Island, Sea Level, and elsewhere. Surf fishing is excellent to fantastic on the Atlantic beaches of the Cape Lookout National Seashore.

◆ **Calico Jack's Inn & Marina.** *Harkers Island Rd., Harkers Island, NC 28531; tel. 919-728-3575. Open daily in fishing season, weather permitting.*

BOATING

◆ **Beaufort Docks.** *Taylor Creek, Beaufort, NC 28516; tel. 919-728-2503. Open daily mid-Apr.-mid-Nov.; limited hours in the off-season.*

◆ **Lookout Cruises.** Catamaran cruises to Shackleford Banks and other destinations. *Beaufort Marina, Beaufort, NC 28516; tel. 919-504-7245. Operates daily, weather permitting.*

DIVING

◆ **Discovery Diving Co.** *414 Orange St., Beaufort, NC 28516; tel. 919-728-2265. Open daily 8-9 Feb.-Oct. and 9-7:30 Nov.-Jan.*

BICYCLING

The village of Beaufort, especially the historic district and environs, is ideal for touring by bike. There is a posted bicycle trail, and many B&Bs and inns in Beaufort rent bikes or provide them free to guests.

GOLF

◆ **Brandywine Bay.** This 18-hole, 6,600-yard, par-71 course, originally designed by Bruce Devlin, is in a residential development but is open to the public. *Rte. 2, U.S. Hwy. 70, Morehead City, NC 28715; tel. 919-247-2541. Open daily.*

Admission. About 5 mi. west of Morehead City on U.S. Hwy. 70.

NATURE

◆ **Cape Lookout National Seashore.** The 28,000 acres of undeveloped barrier islands of the Cape Lookout National Seashore are as wild and beautiful as any place you'll visit on the East Coast. Offers fishing, birding, hiking, primitive camping, and other activities in a serene natural setting. This is the place to get away from everything (*see* "Beaches" and "Attractions" for detailed information). *Visitors Center, 131 Charles St., Harkers Island, NC 28531; tel. 919-728-2250. Open daily.*

◆ **Cedar Island National Wildlife Refuge.** This 12,000-acre reserve at the eastern end of Carteret County's Downeast area is a haven for waterfowl. More than 250 species of birds visit the reserve at one time of year or another. Because of government cutbacks, Cedar Island is no longer staffed, and operations are consolidated at Swan Quarter's Lake Mattamuskeet National Wildlife Refuge. *Hwy. 12, Cedar Island, NC 28520; tel. 919-926-4021. Open daily during daylight hours. Access to most of the refuge's salt marsh wilderness is by boat only. A boat-launching ramp is on Hwy. 12 at the Thorofare Bay Bridge.*

TOURIST INFORMATION

◆ **Cape Lookout National Seashore Visitors Center.** The visitors center and ranger station provide displays and a short video on Cape Lookout history and ecology. Brochures and information on ferries to the national seashore. *131 Charles St., Harkers Island, NC 28531; tel. 919-728-2250. Open daily 8-4:30. The visitors center is at the end of Harkers Island Rd.*

◆ **Crystal Coast Visitors Center.** *U.S. Hwy. 70, Box 1406, Morehead City, NC 28557; tel. 919-726-8148, 800-786-6962. Open Mon.-Fri. 9-5 and Sat.-Sun. 10-5.*

◆ **Beaufort Historical Association.** *138 Turner St., Box 1709, Beaufort, NC 28516; tel. 919-728-5225. Open Mon.-Sat. 8:30-4:30.*

CHAPTER 6

Bogue Banks

Beauty	B
Swimming	B
Sand	B
Hotels/Inns/B&Bs	C
House rentals	B+
Restaurants	C+
Nightlife	C+
Attractions	C+
Shopping	C
Sports	B-
Nature	B

Bogue Banks—named for early settler Josiah Bogue—is a barrier island in Carteret County. About 29 miles long, it runs southwest from Beaufort Inlet near Morehead City across to Bogue Inlet and is separated from the mainland by Bogue Sound. Because the orientation of the island is east-west, you can enjoy both sunrises and sunsets over the ocean from many vantage points.

HOW TO GET THERE

◆ The eastern end of Bogue Banks is 3 hr. by road southeast of Raleigh and 2 hr. northeast of Wilmington.

◆ From Raleigh, take U.S. Hwy. 70 east about 140 mi. to Morehead City, then turn right on the Atlantic Beach Causeway to NC Hwy. 58.

◆ From Wilmington, take U.S. Hwy. 17 north to NC Hwy. 172, connecting with NC Hwy. 24. An alternate route is U.S. Hwy. 17 north to Jacksonville, NC, then Hwy. 24. With either route, from Hwy. 24 turn right on Hwy. 58 after you pass Swansboro, and follow along Bogue Banks.

◆ From Raleigh to the Emerald Isle area at the western end of Bogue Banks, take U.S. Hwy. 70 east to New Bern, then U.S. Hwy. 17 south to Hwy. 58 at Maysville and Hwy. 58 to Bogue Banks. From Wilmington to the Emerald Isle area, follow the directions above going to Atlantic Beach, turning right on Hwy. 58 from Hwy. 24 after you pass Swansboro.

◆ By air, the Morehead City/Beaufort airport has very limited commuter service. Wilmington has commuter and limited jet service. Raleigh-Durham is the closest major airport.

◆ A note on addresses on Bogue Banks: The main road along Bogue Banks, NC Hwy. 58, has several names. Near Fort Macon, it's known as Fort Macon Rd.; at the middle of the island, Salter Path Rd.; and in Emerald Isle, Emerald Dr. For establishments on Hwy. 58, milepost numbers are given: These begin at 0 near Fort Macon and increase as they go westward toward Emerald Isle. Milepost positions are approximate.

"Crystal Coast" is the name given to the general area by marketing types at the local chamber of commerce. This is a beach destination with a split personality. It's a mix of beauty and honky-tonk, crowded day beaches and quiet family spots. Anchoring the area at the eastern end is the most popular state park in North Carolina, Fort Macon, with a nice swimming beach and pleasant natural areas. Near the other end of Bogue Banks is another state park, Hammocks Beach, with one of the most beautiful and undeveloped beaches in the state. In between is Atlantic Beach, an older beach community with development dating from the 1920s; today it's a motley mix of modest motels and strip shopping areas. Then there are several low-key areas: Pine Knoll Shores, which has a collection of hotels, condos, and year-round residences; Salter Path, with older and plainer houses; Indian Beach, which has both upmarket condos and downmarket trailer parks; and Emerald Isle, a popular beach community resolutely suburban in nature.

The gentle south-facing beaches are the big draw of Bogue Banks. And draw beachgoers they do. Fort Macon gets about a million visitors a year, mostly from Memorial Day to Labor Day. Peak season on Bogue Banks is early June to late August, when schools in the region are out, and the area stays busy much of the time from Easter through September.

BEACHES

The beaches we recommend on Bogue Banks are at Fort Macon, Pine Knoll Shores, Salter Path, and Emerald Isle. The main public beach at Atlantic Beach does not meet our standards. Some of the recommended hotels in this chapter have Atlantic Beach addresses, but they are located in Pine Knoll Shores. While Pine Knoll Shores does not have any significant public beach access with parking, there is pedestrian access for those staying in these hotels or renting a house or condo. In addition to the beach access points described below, there are also scores of pedestrian access points, either on a short trail or on a boardwalk (usually marked by signs), along the beach—which, despite the different names, is essentially one long beach. Access to Hammocks Beach State Park on Bear Island is by ferry or private boat only.

FORT MACON STATE PARK BEACH

There are two Fort Macons: the former
military fort and the state park. There is
beach access near the fort, but no swimming is permitted. A regional beach
access point is at Fort Macon State Park.

Beauty	B
Swimming	B
Sand	B-
Amenities	A-

Fort Macon comprises almost 400
acres of maritime forest and wide, south-facing beach. From
certain vantage points, you have a view of Coast Guard cutters
and other ships. *From Morehead City, take the Atlantic Beach
Causeway. Turn left on Hwy. 58 (also known as E. Fort Macon Rd.)
and follow it to the park, which is at Milepost 0. The regional beach
access area is on the right as you enter the park.*

Swimming: Good in designated areas. The gentle slope of the beach
and a protective jetty on the east end contribute to calmer water.
Swim only in areas signed for swimming; other areas may have
strong currents. There are sometimes mud balls in the water because
of channel dredging. In past years, the area has had lifeguards on duty
from 10 a.m. to 5:50 p.m. June through Labor Day, but because of
possible budget cutbacks, check locally. Jellyfish, including the
Portuguese man-of-war, may appear here, especially in June.

Sand: Gray to light-brown sand with many broken shells.

Amenities: An attractive bathhouse with rest rooms, 16 covered
picnic tables, refreshment stand, and nearby nature trails (bathhouse and refreshment stand open June to September).

Sports: Swimming. Surf fishing is good in this area, especially at
the nonswimming beach near the fort.

Parking: The regional beach access point has 300 free paved
parking spaces, but most are filled every day in summer. There
is additional parking at Fort Macon military fort.

PINE KNOLL SHORES

If you're driving along Highway 58
from Atlantic Beach toward Emerald
Isle, you'll see the Sheraton, the
Holiday Inn, and several other hotels
on the beach. This is the main clue
that you're in Pine Knoll Shores rather

Beauty	B
Swimming	B
Sand	B-
Amenities	NA

than Atlantic Beach. (The hotels, though, have Atlantic Beach mailing addresses.)

Aside from the hotels, the North Carolina Aquarium, and the Theodore Roosevelt State Natural Area, Pine Knoll Shores is primarily residential, a combination of low-rise condos and single-family homes, many of them occupied by the owners year-round. The residential areas are mostly hidden in maritime woods of oak, pine, and yaupon holly.

The beach here is attractive, although it varies considerably in appeal as it runs along the shores of Pine Knoll. The beach at the Sheraton is among the best in this area. The rub, however, is that there's really no public beach access at Pine Knoll Shores, since the town limits access by not providing public parking. Residents and renters can either walk to the beach and cross at pedestrian access points or park in lots reserved for local homeowners and guests. If you're staying at one of the hotels, you can access the beach at a hotel and walk anywhere along the beach. *Hotels providing beach access for guests are located on Hwy. 58 around Milepost 5.*
Swimming: Good. The wave action is usually gentle to moderate. No lifeguard. Jellyfish sometimes show up in summer.
Sand: Light tan. The beach slope is moderate.
Sports: Swimming, surf fishing.
Amenities: The only amenities here are at the hotels.
Parking: There is no public parking for beach access in Pine Knoll Shores. Parking lots near the beach are reserved for members of the local residential associations.

SALTER PATH BEACH

Salter Path is an older, more traditional area of Bogue Banks, with quite a few of the residents still involved in fishing.

Beauty	B
Swimming	B
Sand	B
Amenities	B

The access area to Salter Path Beach is one of the nicest in the Carolinas. In fact, the access area is perhaps nicer than the beach! You can park in the shade and walk the attractive boardwalk past live oaks, wax myrtles, and other beachside greenery and across the fairly wide dune field. The 20-

acre Carteret County-owned access area is undeveloped, so houses and condos don't line the beach. However, just a few hundred feet away, the development starts again. *The beach access and parking lot is on Hwy. 58, near Milepost 10 1/4.*

Swimming: Good. The wave action is usually gentle to moderate. No lifeguard. Jellyfish sometimes show up in summer.

Sand: The beach here is more than 150 feet wide at low tide but narrow to nonexistent at high tide. The sand is light tan. The beach slope is moderate, with low dunes and oaks, myrtles, and other trees and shrubs behind the dunes.

Amenities: Rest rooms, showers, vending machines.

Sports: Swimming, fishing.

Parking: More than 50 free parking spaces, some nicely shaded. Demand is high in summer: Arrive early in the morning.

EMERALD ISLE BEACH

Beauty	**B-**
Swimming	**B**
Sand	**B**
Amenities	**B-**

The town of Emerald Isle is about 12 miles long, and for virtually all of that distance the beach is lined with cottages, most built since the mid-1950s, when Highway 58 was extended from Salter Path to Emerald Isle. Beachfront construction is mostly single-family homes and duplexes, with a few low-rise condos. *Residential* is the key word here—there are only a few small motels. Commercial areas are concentrated on Highway 58.

The beach is pleasant, with a gentle slope and occasional low dunes, but the unrelenting rows of beach houses on the water, with few undeveloped areas, doubtless look better to a real-estate broker than to a naturalist. Still, the beach is seldom really crowded, even in summer, since the number of day visitors is limited by lack of parking. *The regional beach access point is on Hwy. 58 at Emerald Isle, near Milepost 15.*

Swimming: Good. The wave action is usually gentle to moderate. Check locally on current lifeguard status. Jellyfish sometimes show up in the warm-weather months.

Sand: The beach is fairly wide at low tide but narrow at high tide. The sand is tan.

Amenities: Rest rooms at the regional beach access point.
Sports: Swimming, fishing, surfing.
Parking: Because this is a residential (not a day) beach area, temporary parking is extremely limited. There are about 75 free parking spaces at the regional beach access point. Pedestrian beach access points are plentiful along the beach—there's one at least every 500 feet—but there are almost no parking spaces for cars.

HAMMOCKS BEACH STATE PARK, BEAR ISLAND

Bear Island, home of Hammocks State Park, is a barrier island almost three and a half miles long and three-quarters of a mile wide. It has a wilderness quality, allowing visitors to see what the area must have been like

Beauty	A
Swimming	B
Sand	A
Amenities	B+

before *Homo sapiens* invented condominiums. Because there hasn't been much overwash of the island in recent years, high dunes have accumulated, some more than 50 feet tall. Together, they make up one of the largest areas of natural dunes in the region. In the center of the island is a maritime forest.

Access to the 900-acre island is by private boat or ferry only. Since each ferry can take fewer than 40 people, this limits the number of visitors. Even on peak summer weekends, the island never seems overrun, and you can easily find your own private piece of beach. *For ferry and private boat landing information, see the Hammocks Beach State Park listing under "Nature," below. From the ferry landing on the island, walk 1/2 mi. on the beach access trail to the designated swimming beach.*

Swimming: Swimming is good but permitted only in the designated, signed area. Lifeguard on duty in summer.
Sand: Beautiful tan to light-gray sand backed by high dunes.
Amenities: The large bathhouse has rest rooms and showers (those on the lower level are free; a fee is charged for those on the upper level), snack bar, picnic tables, small interpretive center. These facilities are closed when the ferry isn't running. Primitive campsites available.
Sports: Swimming, fishing, shelling, birding, hiking on a few

trails (walking on the dunes is also permitted here).

Parking: Leave your car in the large free paved lot at the ferry embarkation point; private vehicles are not allowed on the island.

HOTELS/INNS/B&BS

Except around Atlantic Beach, where there's a mix of independent and chain motels, you'll find slim pickings in overnight accommodations on Bogue Banks. The better motels are mostly in Pine Knoll Shores but have Atlantic Beach addresses.

◆ **Harborlight Guest House** (expensive). Want to stay in a B&B on Bogue Banks? This modern three-story inn is your best bet. It's on Bogue Sound, with water on three sides and a great view of Emerald Isle. Spring for the water-front suites with king-size beds; with a fireplace, two-person whirlpool tub, wet bar, fridge, views of the sound, and breakfast in the room (if you like), they're perfect for a romantic getaway. All seven rooms have private bath. Deluxe breakfast. No kids under 16. *332 Live Oak Dr., Cape Carteret, NC 28584; tel. 919-393-6868, 800-624-8439. Turn right at Hwy. 24, then right on Bayshore Dr. Make a left onto Edgewater Ct. and go right on Live Oak Dr. to the inn on the water.*

◆ **Holiday Inn Atlantic Beach** (expensive). This four-story beachfront motel has seen better days, but because of its location near popular Atlantic Beach, it stays booked all summer and many weekends off-season. Beach-view rooms—those ending in numbers 26 to 30 on the second to fourth floors—are your best bet. *Salter Path Rd. (Hwy. 58), Atlantic Beach, NC 28512; tel. 919-726-2544, 800-465-4329; fax 919-726-6570. In Pine Knoll Shores near Milepost 5.*

◆ **Sheraton Resort and Conference Center** (expensive). If you like high-rises, this nine-story Sheraton is a good choice. All rooms are either ocean view or ocean front. Great sunrises and sunsets on the water. Two pools, including one indoor. The resort is on one of the best stretches of beach on Bogue Banks. *Salter Path Rd. (Hwy. 58), Atlantic Beach, NC 28512; tel. 919-240-1155, 800-325-3535; fax 919-240-1452. In Pine Knoll Shores near Milepost 5.*

◆ **Parkertown Inn** (moderate). This modern motel has clean, attractive rooms, and with rates as low as $35 off-season and $60 in summer, it's an excellent value. No views, but convenient to Hammocks Beach State Park and Emerald Isle. Continental breakfast. Pool. *1184 Hwy. 58, Cape Carteret, NC 28584; tel. 919-393-9000, 800-393-9909.*

HOUSE RENTALS

Most travelers to Bogue Banks opt to rent a beach house. Emerald Isle has the largest number of rental houses; one reason for its popularity is that rentals here, even beach-front ones, generally go for less than in most other destinations in North Carolina. Expect to pay about $800 to $1,500 a week for a two- to four-bedroom ocean-front house in Emerald Isle during peak season (early June to late August). Newer and larger homes cost more. Even one or two lots back, most of these rent for less than $1,000. Two- and three-bedroom condos, even those on the water, go for less than $1,000 a week in the high season. Rates drop by up to a third during May and from late August through September and by as much as half or more at other times.

◆ **Emerald Isle Realty.** Rentals in Emerald Isle. *7501 Emerald Dr., Emerald Isle, NC 28594; tel. 919-354-3315, 800-849-3315. Open daily.*

◆ **Sun Surf Realty.** Rentals in Emerald Isle and elsewhere on Bogue Banks. *7701 Emerald Dr., Emerald Isle, NC 28594; tel. 919-354-2658, 800-553-7873. Open daily.*

RESTAURANTS

For additional restaurant choices, drive to Morehead City or Beaufort (*see* Chapter 5).

◆ **Bistro by the Sea** (moderate). This tiny café is about the only Atlantic Beach restaurant that attracts locals from Beaufort and Morehead City. Instead of the usual beach fare, it serves pasta and beef. Limited parking, not much atmosphere, no view—you come here for the food. *401 Money Island Rd., Atlantic Beach, NC 28512; tel. 919-247-2777. Open Tue.-Sat. for dinner. Closed mid-Dec.-early Feb. Near Milepost 1 1/4 at Sportsman's Pier.*

◆ **Bushwhackers** (moderate). Very casual seafood dining directly on the water. Surfing decor. Emphasis at this popular, heavily advertised spot is on broiled fresh fish and shrimp. The flounder stuffed with crab or shrimp is a specialty, and the fish of the day, under $10, is a good value. *Bogue Inlet Pier, Emerald Isle, NC 28594; tel. 919-354-6300. Open daily Mar.-Nov. Near Milepost 19 1/2.*

◆ **Big Oak Drive-In** (inexpensive). Walk up to the window and order the shrimp burger, one of the best you'll ever taste. The Big Oak also has pizza, burgers, and barbecue sandwiches. No indoor seating. *Salter Path Rd. (Hwy. 58), Salter Path, NC 28575; tel. 919-247-2588. Open daily for lunch and dinner Apr.-Thanksgiving. Near Milepost 10 1/2.*

◆ **Yanna's Ye Olde Drugstore Restaurant** (inexpensive). The drugstore memorabilia and neo-hippie decor make this one of the most interesting places to eat in the region. Try the Bradburger, a hamburger with egg, bacon, and cheese. *Front St., Swansboro, NC 28584; tel. 910-326-5501. Open daily for breakfast and lunch.*

NIGHTLIFE

◆ **DJ Shooters.** Recorded Top 40, beach, and country music. *Hwy. 58, Atlantic Beach, NC 28512; tel. 919-247-7468. Open daily. Across from the Sheraton near Milepost 5.*

◆ **Woody's II On the Beach.** Ocean-front club at the Sheraton, with recorded music. *Salter Path Rd. (Hwy. 58), Atlantic Beach, NC 28512; tel. 919-240-1155. Open nightly 9 p.m.-2 a.m. Memorial Day-Labor Day and weekend nights the rest of the year. Near Milepost 5.*

ATTRACTIONS

◆ **Fort Macon State Park.** At the start of the Civil War, North Carolina seized this five-sided military fort dating from 1826, but Union forces recaptured it in 1862 and held it until the end of the war. Guided and self-guided tours, plus swimming (*see* "Beaches") and hiking on nature trails (*see* "Nature"). *Box 127, Atlantic Beach, NC 28512; tel. 919-726-3775. Open daily 8-9 Jun.-Aug., 8-8 Apr.-May and Sep., 8-7 Mar. and Oct., and 8-6 Nov.-Feb. About 5 mi. west of Atlantic Beach, at Milepost 0.*

◆ **North Carolina Aquarium at Pine Knoll Shores.** This small but educational aquarium is one of three on the coast operated by the state. "Living Shipwreck" exhibit. *Theodore Roosevelt Natural Area, Hwy. 58, Atlantic Beach, NC 28512; tel. 919-247-4003. Open Mon.-Sat. 9-5 and Sun. 1-5. Admission. Near Milepost 7.*

◆ **Worthy is the Lamb.** Religious musical drama on the life of Christ presented in a 2,000-seat theater on the White Oak River. *Crystal Coast Amphitheatre, Peletier, NC 28584; tel. 919-*

393-8373, 800-662-5960. Performances 8:30 p.m. Thu.-Sat. late Jun.-early Sep. and 8 p.m. Fri.-Sat. the rest of Sep. Admission. 3 mi. north of Emerald Isle Bridge, off Hwy. 58.

SHOPPING

The little town of Swansboro has some interesting antiques and boutique shops. Emerald Isle and Atlantic Beach have a few strip shopping centers for basic beach needs.

◆ **Emerald Isle Books.** Nice collection of regional books. *Emerald Plantation Shopping Center, Emerald Isle, NC 28594; tel. 919-354-5323. Open daily. Near Milepost 20.*

◆ **Swansboro Antique Mall.** About 50 dealers. *Hwy. 24, Swansboro, NC 28594; tel. 919-393-6003. Open daily.*

BEST FOOD SHOPS

◆ **Food Lion.** Besides groceries, baked goods, and produce, it also sells beer, wine, and soft drinks. *Emerald Plantation Shopping Center, Emerald Isle, NC 28594; tel. 919-354-4270. Open daily. Near Milepost 20.*

SANDWICHES: ◆ **The Flying Bridge Deli.** *Hwy. 24 E., Cedar Point, NC 28564; tel. 919-393-6411. Open daily.*

SEAFOOD: Salter Path is the fishing village of Bogue Banks. There are several seafood stores here, as well as some in the Cedar Point area on Highway 24 near Swansboro.

◆ **Willis Seafood Market.** *Salter Path, NC 28575; tel. 919-247-2752. Open daily Easter-Thanksgiving. Near Milepost 10 1/2.*

BEVERAGES: ◆ **ABC Store.** Liquor—no beer or wine. *Hwy. 58, Emerald Isle, NC 28594; tel. 919-354-6000. Open Mon.-Sat. Near Milepost 20. Additional locations in Atlantic Beach and Swansboro.*

SPORTS
FISHING

Bogue Banks fishing is excellent. There are seven fishing piers from Fort Macon to Emerald Isle, and surf fishing is possible all along the beaches. Charter boats will take you out to the Gulf Stream for tuna, sea bass, snapper, and even white and blue marlin. You can also fish Bogue Sound.

◆ **Capt. Stacy Fishing Center.** The *Capt. Stacy IV* party boat goes to the Gulf Stream. *Atlantic Beach Causeway, Atlantic Beach, NC*

28512; tel. 919-247-7501, 800-533-9417. Operates daily in season, weather permitting.

◆ **Island Harbor Marina.** Rents skiffs, pontoon boats, and Waverunners; offers charters. *Old Ferry Rd., Emerald Isle, NC 28594; tel. 919-354-3106. Open daily. At the end of Old Ferry Rd., 1 1/2 mi. east of the Emerald Isle Bridge.*

BOATING

Bogue Sound is a quieter body of water than the Atlantic and offers windsurfing and recreational boating.

◆ **Club Nautico.** Rents motorboats. *Crow's Nest Marina, Atlantic Beach Causeway, Atlantic Beach, NC 28512; tel. 919-726-1616. Open daily. Closed Mon. mid-Oct-Easter.*

SURFING

◆ **Sweet Willy's Surf Shop.** Maintains a "mobile surf shop," a painted bus straight out of the 1960s. *Surfside Plaza, Emerald Dr. (Hwy. 58), Emerald Isle, NC 28594; tel. 919-354-4611. Open daily Apr.-Nov. and Fri.-Sun. the rest of the year. Near Milepost 19 1/2.*

GOLF

◆ **Bogue Banks Country Club.** An 18-hole, par-72 course with views of Bogue Sound. Open to the public. *152 Oakleaf Dr., Pine Knoll Shores, NC 28512; tel. 919-726-1034. Open daily. Admission.*

TENNIS

Tennis courts at several area golf clubs are open to the public.

◆ **Bogue Banks Country Club.** *152 Oakleaf Dr., Pine Knoll Shores, NC 28512; tel. 919-726-1034. Open daily. Admission. Near Milepost 5.*

◆ **Silver Creek Golf Course.** *Hwy. 58, Swansboro, NC 28584; tel. 919-393-8058. Open daily. Admission.*

NATURE

◆ **Croatan National Forest.** Covering about 157,000 acres, Croatan is a mix of swamp, bogs, pine forest, lakes, and other coastal environments. Hiking, boating, and primitive camping. *U.S. Forest Service, 141 E. Fisher Ave., New Bern, NC 28560; tel. 919-638-5628. Open daily. Parts of the National Forest are closed in* *winter—check with the Forest Service. U.S. Hwys. 70 and 17, as well as Hwys. 24 and 58, go through or near Croatan.*

◆ **Fort Macon State Park.** Surf fishing, crabbing, picnicking, birding, and hiking on nature trails at this 389-acre park. *Box 127, Atlantic Beach, NC 28512; tel. 919-726-3775. Open daily 8-9 Jun.-Aug., 8-8 Apr.-May and Sep., 8-7 Mar. and Oct., and 8-6 Nov.-Feb. At Milepost 0.*

◆ **Hammocks Beach State Park.** Swimming, hiking, shelling, birding, fishing, and other activities at this beautiful park on Bear Island, accessible by ferry or private boat only (for more information, *see* "Beaches"). *1572 Hammocks Beach Rd., Swansboro, NC 28584; tel. 910-326-4881. A 36-passenger pontoon ferry ($2 per adult, $1 per child) makes the 25-min. trip to Bear Island; call for the schedule. In summer the ferry may stop accepting passengers in the early afternoon, because otherwise it wouldn't be possible to get everyone back from the island. For those arriving by private boat, the park is open daily 8-7 Jun.-Aug. and 8-6 Sep.-May. Admission. From Hwy. 24 west of Swansboro, take Hammocks Beach Rd. (State Rd. 1511) to the ferry.*

◆ **Theodore Roosevelt State Natural Area.** This 265-acre natural area has trails along the sound. *Hwy. 58, Atlantic Beach, NC 28512; tel. 919-726-3775. Open daily sunrise to sunset. Near Milepost 7.*

TOURIST INFORMATION

◆ **Crystal Coast Visitors Center.** *3409 Arendell St. (U.S. Hwy. 70), Box 1406, Morehead City, NC 28557; tel. 919-726-8148, 800-786-6962. Open Mon.-Fri. 9-5 and Sat.-Sun. 10-5. Open until 6 Fri. Easter-Sep.*

◆ **Crystal Coast Visitors Center—Emerald Isle Branch.** *Hwy. 58, Cape Carteret, NC 28584; tel. 919-393-3100. Open daily 10-5 Easter-Sep. and Fri.-Sun. 10-5 the rest of the year.*

CHAPTER 7

Wilmington

Beauty	B
Swimming	B
Sand	B
Hotels/Inns/B&Bs	B+
House rentals	B
Restaurants	B+
Nightlife	B
Attractions	A-
Shopping	B
Sports	B
Nature	B-

Can the town where Michael Jordan grew up help but be a cool vacation spot? Could the town where the Teenage Mutant Ninja Turtles movies were filmed be anything but a cowabunga place for a beach vacation? Before you answer, let's take a little journey back through the fall and rise of Wilmington as a hip coastal city and hot beach destination.

The largest city in North Carolina during the 19th

century, Wilmington failed to share in the prosperity and growth of other areas of the state during the first two-thirds of the 20th century. Provincial local leadership and bad economic luck combined to stagnate the area. In the 1960s and 1970s, the downtown became almost a ghost town. A few tourists, driving the back roads, found their way here for an inexpensive beach vacation but little else.

Today, Wilmington is a different place, thanks to three factors: the completion of the last leg of I-40, which in 1991 opened Wilmington and its beaches to the state's population centers around Charlotte, the Raleigh Triangle, and the Greensboro/High Point/Winston-Salem triad; the booming North Carolina economy, which lures new industry like crazy; and a new generation of mobile yuppies who discovered that coastal Carolina was a good place to live or retire. The Cape Fear Coast—Wilmington and the areas along the Cape Fear River—is now one of the fastest-growing regions in the South. The historic district, full of beautiful 18th- and 19th-century homes, can give Charleston's and Savannah's preservationists a run for the visitor dollar. The Cape Fear River water front is alive with shops and restaurants. A once-decaying downtown is home to trendy new restaurants and not one but three gourmet

HOW TO GET THERE

◆ By car, Wilmington is about 2 1/2 hr. southeast of Raleigh and about 1 1/2 hr. north of Myrtle Beach.

◆ From Raleigh, take I-40 southeast.

◆ From I-95, the major north-south route up the Eastern seaboard, connect with I-40 at I-95 Exit 80; from there it's about 92 mi. to Wilmington.

◆ From Myrtle Beach, take U.S. Hwy. 17 north.

◆ Wilmington has commuter and limited jet service at the optimistically named New Hanover International Airport. Raleigh-Durham is the nearest major airport.

coffeehouses. Local beaches, some of them excellent, are again taking their place in the sun.

Film and TV watchers may see a lot of familiar faces—and scenery—around Wilmington. The area's film industry is a leading producer of made-for-TV movies and series. North Carolina native Andy Griffith's *Matlock* was shot here, along with many feature films, including *Sleeping with the Enemy*, *Crimes of the Heart*, *Blue Velvet*, and Ninja Turtle flicks. In some years, more movies are produced in Wilmington than in any U.S. city except Los Angeles and New York.

For the visitor who wants a beach but more than *just* a beach, who wants bright lights, good food, and a lot to do and see, Wilmington makes for a remarkably appealing alternative to Savannah and Charleston.

Summer is the peak visitor season around Wilmington, when the average high is 88 degrees, with ocean temperatures in the high 70s or above from June to October. Spring and fall, though, are the most pleasant months in terms of weather. March through May, and October and November, are perfect for sightseeing and outdoor sports, with average temperatures in the 60s and 70s. Flowers bloom from March to November, and the Azalea Festival in April paints the city with color. Winters are a touch too cool for most beach-seeking visitors, with lows averaging in the mid-30s.

BEACHES

There are four main public beaches to consider in the Wilmington area: Wrightsville Beach, Carolina Beach, Kure (*CURE-ree*) Beach, and Fort Fisher. Tourism promoters have dubbed the last three Pleasure Island. Locals, however, still refer to these beaches using their original names.

Despite its rapid growth in recent years, drawing new residents and real-estate investors, Carolina Beach does not meet the minimum qualifications for inclusion in this guide. The gussied-up public-relations pictures paint a different story, but we find Carolina Beach an unappealing blend of high-rise condos, rundown shops, and downmarket beach houses. Kure Beach is a little better, but North Carolina has many beaches that surpass it in every way.

Wrightsville Beach and Fort Fisher, however, are a different matter. Wrightsville, though heavily developed, has managed to maintain a low-key, family appeal. Fort Fisher simply has a beautiful stretch of beach by any standard.

Figure Eight Island, just to the north of Wrightsville Beach, has a good stretch of beach, but the island is a private, gated development not open to the public (*see* "House Rentals"). Masonboro Island, immediately south of Wrightsville Beach, has one of the most pristine beaches in southern North Carolina, but it's accessible only by private boat (for details, *see* "Nature"). The Cape Fear River has swift currents, not to mention alligators, and is not suitable for swimming.

WRIGHTSVILLE BEACH

Known locally as Shell Island, Wrightsville Beach is a predominantly residential area about 15 minutes from downtown Wilmington. It's partly a bedroom community for Wilmington and partly a seasonal beach resort.

Beauty	**B**
Swimming	**B+**
Sand	**C+**
Amenities	**B**

Although heavily developed with many mid- and high-rise con-dos, most of the island has a relaxed, upscale feel, with few tacky shops or low-rent motels.

The beach here, about five miles long, is hardly spectacular, but it's user-friendly, clean, and enjoyable. Animals are not allowed on the beach April through September. No vehicles are allowed at any time. *From Wilmington, take U.S. Hwy. 74 (also known as Eastwood Rd.) east or U.S. Hwy. 76 (also known as Wrightsville Ave.). Once you cross the drawbridge over the Intracoastal Waterway, you're on Harbor Island. You can either go straight on U.S. Hwy. 76 or bear left on U.S. Hwy. 74. Both take you across the sound to the main streets that parallel the beach on Shell Island (Wrightsville Beach). To the north, N. Lumina Ave. is the only north-south road. To the south, Waynick Blvd. is the main through street along the sound, with a number of short east-west streets going to the beach. S. Lumina Ave., on the south end of the island, is the street closest to the ocean, but it is not a through street and is a one-*

way at some points. Signs for the regional and neighborhood access points are posted on N. Lumina Ave. and on Waynick Blvd.

Swimming: Very good. The wave action is usually moderate to gentle, making it good for kids. The water is slow to warm up—temperatures don't reach the high 70s until June—but it stays swimmable until around October. Lifeguards are on duty from May to early September, but not all sections of the island have them—check locally. Because of dangerous currents, swimming is not permitted at the inlets at the north and south ends of the island.

Sand: The beach has a gentle slope. It's moderately wide even at high tide, typically about 100 to 150 feet; at low tide, it's 300 feet wide or greater in many spots. The beach is widest at the north and south ends of the island. The sand is light gray, with many broken shells. There are few sand dunes. Beach erosion is a recurring problem, especially in the central part of the island; parts of the southern end are accreting beach.

Sports: Surf and pier fishing, surfing (restrictions apply; *see* "Surfing").

Amenities: Rest rooms are at some regional access points; a few restaurants, bars, and stores are within walking distance of the beach.

Parking: On peak summer weekends, competition for the 2,000 parking spaces is intense. There are four regional access points (look for the orange, blue, and brown regional access signs) with metered parking. From north to south, they are at the north tip of the island next to Dune Ridge condominiums (about 70 spaces), next to the Holiday Inn Sunspree Resort (about 40 spaces), at Salisbury Street near the end of U.S. Highway 74 (about 100 spaces), and near the Oceanic Pier (90 spaces). There are also many neighborhood access points, about one every block, but these have few spaces.

FORT FISHER STATE RECREATION AREA

At the southern tip of Pleasure Island, about half an hour from Wilmington, is Fort Fisher. There are actually several Fort Fishers. One is a small recreational, training, and lodging facility for military personnel that's not open to the

Beauty	A-
Swimming	B
Sand	B+
Amenities	B+

general public. Another is the Civil War fort itself, with its adjoining museum (*see* "Attractions"). Finally, there's the Fort Fisher State Recreation Area, just to the south of the fort. This is the main beach area.

After the overwrought commercialism of Carolina Beach and the unprepossessing Kure Beach, the beach at Fort Fisher State Recreation Area is a very pleasant surprise. A lovely beach, it stretches for some four undisturbed miles south of Fort Fisher, a respite from the ugly development of the rest of so-called Pleasure Island. Walk south on this beach and, before long, you're away from the crowds, even in summer. *From Wilmington, take U.S. Hwy. 421 south to Pleasure Island. Go through Atlantic Beach and Kure Beach. About 1/10 mi. past Fort Fisher itself, turn left on State Rd. 1713 to the regional beach access and parking lot.*

Swimming: Good, although rip tides and undertows may be present. The wave action is usually moderate. Jellyfish, including the Portuguese man-of-war, sometimes visit during warm-weather months. The beach has lifeguards on duty in summer, but because of budget cuts, it's a good idea to check locally.

Sand: The wide beaches have soft light-tan sand. The slope is moderately steep in places. There is no shade on the beach.

Sports: Swimming, surf fishing, surfing.

Amenities: Rest rooms, showers, refreshment stand, sun shelter (a small covered picnic area).

Parking: About 200 free parking spaces are available in a paved lot on State Road 1713, but in summer these fill up early.

HOTELS/INNS/B&BS

The historic district has about a dozen B&Bs. In and near the downtown are many chain motels and hotels. The nicest beach lodgings are at Wrightsville Beach, which has about ten properties.

◆ **Blockade Runner** (expensive). If you're looking for a full-service resort, this 150-room four- to seven-story hotel, still privately owned and not part of a chain, is about as close as you'll get on these beaches. Rooms 210, 310, and 410 (very expensive) are the nicest suites—410 even has a Jacuzzi. The hotel offers an indoor-outdoor pool, sailing center, exercise room, restaurant, kids' program in summer, live entertainment some nights, and myriad package plans. Given the summer rates, the resort could use a bit of sprucing up. The beach front is wide and sandy. An old beach house next door, The Cottage, is operated by the hotel, with 13 rooms rented mostly to groups that take the entire house. *275 Waynick Blvd., Box 555, Wrightsville Beach, NC 28480; tel. 910-256-2251, 800-541-1161; fax 910-256-5502. From Wilmington, take U.S. Hwy. 74 (also known as Eastwood Rd.) east. After you cross the drawbridge to the island, go straight on U.S. Hwy. 76. Turn right on Waynick Blvd.*

◆ **Holiday Inn Sunspree Resort** (expensive). This four-story, 144-room beach-front motel, renovated in 1995, is now the nicest place to stay on Wrightsville Beach. Most rooms have ocean views from small balconies or patios; all have a small fridge, a coffee maker, and a microwave. Get a poolside room and save $20 to $30 over the oceanview rooms (poolside rooms on the second to fourth floors also have ocean views). Beautiful pool, bright and attractive public areas. Kids' program in summer. The beach here is pretty good, although there's some erosion. *1706 N. Lumina Ave., Wrightsville Beach, NC 28480; tel. 910-256-2231, 800-532-5362; fax 910-256-9208. From Wilmington, take U.S. Hwy. 74 (also called Eastwood Rd.). As you enter the island, stay left on U.S. Hwy. 74 to N. Lumina Ave. Turn left on N. Lumina.*

◆ **Inn at St. Thomas Court** (expensive). This all-suites place close to downtown stays nearly full most of the time, and no wonder. The large one- and two-bedroom suites, most carved out of a cluster of old buildings, are attractively decorated in varying styles, ranging from country French to American Southwest. All are bright, spotlessly clean, and well-maintained by the on-site owner. Some have full kitchen and washer/dryer. *101 S. Second St., Wilmington, NC 28401; tel. 910-343-1800, 800-525-0909. About 2 blocks from the Cape Fear River water front.*

◆ **Ocean Princess Inn** (moderate). Billed as "an adult B&B" (i.e., no children), the Ocean Princess opened in 1995 in a modern house across the road from the ocean at Kure Beach, close to Fort Fisher. It has nine rooms, seven with private bath. Two of the rooms have Jacuzzis. Attractive pool. *824 Ft. Fisher Blvd., Kure Beach, NC 28449; tel. 910-458-6712, 800-762-4863.*

◆ **Taylor House Inn** (moderate). This 1905 house once owned by a prominent local merchant has been turned into a pleasant B&B by innkeeper Glenda Moreadith. The public areas downstairs are delightful, with oak paneling, stained glass, and pine floors. The Jacobean Room is the top pick of the inn's four rooms, with a canopied king-size bed. *14 N. Seventh St., Wilmington, NC 28401; tel. 910-763-7581, 800-382-9982. In the historic district, about 7 blocks from the Cape Fear River water front.*

◆ **Worth House** (moderate). The exterior of this Queen Anne-style house is Victorian with a capital V: curving turrets, wood shakes, and wraparound porch. Inside, it's comfy rather than luxurious, with seven appealing rooms. The second-floor rooms are nicest. For romance, come up with $110 for No. 4—it has a king-size canopy bed and a fireplace. Full breakfast included. *412 S. Third St., Wilmington, NC 28401; tel. 910-762-8562, 800-340-8559; fax 910-763-2173. In the heart of the historic district, about 3 blocks from the Cape Fear River water front.*

HOUSE RENTALS

Ocean-front two- and three-bedroom condos on Wrightsville Beach typically go for $1,200 to $2,000 a week from early June through mid August. Cottages and condos off the water are cheaper. Rates for periods other than the peak summer season are less

A few luxury rental homes, on and near the beach, are available on Figure Eight Island, a private island with gated access to the 375 or so homes. About 75 of these are available for weekly rentals, with beach-front four- and five-bedroom houses going for $2,000 to $4,000 a week in summer.

◆ **Bryant Real Estate.** Rents houses and condos on Wrightsville Beach. *1001 N. Lumina Ave., Box 899, Wrightsville Beach, NC 28480; tel. 910-256-3764, 800-322-3764; fax 910-256-2633. Open daily.*

◆ **Figure Eight Realty.** Rents homes on Figure Eight Island. *15 Bridge Rd., Wilmington, NC 28405; tel. 910-686-4400. Open Mon.-Sat. and Sun. by appointment.*

RESTAURANTS

Wilmington may not be in the same class as Charleston for restaurants, but with an active fishing and shrimping fleet, it serves up plenty of fresh seafood. Oyster roasts are a local tradition in the spring and fall.

◆ **Caffe Phoenix** (moderate). This is not your ordinary downtown restaurant. Light Italian and Mediterranean dishes are featured, with olive oil for dipping the fresh-baked bread. Known for its soups and salads, Caffe Phoenix is a bright, busy bistro that would be at home on New York's Upper West Side. *9 S. Front St., Wilmington, NC 28401; tel. 910-343-1395. Open daily for dinner and Mon.-Sat. for lunch. Downtown Wilmington.*

◆ **Gardenias** (moderate). It has some of Wilmington's most interesting cooking, but this is not innovation for its own sake. Such traditional fare as a veal chop with mashed potatoes comes out perfectly prepared and creatively presented; with a fine red wine—the wine list is exceptional—even this simple veal dish is raised to new heights. Outside, Gardenias looks nondescript; inside, the atmosphere is cozy and candlelit, the service friendly and professional. If you dine only once in Wilmington, make it here. *7105 Wrightsville Ave., U.S. Hwy. 76, Wilmington, NC 28403; tel. 910-256-2421. Open Mon.-Sat. for dinner. Immediately west of the Intracoastal Waterway.*

◆ **Oceanic** (moderate). You gotta love this big, classic seafood restaurant with a knock-'em-dead location on the water. Fabulous views from window tables on two floors; on nice days, you can dine on the Oceanic Pier, which extends 700 feet out over the Atlantic from the restaurant. The seafood, grilled or fried, is fresh and always excellent. *703 S. Lumina Ave., Wrightsville Beach, NC 28480; tel. 910-256-5551. Open daily for lunch and dinner.*

◆ **Pilot House** (moderate). Not a lot of razzmatazz here, just well-prepared seafood and regional dishes in a choice setting in an 1870 house overlooking the Cape Fear River. The crab cakes are unusually good. Elijah's, next door, is under the same ownership and serves similar regional dishes and seafood (it's famous for its crab dip). *2 Ann St., Wilmington, NC 28401; tel. 910-343-0200. Open Mon.-Sat. for lunch and dinner. Downtown, on the river front in Chandler's Wharf.*

◆ **Middle of the Island** (inexpensive). In this no-frills joint, the kiss-my-grits waitresses call you "Hon" and do a great job of serving truckloads of locals. Many regulars come in every day. The Mid, or the MOI, as it's variously known, is the No. 1 spot in the Wilmington area for a high-cholesterol, and absolutely delicious, breakfast. *216 Causeway Dr., Wrightsville Beach, NC 28480; tel. 910-256-4277. Open daily for breakfast, lunch, and dinner.*

NIGHTLIFE

◆ **Ice House.** The best-known Wilmington club. Live blues, rock, and jazz. No cover. *115 S. Water St., Wilmington, NC 28401; tel. 910-763-2084. Open daily May-Nov. Closed Mon. in the off-season. On the Cape Fear River water front in the historic district.*

◆ **Thalian Hall Center for the Performing Arts.** Wilmington's major venue for live theater and performance. *310 Chestnut, Wilmington, NC 28401; tel. 910-343-3660, 800-523-2820. Performance dates vary. Admission. In the downtown historic district.*

ATTRACTIONS

◆ **Airlie Gardens.** These privately owned gardens, once the estate of a wealthy 19th-century rice magnate, have expansive plantings of azaleas, camellias, and other flowering shrubs and trees. *Airlie Rd., Wilmington, NC 28403; tel. 910-763-4646. Open late Mar.-early May. Admission. From Wilmington, take U.S. Hwy. 76.*

◆ **Battleship North Carolina.** The "Showboat," considered the world's great sea weapon during World War II, served in every major naval offensive in the Pacific. It takes about two hours for a self-guided tour of this fascinating ship, which is preserved as it was in WWII. *Box 480, Wilmington, NC 28402; tel. 910-350-1817, 910-251-5797. Open daily 8-8 mid-May-mid-Sep. and daily 8-5 the rest of the year. Admission. Located on U.S. Hwy. 421 N. at the intersection of U.S. Hwys. 17, 74, 76, and 421.*

◆ **Cape Fear Museum.** Although the museum has many displays on area history and nature, most visitors come just to see the basketball memorabilia of Michael Jordan, who grew up in Wilmington. *814 Market St., Wilmington, NC 28401; tel. 910-341-4350. Open Tue.-Sat. 9-5 and Sun. 2-5. Admission.*

◆ **Fort Fisher.** This Civil War fort, controlled by the Confederates for most of the war, helped the port of Wilmington to stay open, supplying food, clothing, and munitions to the South. A small museum and the remains of the fort are open to the public. *U.S. Hwy. 421, Box 169, Kure Beach, NC 28449; tel. 910-458-5538. Open Mon.-Sat. 9-5 and Sun. 1-5 Apr.-Oct. and Tue.-Sat. 10-4 and Sun. 1-4 the rest of the year. From Wilmington, take U.S. Hwy. 421 south to Pleasure Island. Go through Atlantic and Kure beaches. Fort Fisher is near the end of U.S. Hwy. 421, before you get to the Fort Fisher-Southport ferry.*

◆ **North Carolina Aquarium at Fort Fisher.** A small but good aquarium with a shark tank, a touch tank, and a skate and ray exhibit. *2201 Fort Fisher Blvd., Kure Beach, NC 28449; tel. 910-458-8257. Open Mon.-Sat. 9-5 and Sun. 1-5. Admission.*

◆ **Wilmington Historic District.** It's the largest in North Carolina, with scores of homes and buildings from the 18th and 19th centuries. Highlights include the Bellamy Mansion Museum, a restored 1859 home that is now a history and design arts museum; the Burgwin-Wright House and Garden, a "Colonial gentleman's town house" dating from 1770; the Latimer House, a Victorian/Italianate-style house now the headquarters of the Lower Cape Fear Historical Society. Besides self-guided walking tours (for maps and information, visit the Cape Fear Coast Convention & Visitors Bureau—*see* "Tourist Information"), horse-drawn carriage tours are offered (Springbrook Farms; tel. 910-251-8889).

◆ **Wilmington Railroad Museum.** This small museum tells the history of railroading in Wilmington, with photos and mementos of the days when the railroad was the area's chief industry. Upstairs, there's an elaborate model-train layout. Steam engine and caboose on display next to the museum. *501 Nutt St., Wilmington, NC 28401; tel. 910-763-2634. Open Tue.-Sat. 10-5 and Sun. 1-5. Closed early Jan. Admission. At the north end of the downtown historic district, on the Cape Fear River water front.*

SHOPPING

Wilmington is a good spot for antiquing. There are about 20 antiques shops downtown alone, mostly along Front Street, the main downtown shopping corridor.

◆ **Chandler's Wharf.** Small but charming area with specialty shops and restaurants. *2 Ann St., Wilmington, NC 28401. Open Mon.-Sat., with some shops open Sun. On the south end of the Cape*

Fear River water front, in the historic district.

◆ **Old Wilmington City Market.** Permanent "junque" and miscellaneous shops, plus vendors selling fruits and vegetables. *119 S. Water St., Wilmington, NC 28401; tel. 910-763-9748. Open Tue.-Sun. On the Cape Fear River water front, in the historic district.*

◆ **The Cotton Exchange.** More than 30 specialty shops in eight restored brick buildings. *321 Front St., Wilmington, NC 28401; tel. 910-343-9896. Open Mon.-Sat., with some shops open Sun. On the north end of the Cape Fear River water front, in the historic district.*

BEST FOOD SHOPS

◆ **Harris-Teeter.** Besides groceries and produce, it has a good selection of beer, wine, and soft drinks. *6800 Wrightsville Ave., Wrightsville Beach, NC 28480; tel. 910-256-6820. Open daily.*

◆ **Roberts Market.** Longtime local grocery handy to the beach. *32 N. Lumina Ave., Wrightsville Beach, NC 28480; tel. 910-256-2641. Open daily.*

SANDWICHES: ◆ **Wolber's Garden Deli.** *Stone and Lumina Sts., Wrightsville Beach, NC 28480; tel. 910-256-3770. Open daily. Closed in winter.*

SEAFOOD: ◆ **East Coast Seafood.** *1315 Dawson St., Wilmington, NC 28401; tel. 910-763-9589. Open Mon.-Sat.*

BAKERY: ◆ **Normandie Bakery.** Great French bread. *7316 Market St., Wilmington, NC 28405; tel. 910-686-1372. Open Tue.-Sun.*

ICE CREAM: ◆ **Hall's Drug Store.** Real milk shakes and good ice cream at an old-fashioned soda fountain. *Fifth and Castle Sts., Wilmington, NC 28401; tel. 910-762-5265. Open Mon.-Sat.*

BEVERAGES: ◆ **ABC Store.** Liquor—no wine, beer, or soft drinks. *101 Burke Ave., Wilmington, NC 28403. Open Mon.-Sat. On Burke Ave. at Wrightsville Ave. (U.S. Hwy. 76).*

WINE: ◆ **The Wineseller.** Wine and beer. *1207 S. Kerr Ave., Wilmington, NC 28403; tel. 910-799-5700. Open Mon.-Sat.*

SPORTS
FISHING

Fishing is excellent on the Cape Fear coast. You have a choice of pier fishing (there are two piers at Wrightsville Beach, three at Carolina Beach, and one in Wilmington), surf fishing, river and creek fishing, and inshore and offshore fishing.

◆ *Flapjack* and *Gung Ho.* Inshore and Gulf Stream charters. *Box 2140, Carolina Beach, NC 28428; tel. 910-458-4362, 800-288-3474. Operates daily, weather permitting.*

◆ **Whipsaw Charters.** The oldest charter operation in Wrightsville. *546 Long Leaf Acres Dr., Wilmington, NC 28405; tel. 910-791-0555. Operates daily in season, weather permitting. In the Seapath Yacht Club on Wrightsville Beach.*

BOATING

With the Intracoastal Waterway, the Cape Fear River, and the Atlantic Ocean all at hand, Wilmington has big-time boating.

◆ **Dockside Watersports.** Boat and Waverunner rentals. Parasailing. *Snow's Cut Marina, 100 Spencer-Farlow Dr., Carolina Beach, NC 28428; tel. 910-458-0220. Open daily.*

SURFING

The best surfing around Wilmington is off the north end of Masonboro Island (*see* "Nature"), in the area south of the jetty. Another surfing spot is off Fort Fisher State Recreation Area. Surfing is also fairly popular on Wrightsville Beach, but there are strict rules limiting where and when: No surfing is allowed between 11 and 4 in summer, except in two-block surf zones, which move daily (ask a lifeguard for information). Surfing is also prohibited at all times within 500 feet of fishing piers and the jetty at Masonboro Inlet.

◆ **Surf City Surfshop.** Sells surfing gear and accessories. Rents surfboards. Provides a surfing report, updated at least daily (tel. 910-256-4353). *Landing Shopping Center, 530 Causeway Dr., Wrightsville Beach, NC 28405; tel. 910-256-2265. Open daily.*

DIVING

Despite visibility averaging only 20 to 50 feet, wreck diving is increasingly popular here. Running the Union naval blockade to bring in supplies was a leading industry in Wilmington waters during the Civil War. Many of these blockade runners didn't make it, and the remains of these ships, plus other wrecks lost in Atlantic storms, are scattered around the ocean floor.

◆ **Aquatic Safaris.** Equipment rentals, sales, daily dive charters.

5751-4 Oleander Dr., Wilmington, NC 28403; tel. 910-392-4386. Open daily in summer and Mon.-Sat. the rest of the year.

BICYCLING

Biking is good around the historic district in Wilmington, on Wrightsville Beach, and in the quieter areas of Kure Beach and Fort Fisher. For a free Wilmington bike map, contact the Wilmington Traffic Safety Department (tel. 910-341-7888).

◆ **Bicycle Works.** Rentals. *4547 Fountain Dr., Wilmington, NC 28403; tel. 910-313-1415. Open daily.*

GOLF

◆ **Beau Rivage Plantation.** At this par-72, 6,709-yard semiprivate course, lakes come into play on some holes. *6230 Carolina Beach Rd., Wilmington, NC 28412; tel. 910-392-9022. Open daily. Admission. South of Wilmington, off U.S. Hwy. 421.*

◆ **Landfall Club.** The two courses here are the best in Wilmington. The Jack Nicklaus Course, built in 1989, plays to 7,142 yards at par 72. The Pete Dye Course, built in 1987, is a 6,997-yard, par-72 course. Although the Landfall Club is private, reciprocity with other clubs is allowed, and many visiting golfers get a chance to play here. Greens fees are steep (more than $100). *2015 Pembroke Jones Dr., Wilmington, NC 28405; tel. 910-256-6111. Open daily. Admission. Off U.S. Hwy. 74, north of Wilmington.*

TENNIS

◆ **Cape Golf & Racquet Club.** *535 The Cape Blvd., Wilmington, NC 28412; tel. 910-799-3110. Open daily. Admission. South of Wilmington, off U.S. Hwy. 421.*

◆ **Greenfield Park.** Wilmington's nicest public park has lighted tennis courts. *Carolina Beach Rd., U.S. Hwy. 421, Wilmington, NC 28412; tel. 910-341-7855. Open daily.*

NATURE

◆ **Carolina Beach State Park.** This 1,770-acre park includes a maritime forest of long-leaf pines and oak, five miles of hiking trails, a picnic area, and a campground. No beach, but a nice marina. *Dow Rd., Box 475, Carolina Beach, NC 28428; tel. 910-*

458-8206. Open daily 8-10 May-Aug., 8-8 Apr. and Sep., 8-7 Mar. and Oct., and 8-6 Nov.-Feb. About 10 mi. south of Wilmington. Take U.S. Hwy. 421 to the city limits of Carolina Beach, then turn right on Dow Rd. and follow signs.

◆ **Masonboro Island Estuarine Reserve.** This nine-mile long barrier island, immediately south of Shell Island (Wrightsville Beach), is a haven for nature lovers. It has one of the best beaches on the southern coast of North Carolina. A part of the North Carolina National Estuarine Research Reserve, it's a wonderful place for birding, beach-walking, and swimming (exercise caution, though, since currents can be strong, with hidden rips). It's also the best spot for surfing, with favorite areas being at the north end. You must pack in everything you need, including water. Primitive camping is presently permitted. (A small part of the island, at the north end, is privately owned—respect the no-trespassing signs.) What's the catch? It's accessible only by boat. You'll need to have your own or rent one to get here (*see* "Boating"). *North Carolina Estuarine Research Reserve, 7205 Wrightsville Ave., Wilmington, NC 28403; tel. 910-256-3721. Open daily.*

◆ **Zeke's Island.** This small, sandy island is one part of the 1,165-acre Zeke's Island National Estuarine Research Reserve. Zeke's is a loggerhead turtle nesting area and a haven for shorebirds. Access is by boat or, at low tide, you can walk to the low-lying island (from the end of U.S. Highway 421 near the Fort Fisher-Southport ferry landing) over what are called The Rocks. Note that The Rocks are covered with water at high tide, and they're slippery. *North Carolina Estuarine Research Reserve, 7205 Wrightsville Ave., Wilmington, NC 28403; tel. 910-256-3721. Open daily. To reach The Rocks from Wilmington, take U.S. Hwy. 421 south to Pleasure Island. Go to the end of U.S. Hwy. 421 at the Fort Fisher-Southport ferry landing. The Rocks are southwest of the ferry ramp.*

TOURIST INFORMATION

◆ **Cape Fear Coast Convention & Visitors Bureau.** *24 N. Third St., Wilmington, NC 28401; tel. 910-341-4030, 800-222-4757. Open daily.*

CHAPTER 8

Bald Head Island

Beauty	A
Swimming	B+
Sand	B+
Hotels/Inns/B&Bs	B
House rentals	A
Restaurants	B
Nightlife	C-
Attractions	C
Shopping	C
Sports	B
Nature	B

$\mathcal{S}$mith Island, a semi-tropical island at the extreme southern end of coastal North Carolina, was long considered to have some of the most beautiful beaches in the entire Southeast. Its semitropical shoreline and maritime forests and marshes, warmed by the nearby Gulf Stream, were renowned but relatively little visited, because the island was undeveloped and accessible only by boat. Wilmington residents knew it as a

HOW TO GET THERE

◆ The nearest mainland town to Bald Head Island is Southport, about 3 1/4 hr. (153 mi.) southeast of Raleigh and about 45 min. (26 mi.) south of Wilmington via the land route. From Raleigh, take I-40 east to Wilmington, then U.S. Hwy. 17 south 9 mi. to Winnabow. Turn left on NC Hwy. 87 and follow it about 17 mi. to the junction of NC Hwy. 211 at Southport.

◆ An alternative route from Wilmington to Southport is via the Fort Fisher car ferry. From Wilmington, take U.S. Hwy. 421 south to its end at Fort Fisher. The state toll ferry to Southport runs—on a first-come, first-served basis—about every 50 min. between 8:50 a.m. and 6:50 p.m. Apr.-Oct., with less frequent service Nov.-Mar. The crossing takes 30 min. For information, call 919-726-6446 or 800-293-3779.

◆ The only access to Bald Head Island is by boat, and private cars are not allowed on the island. The private pedestrian ferry from Southport to Bald Head adds another 20 min. travel time, plus the wait. The ferry to Bald Head Island runs hourly (except noon) from 8 a.m. to 6 p.m.; by advance reservation only after those hours during summer; schedules reduced in winter. Round-trip: $15 for adults, $8 for children under 12, under 2 free. If you leave your car at the ferry landing, there is a $4 daily parking fee. Ferry departs from Indigo Plantation, off W. 9th St. (from Hwy. 211, which turns into Howe St., turn at W. 9th St. and follow ferry signs). For ferry reservations (strongly advised) and information, call Bald Head Island Information Center (tel. 800-234-1666). Once on the island, connecting transportation via tram is provided to those staying there.

◆ The nearest major commercial airports are at Raleigh, Wilmington, and Myrtle Beach. From the last two, you can reach Southport via limousine service (call 800-234-1666 for current selection)—a convenient option that eliminates the need for renting a car.

fine spot for picnics or crabbing expeditions. Sailors remembered the island mostly for its lighthouse, Old Baldy, the oldest standing lighthouse in North Carolina, and also for its southeast point, Cape Fear: the site of many a shipwreck.

Although development did come, inevitably, in the early 1980s, the result has been as good as one could hope; every effort was made to preserve the ecology. Bald Head Island, as the southern portion of the island is now called, is today one of the region's most attractive vacation destinations, especially for those who want a quiet, upmarket getaway in a beautiful setting. The island's beaches, about 14 miles of them, remain stunningly scenic. The maritime forest, tidal creeks, and marshland are mostly unspoiled. The development that did take place has been on a small scale: The island has some 400 luxury homes and condominiums, about 90 permanent residents, a golf course, a small inn, a B&B, several restaurants, a general store, and a post office (open one full hour a day, except Sunday).

Except for fire trucks and other official vehicles, no gas-powered cars or trucks are permitted on the island—which helps maintain the clean, quiet atmosphere. You get around by golf cart, bicycle, or foot. Bikes and golf carts are available for rent by the hour, day, or week at the ferry landing on the island. Bald Head Island promotes itself as a private resort, but anyone with the money can rent a home or condo here. Anyone who stays on the island, either in a rental or in the B&B or the inn, automatically receives temporary membership in the Bald Head Island Club, which conveys certain privileges, including club dining and discounts on activities such as golf. You don't have to stay on the island to use the beaches, however, and many visitors do come just for the day via the ferry.

Bald Head Island is 20 minutes by private passenger ferry from the town of Southport, directly across the Cape Fear River and the Intracoastal Waterway. Southport itself has much to offer, although there are no good swimming beaches in town. With its historic district, oak-shaded lanes, and fishing-village ambience, Southport may remind some of a slightly smaller Beaufort, North Carolina (*see* Chapter 5). Southport is a good spot for antiques hunters: It claims to have 75 dealers. The town has several no-frills motels, a couple of pleasant B&Bs, and a surprising number of good restaurants. Only the fact that Southport remains a working fishing town and that it lies in the shadow of a nearby Carolina Power and Light nuclear power plant keep it from qualifying as quaint.

The season in this area runs primarily from Memorial Day to Labor Day; spring and fall are popular for golf and fishing.

BEACHES

Bald Head Island offers some beautiful beaches. They are wide and sandy, and even on summer weekends they're not crowded. Although there are homes along the beach, in most places they do not mar the natural setting.

Beauty	A
Swimming	B+
Sand	B+
Amenities	D

Swimming: Atlantic swimming is excellent, in waters that are generally warmer than elsewhere in North Carolina (over 80 degrees in summer). Caution is always advised for rip currents. No lifeguard.

Sand: Wide golden-sand beaches stretch for miles along the Atlantic.

Amenities: Since most visitors stay in rented houses, there are no bathhouses or rest rooms on the beaches. Day visitors can change at facilities at the ferry landing.

Sports: There is excellent surf and sound fishing on the Atlantic, especially in fall and spring. A fishing rodeo is held on the island in the spring, a sailing regatta in the fall.

Parking: No private vehicles allowed on the island. Park your rented golf cart or bike just a few yards from the beach.

South Beach

South Beach faces the Atlantic and offers the best swimming and most beautiful scenery of the island's beaches. Loggerhead turtles nest here, as well as elsewhere on Bald Head Island, representing as much as one-half of all the eggs laid in North Carolina. *From the ferry landing, take W. Bald Head Island Wynd, which becomes S. Bald Head Island Wynd. There are about a dozen beach access points on South Beach, marked on maps available at the Bald Head Island offices at the ferry landing.*

West Beach

West Beach fronts on the mouth of the Cape Fear River, just around the corner of the island from the Atlantic. As a result, the surf is slightly calmer here, but water from the river can be murky, so the swimming is not as good as on the Atlantic side of the island. Beware of river currents. The beach is attractive; as on South Beach, homes do not mar the natural setting. Crabbing and clamming are good in this area. *From the ferry landing, take W. Bald Head Island Wynd. There are at least 3 beach access points on West Beach, marked on maps available at the Bald Head Island offices at the ferry landing.*

HOTELS/INNS/B&BS

Hotel accommodations on Bald Head Island are limited to one B&B and one small inn, both of which opened in 1995. Southport has a few independent motels and small B&Bs. With so few rooms available, most are heavily booked in season, especially on weekends.

◆ **Marsh Harbour Inn** (very expensive). Opened in late 1995, this inn offers 16 deluxe rooms. For a water view, ask for a marina-front room. Rates include full breakfast and use of electric carts and bikes. *Harbour Village, Bald Head Island, NC 28461; tel. 800-234-1666.*

◆ **Theodosia's** (expensive). This extremely attractive ten-room B&B is located on the harbor front on Bald Head Island, at the mouth of the Cape Fear River. Most of the rooms are in a three-story Victorian-inspired home built as a B&B and opened in early 1995, with the rest in a carriage house. Some guest rooms are decorated in bright West Indies colors with beautiful wood floors and woodwork. There's a piano and a fireplace in the sitting room, Beethoven on the CD player. Owners Lydia and Frank Love are long-time Bald Head residents, so they know the area well. *2 Keelson Rd., Harbour Village, Box 3130, Bald Head Island, NC 28461; tel. 910-457-6563, 800-656-1812; fax 910-457-6055. Closed Dec.-Jan.*

◆ **Indian Oak Inn** (moderate). This B&B in an 1886 Victorian home in the Southport historic district sparkles with charm and comfy appeal. Rocking chairs on the porch entice guests to sit a spell and enjoy the small-town atmosphere. With the conversion of two smaller rooms to a large wedding suite with whirlpool and bath, all three rooms now have private baths. Helpful owner Norma Kluttz prepares a full breakfast every morning and proffers home-made chocolate-chip cookies and decaf coffee in the evening. *120 W. Moore St., Southport, NC 28461; tel. 910-457-0209, 800-513-3996; fax 910-457-5009, 800-457-1152. Closed Thanksgiving–early January.*

◆ **Riverview Inn** (moderate). This restored 19th-century home became a B&B in 1995, with four pleasant rooms. The Riverview indeed has views of the Cape Fear. Full breakfast included. Within walking distance of most Southport historic sites. Don't confuse it with the Riverside Motel, which is directly across the street. *106 W. Bay St., Southport, NC 28461; tel. 910-457-6701.*

◆ **Sea Captain Motor Lodge** (inexpensive). This is Southport's largest motel, with 96 rooms, mostly standard-issue motel quarters but some two-bedroom efficiencies. Refrigerators in most rooms. Large pool, restaurant on premises. Nothing quaint or au courant about this place, but it's a decent value with appeal to anglers and families. *608 W. West St., Southport, NC 28461; tel. 910-457-5263, 800-554-5205.*

HOUSE RENTALS

Many of the luxurious private homes on Bald Head Island are available for weekly rental, under the management of the island's development company. Some of the ocean-front homes go for more than $3,000 a week in summer, but condos are in the $1,000 to $1,600 range (some condos are also available on a daily basis). Off-season, rates drop by as much as 50 percent.

◆ **Bald Head Island Management.** *5079 Southport-Supply Hwy., Southport, NC 28461; tel. 800-234-1666. Open daily.*

RESTAURANTS

There are only three restaurants on Bald Head Island. Since the island remains geared to those in beach houses or condos, restaurants are open only on a limited schedule, especially in the off-season. There are more dining choices in Southport, but once you're on Bald Head Island, getting back to the mainland by ferry for dinner is time-consuming and expensive.

◆ **Bald Head Island Club** (expensive). Dine in a country club setting at the golf course. Doing so requires at least temporary membership in the Bald Head Island Club, but this is automatic with rentals or stays at the island's B&B or inn. Grilled seafood and steaks are specialties. *S. Bald Head Wynd, Bald Head Island, NC 28461; tel. 910-457-7300. Open daily except Mon. for dinner in season. Closed Jan. and part of Feb. Schedules vary in spring and fall.*

◆ **Mister P's Bistro** (moderate). This new restaurant already has won the hearts and stomachs of many locals, and quite a number consider it the best restaurant in town. It serves such Cape Fear regional dishes as shrimp grits. Attractive, friendly spot. *309 N. Howe St., Southport, NC 28461; tel. 910-457-0832. Open daily for dinner.*

◆ **River Pilot Cafe and Lounge** (moderate). This casual café offers soups, sandwiches, pizza and simple seafood, and other dishes. *Ferry Landing and Marina, Bald Head Island, NC 28461; tel. 910-457-7390. Open daily for breakfast, lunch, and dinner; no Sun. dinner in the off-season.*

◆ **Thai Peppers** (moderate). For a real change of pace, try this authentic Thai spot that gets high marks from locals and visitors alike. All your fave Thai dishes are prepared to order here, including curries and satay. *115 E. Moore St., Southport, NC 28461; tel. 910-457-0095. Open daily for dinner; Mon.-Fri. for lunch.*

◆ **Eb & Flo's** (inexpensive). This cleverly named spot at the marina offers steamed oysters, clams, and other seafood in an informal dockside atmosphere. *Ferry Landing and Marina, Bald Head Island, NC 28461; tel. 910-457-7217. Open for lunch and dinner Thu.-Sun. Closed in the off-season.*

NIGHTLIFE

Nightlife is minimal to nonexistent in this area. Wilmington (*see* Chapter 7) is your best bet for evening action.

ATTRACTIONS

◆ **Old Baldy Lighthouse.** Although decommissioned in 1903, Old Baldy remains one of the landmarks of the Cape Fear region. Visitors to Bald Head Island can climb to the top of the 110-foot brick structure, the oldest standing lighthouse in North Carolina, for a panoramic view of the island, the Cape Fear River, and the Atlantic. Watch out for the last few steps—up a steep ladder. *N. Bald Head Wynd, Bald Head Island, NC 28461; tel. 910-457-5003 (for information about transportation to the lighthouse). Open daily during daylight hours.*

◆ **Orton Plantation Gardens.** There are 20 acres of beautiful formal and informal gardens at this antebellum rice plantation rich with Low Country history. Spring to early summer is the best time to enjoy the gardens in bloom. *9149 Orton Rd. S.E., Winnebow, NC 28479; tel. 910-371-6851. Open daily 8-6 Mar.-Sep. and 10-5 Oct.-Nov. Admission. Take Hwy. 133 north from Southport about 14 mi.*

◆ **Southport Maritime Museum.** Small museum devoted to the maritime history of Southport and the Lower Cape Fear area. *116 N. Howe St., Southport, NC 28461; tel. 910-457-0003. Open Tue.-Sat. 10-4. Admission.*

SHOPPING

Despite its reputation as an upscale destination, Bald Head Island has virtually no stores. In Southport, antiques are the thing, with dozens of professional and semiprofessional dealers.

◆ **Antique Mall.** About two dozen antiques dealers operate from this group of buildings. *108 E. Moore St., Southport, NC 28461; tel. 910-457-4982. Open Mon.-Sat.*

BEST FOOD SHOPS

Once you're on Bald Head Island, there's only one place to shop for food: the grocery-cum-general store called The Island

Chandler. Many renters bring their own provisions from super-markets on the mainland. Ferry staff see that these items are delivered to your house.

◆ **The Island Chandler.** Groceries, deli, beer, wine. *Ferry Landing and Marina, Bald Head Island, NC 28461; tel. 910-457-7450. Open daily.*

◆ **Food Lion.** Full range of supermarket items, including beer and wine. *River Run Shopping Center, Southport, NC 28461; tel. 910-457-9099. Open daily.*

SPORTS
FISHING

Fishing in the Cape Fear River and the Atlantic around Southport is, in a word, excellent. Fall is the big fishing season here, with flounder, drum, croakers, and trout all likely to be hitting in the river channels and sounds. Early fall is also the time for Spanish and king mackerel in the Atlantic and Cape Fear channel. There's a small municipal pier at Waterfront Park in Southport, good for casual fishing and crabbing. Bald Head Island offers fine surf fishing on the Atlantic beaches and good crabbing and clamming on the river front.

◆ **Sure Catch Tackle.** Tackle shop with information on charters. *Southport Boat Harbor, Southport, NC 28461; tel. 910-457-4545. Open daily, weather permitting.*

◆ **Island Wheels.** Rents crab traps and clam rakes. *Ferry Landing and Marina, Bald Head Island, NC 28461; tel. 910-457-4944. Open daily.*

BOATING

◆ **Bald Head Island Marina.** *Ferry Landing and Marina, Bald Head Island, NC 28461; tel. 910-457-7380. Open daily.*

◆ **Island Wheels.** Canoes for rent, basic instruction, tour guides on request. *Ferry Landing and Marina, Bald Head Island, NC 28461; tel. 910-457-4944. Open daily.*

◆ **Southport Marina.** *606 W. West St., Southport, NC 28461; tel. 910-457-5261. Open daily.*

BICYCLING

The flat terrain in this part of North Carolina makes it a popular spot for biking. Since cars are not permitted, Bald Head

Island is ideal for two-wheeling, and Southport, with its quiet village streets, is also bicycle-friendly.

◆ **Island Wheels.** Bicycle and golf cart rentals. *Ferry Landing and Marina, Bald Head Island, NC 28461; tel. 910-457-4944. Open daily.*

GOLF

◆ **Bald Head Island Club.** With its scenic ocean and maritime forest setting, this George Cobb-designed course is considered one of the best in the Carolinas. Par 72. The wind can be a killer here. *Bald Head Island, NC 28461; tel. 910-457-7310. Open daily. Admission.*

TENNIS

◆ **Bald Head Island Club.** Four all-weather courts are available to those staying on the island. *S. Bald Head Wynd, Bald Head Island, NC 28461; tel. 910-457-7300. Open daily. Admission.*

NATURE

Since much of Bald Head Island is still undeveloped and in its natural state, there's plenty for nature-lovers to enjoy, including a maritime forest preserve and salt marshes with egrets and blue herons. You can explore Bald Head Creek and the marshes by canoe or kayak (in addition to the listing below, *see* Island Wheels under "Boating").

◆ **Laughing Gull Expeditions.** Salt marsh tours by boat and kayak. *Box 3040, Bald Head Island, NC 28461; tel. 910-457-9257.*

TOURIST INFORMATION

◆ **Bald Head Island Information Center.** This is the information and rental center for the private company that is developing Bald Head Island. Ask for the "Armchair Guide to Bald Head Island." *5079 Southport-Supply Hwy., Southport, NC 28461; tel. 800-234-1666. Open daily 9-5.*

◆ **Southport Visitors Information Center.** *109 E. Nash St., Southport, NC 28461; tel. 910-457-7927. Open Mon.-Fri. 10-4, Sat. in spring and summer.*

CHAPTER 9

Brunswick Isles

Beauty	B
Swimming	B
Sand	B-
Hotels/Inns/B&Bs	C-
House rentals	A
Restaurants	C
Nightlife	D
Attractions	C
Shopping	C-
Sports	B
Nature	D

he Brunswick Isles, as they're popularly known, lie in Brunswick County, at the southernmost tip of coastal North Carolina. This part of the coast curves back almost due west, and the four main islands here—Oak Island, Holden Beach, Ocean Isle, and Sunset Beach—are arranged in a gentle east-west arc along the Atlantic Ocean, narrowly separated from the mainland by the Intracoastal Waterway. Because of the east-west orientation of the islands, from many vantage points you can enjoy both sunrises and sunsets over the ocean.

Once remote and little-known, the Brunswick islands, especially the three westernmost ones, have grown rapidly in the last decade, benefitting from their proximity to Myrtle Beach, less than an hour south. Suddenly, instead of pine trees and subsistence farms, golf courses are everywhere. At last count, there were 20 courses around the Brunswick coast, with more being planned. Golf course retirement homes and $250,000 beach

HOW TO GET THERE

◆ The Brunswick Isles are on the southwest end of the North Carolina coast, roughly 45 min. south of Wilmington, 45 min. north of Myrtle Beach, and 3 hr. southeast of Raleigh (depending on where in Brunswick County you are going, the time can vary).

◆ From Raleigh, take I-95 east to Wilmington, then U.S. Hwy 17 south. From Wilmington, take U.S. Hwy. 17 south. From Myrtle Beach, take U.S. Hwy. 17 north.

◆ From U.S. Hwy. 17 to Holden Beach, take NC Hwy. 130; to Ocean Isle Beach, take Ocean Isle Beach Rd.; to Sunset Beach, take NC Hwy. 904 to NC Hwy. 179. (Beach exits off U.S. Hwy. 17 are well marked—just follow signs to your destination.)

◆ The town of Shallotte has a roughly central location, on NC Hwy. 130 just off U.S. Hwy. 17.

◆ By air, there is limited jet service to the Wilmington airport (35 mi. north of Shallotte) or the Myrtle Beach airport (35 mi. south of Shallotte). For more jet service, the Raleigh-Durham airport is about 165 mi. northwest of Shallotte.

cottages are going up at a record pace.

Even so, most of Brunswick County retains a definite rural feel. Development, even close to the beaches, has been essentially residential in nature, rather than commercial. These are not busy day beaches but places where families stay in rental homes and walk to the beach. Far from being another Myrtle Beach, Brunswick has no big malls or bustling entertainment complexes. The only town of any size in this area is Shallotte (it rhymes with *afloat*), which is hardly more than a wide place in the road with several chain restaurants and some small businesses.

While no longer remote, the Brunswick islands are hardly on the beaten path. The area is away from interstate routes, the closest being I-40 in Wilmington. Getting to the islands, and going from one to another, means a drive along a two-lane country road.

Of the Brunswick islands, the three westernmost ones—Holden Beach, Ocean Isle, and Sunset Beach—offer the better beach vacation destinations. Each of the beach areas is a little different and attracts a slightly different crowd. These are not the wildly beautiful beaches of the Outer Banks or Cape Lookout National Seashore, nor are they the master-planned beaches of nearby Bald Head Island. Instead of superlatives, they offer casual comfort and an agreeably relaxing, if not exciting, beach experience.

Holden Beach is a collection of attractive, upscale beach homes, most built since the 1970s. The island has a permanent population of about 700 and a summer population of about 25,000. There's a fishing pier and a few shops and restaurants. You enter the island over a high bridge, completed in 1986, that curves like a clamshell, giving you a dramatic view of some nine miles of beach, with houses shoulder-to-shoulder along the ocean.

Ocean Isle, just west of Holden Beach, is the most developed of the Brunswick islands, but even here development is totally low-key compared with Myrtle Beach. The island has about 600 year-round residents, a number that jumps manyfold in summer. Besides miles of second homes, there are several motels here, some restaurants, and a few stores, all convenient to the eight miles of oceanfront beach. The only high-rise residential building on the Brunswick islands is a condo on the western tip of Ocean Isle.

Sunset Beach, only about three miles long, is the smallest

Brunswick island. Access is over a one-lane pontoon bridge, which swings open on the hour to allow private boats passage and opens on demand for commercial boats, so cars sometimes have to wait. Once on the island, you'll see that the narrow bridge has not stopped development. Second homes and rental houses, many of them large and luxurious, cover much of the available land. But because the homes are set well back from the ocean, behind wide rows of dunes, the island retains a sense of space, especially when you're on the beach.

A few miles toward South Carolina from Sunset Beach is Calabash. This town of 1,200 residents boasts more than 20 seafood restaurants and bills itself as the fried-seafood capital of the world. "Calabash-style" seafood, common not just in Calabash but all along the coast of North Carolina and south to Myrtle Beach, means that oysters, fish, shrimp, and scallops have been fried in a cornmeal batter and served (usually) with hush puppies, french fries, and cole slaw. In season, the Calabash restaurants—many of which are garishly lit at night, like the small casinos in Las Vegas—serve tons of seafood, mostly to visitors from Myrtle Beach and busloads of package tourists.

The prime beach season on the Brunswick islands is Memorial Day to Labor Day, but golf, fishing, and other out-door activities attract many spring and fall visitors. The climate is moderate most of the year, with an average year-round temperature of 74 degrees and an average water temperature of 69 degrees. Summer days are in the 80s and humid, though at the beach, temperatures are moderated by ocean breezes. Spring and fall highs are usually in the 70s. Winters are brief, and golf and other outdoor sports are possible most days.

BEACHES
HOLDEN BEACH

Holden is a resolutely middle-class summer beach area that has built up mostly in the past two decades. It holds great appeal for families, especially because of its gentle surf. However, it's rarely crowded, even in sum-

Beauty	B-
Swimming	B
Sand	B
Amenities	D

mer, owing to its residential nature. *Follow Hwy. 130 over the "high-rise" bridge to the island. Ocean View Dr. turns left, to the east end of the island, paralleling the Atlantic, and Ocean Blvd. turns right along the longer, western end of the Atlantic, also paralleling the ocean.*

Swimming: Swimming is good. The wave energy here is usually low, making for a gentle surf.

Sand: Light gray to tan sand. Erosion is a problem along parts of this beach.

Sports: Surf and pier fishing.

Amenities: Few. Most visitors stay in rental homes and thus don't require public rest rooms and other amenities.

Parking: There's a free parking lot for beach access just after you cross the bridge to the island—watch for signs.

OCEAN ISLE BEACH

Ocean Isle is the most built up and, relatively speaking, the "hot spot" of the Brunswick islands: It has a bar or two, some restaurants, and even a small water slide. *From Ocean Isle Beach Rd., cross the bridge over the*

Beauty	**B-**
Swimming	**B**
Sand	**B-**
Amenities	**C-**

Intracoastal Waterway. Turn right on First St. to go to the beach areas at the west end of the island, left to go to the east end.

Swimming: Swimming is good. The wave energy here is usually low, making for gentle to moderate surf. The beach slope is mild, and many kids swim here. No lifeguard.

Sand: Light gray sand. Erosion is a problem at the east end of the island, especially near the Shallotte River Inlet. At most points the beach is very narrow at high tide: only a few feet wide.

Sports: Surf fishing.

Amenities: The main parking area just after you cross the bridge offers access to a few restaurants, a water slide, and some beach shops.

Parking: There are small designated free parking areas about every six blocks along First Street, the east-west beach-front road along the island.

SUNSET BEACH

Of the Brunswick islands, Sunset features the most attractive and appealing beach. Wide to begin with, the beach has been accreting sand, and this, plus the fact that homes are set well back behind the dunes, means that the beach

Beauty	**B+**
Swimming	**B**
Sand	**B**
Amenities	**C**

has a spacious, open feel. At low tide, it's more than 300 feet wide in most places, and the low dunes stretch another several hundred feet. At low tide, it's possible to wade across Mad Inlet at the west end of Sunset Beach to small, privately owned Bird Island. *From Hwy. 904 (also known as Seaside Rd.) turn right on Sunset Blvd. and follow it to Sunset Beach. A single-lane pontoon bridge that opens on the hour for private boat traffic and on demand for commercial traffic can delay your crossing of the Intracoastal Waterway. On the island, Sunset Blvd. dead-ends at Main St., the east-west street that parallels the Atlantic.*

Swimming: Swimming is good. The wave energy here is usually low, making for a gentle surf. Check locally on status of lifeguarding in summer.

Sand: Wide expanses of light gray sand.

Sports: Surf and pier fishing.

Amenities: Few, except rest rooms at the pier.

Parking: Parking is available at a pay lot near the Sunset Pier. There are also about two dozen access points along Main Street, the east-west street paralleling the ocean.

HOTELS/INNS/B&BS

◆ **Sea Trail Plantation & Golf Resort** (very expensive). Sea Trail is a 2,000-acre condo villa resort with three golf courses. It's on the mainland side of the bridge to Sunset Beach and not on the ocean. Attractively furnished two- and three-bedroom villas with full kitchens overlook one of the golf courses or Calabash Creek. Swimming pools, restaurants, tennis, hike-and-bike trails, and other resort facilities. *211 Clubhouse Rd., Sunset Beach, NC 28468; tel. 910-287-1100, 800-624-6601; fax 910-287-1104. From U.S. Hwy. 17 at Shallotte, take Hwy. 904. Follow signs to Sea Trail.*

◆ **The Winds Clarion Inn** (expensive). This is an attractive complex on the beach with 11 different types of motel and villa units, ranging from standard rooms to four-bedroom houses (very expensive). The ocean-front rooms and efficiencies have nice views but are small. The two-and three-bedroom suites on the ocean and the villas across the street are good choices for families. A two-bedroom penthouse has a whirlpool and a wet bar in the master bedroom and great views. All units have refrigerators and microwaves; some have full kitchens. Heated pool (enclosed in winter), sauna, cookout areas, and exercise room. The beach here has suffered erosion and is narrow at high tide. Golf packages available. Free tennis at courts nearby. *310 E. First St., Ocean Isle Beach, NC 28469; tel. 910-579-6275, 800-334-3581; fax 910-579-2884. At Ocean Isle Beach, cross the bridge to the ocean front. Turn left and go 1 1/2 mi.*

◆ **Ocean Isle Inn** (moderate). In this pleasant two-story motel on the beach, all rooms have either an ocean or a sound view—the views from the oceanside rooms are worth the extra ten bucks. Two pools, one indoor and heated. Good beach in front of the motel. Golf packages available. *37 W. First St., Ocean Isle Beach, NC 28469; tel. 910-579-0750, 800-352-5988. At Ocean Isle Beach, cross the bridge to the ocean front, turn right, and go 2 blocks.*

HOUSE RENTALS

A rental house is absolutely the best way to go on the Brunswick islands. Although the exact dates vary from one realty company to another, the highest rental rates in this area are from early June to late August. Shoulder seasons—from April to early June and from late August to late September—typically offer discounts of a third or more off peak rates. Off-season (October to March, more or less) sees discounts of about half. Expect to pay $1,000 to $2,000 per week in season for an ocean-front three- or four-bedroom home on Holden Beach. Rentals are generally somewhat higher at Sunset Beach, which has some of the most luxurious rentals on the Brunswick islands, and slightly lower at Ocean Isle. Note that even ocean-front rentals on Sunset Beach are a good hike from the beach because of the wide dune zone. Rental homes book up early, with many families reserving their favorite house a year in advance. If you have trouble finding a rental, try calling in mid or late January: Some rental companies require that significant deposits on advance rentals be made by that time, and there are usually cancellations owing to deposits not being received.

◆ **Alan Holden Realty.** Rents houses on Holden Beach. *128 Ocean Blvd., W. Holden Beach, NC 28462; tel. 910-842-6061, 800-720-2200; fax 910-842-8292. Open daily.*

◆ **Sloane Realty.** Rents houses on Ocean Isle. *16 Causeway Dr., Ocean Isle Beach, NC 28469; tel. 910-579-6216, 800-843-6044. Open daily.*

◆ **Sunset Properties.** Rents houses on Sunset Beach. *419 S. Sunset Blvd., Sunset Beach, NC 28468; tel. 910-579-9900, 800-525-0182. Open daily.*

RESTAURANTS

You won't find any gourmet restaurants on the Brunswick islands, but you'll discover plenty of fresh seafood at low to moderate prices.

The little town of Calabash is regionally famous for its fried seafood, which is served in large portions at modest prices in about 20 restaurants, all clustered in a one-square-mile area on Highway 179 and on the water front. Calabash is definitely touristy, and there is a limit to how much cornmeal-battered shrimp you can eat before you hit overload. Nevertheless, the town and the style of seafood preparation are part of the Carolina beach experience. We've listed a couple of the best Calabash restaurants, but, frankly, there's not much difference among them. Since they're all in the same area, just look for the ones with the most cars parked out front and you'll likely get a big, filling meal for less than $12 per person.

◆ **Crabby Oddwaters** (moderate). It's on the second floor, above Bill's Seafood Market, and all the seafood is fresh from the market and not prepared until it's ordered. Throw your crab and shrimp shells in the hole in the center of the table. Lots of good local seafood, with daily specials. *310 Sunset Blvd., Hwy. 179, Sunset Beach, NC 28469; tel. 910-579-6372. Open for dinner daily Mar.-Oct. and Thu.-Sat. Nov.-Feb. On the left on the mainland, just before you cross the pontoon bridge to Sunset Beach.*

◆ **Ella's of Calabash** (moderate). Archetypal Calabash restaurant serving huge portions of well-prepared and very fresh seafood in a casual, Formica-top-table atmosphere. Ella's has been doing a great job with seafood since 1950. *148 River Rd., Calabash, NC 28467; tel. 910-579-6728. Open daily for lunch and dinner. Turn off Hwy. 179 toward the Calabash water front. Ella's is on the right, about halfway to the water.*

◆ **Twin Lakes Seafood Restaurant** (moderate). One of the best restaurants in Brunswick County. Try Grouper in a Garden (of fresh vegetables), the Steamed Seafood Feast (three crabs, half a pound of shrimp, a half-dozen clams, corn on the cob, and potato for about $16), or any of the daily specials. Friendly service in a pleasant, comfortable setting overlooking the Intracoastal Waterway. *Sunset Blvd., Hwy. 179, Sunset Beach, NC 28469; tel. 910-579-1067. Open daily for dinner Feb.-Thanksgiving. On the Intracoastal Waterway, on the left just before you cross the pontoon bridge to Sunset Beach.*

◆ **Larry's Calabash Seafood** (inexpensive). A Calabash-style place with a popular all-you-can-eat seafood buffet. *Hwy. 179, Calabash, NC 28467; tel. 910-579-6976. Open daily for dinner Mar.-Nov. In the heart of the main drag (Hwy. 179) through Calabash, on the right as you drive south.*

NIGHTLIFE

Being quiet and family-oriented, the Brunswick islands offer very limited nightlife. Ocean Isle has the most. For a bit more excitement, head north to Wilmington (*see* Chapter 7). For full-bore beach action, drive south to Myrtle Beach (*see* Chapter 10).

◆ **Steamers Restaurant & Lounge.** Live entertainment most nights in season: rock bands, karaoke, shag dancing. *8 Second St., Ocean Isle Beach, NC 28469; tel. 910-579-0535. Open daily.*

ATTRACTIONS

This area is devoted to relaxing, not sightseeing. If you get bored, drive south to Myrtle Beach (*see* Chapter 10), east to Southport (Chapter 8), or north to Wilmington (Chapter 7).

◆ **Museum of Coastal Carolina.** Small but interesting museum focusing on the natural history of coastal North and South

Carolina. Its shell collection includes nearly all 200 shells found on the Carolina coast. There's also a shark jaw display and a large diorama of an ocean reef. Children's program daily at 2 p.m. in summer. *Ocean Isle Beach, NC 28469; tel. 910-579-1016. Open Mon.-Wed. and Fri.-Sat. 9-5, Thu. 9-9, and Sun. 1-5 Memorial Day-Labor Day; open Sat. 9-5 and Sun. 1-5 the rest of year. Admission. From the bridge onto the island, turn left on Second St. at the water slide. The museum entrance is on the left.*

SHOPPING

Although the Brunswick islands are physically close together on the coast, getting from one to another by land involves a fairly long drive. Most of the shops included here are more or less centrally located in and around Shallotte. Depending on which island you're staying on, however, you may find an adequate substitute close by.

◆ **Calabash Nautical Gifts.** Beach "junque" and a million Christmas ornaments. *9973 Beach Dr. (Hwy. 179), Calabash, NC 28467; tel. 910-579-2611. Open daily. At the stop light in Calabash.*

◆ **L. Bookworm.** Small bookstore with southern authors section. *3004 Holden Beach Rd. S.W., Supply, NC 28462; tel. 910-842-7380. Open daily 10-9 Memorial Day-Labor Day and Mon.-Sat. 10-6 Labor Day-Memorial Day.*

BEST FOOD SHOPS

◆ **Food Lion.** Besides groceries, baked goods, and produce, it carries beer, wine, and soft drinks. *Twin Creek Plaza, U.S. Hwy. 17, Shallotte, NC 28462; tel. 910-754-9992. Open daily 24 hr.*

Sandwiches: ◆ **Roberto's Pizzeria & Restaurant.** Hand-tossed pizza, hoagies, and Philly cheese steaks. *Hwy. 179, Ocean Isle Beach, NC 28469; tel. 910-579-4999. Open daily. A second location on Holden Beach is open daily Mar.-Nov.*

Seafood: ◆ **Bill's Seafood.** *310 Sunset Blvd., Hwy. 179, Sunset Beach, NC 28469; tel. 910-579-6372. Open Mon.-Sat.*

Ice Cream: ◆ **Julie's Sweet Shop.** *2 Main St., Sunset Beach, NC 28469; tel. 910-579-1211. Open daily Mar.-Nov.; hours vary in off-season.*

Beverages: ◆ **ABC Store.** Liquor only (no wine, beer, or mixers). *Holden Beach Rd., Shallotte, NC 28462; tel. 910-842-8839. Open*

Mon.-Sat. Other locations near several of the Brunswick beaches.

SPORTS

Golf courses are going up right and left in Brunswick County, making it one of the leading golf destinations in the state, with 20 courses at last count. Most of these are associated with residential subdivisions but are open to the public. Fishing is good to excellent off the coast. The gentler waters here make for generally mediocre to poor surfing, except when a storm is blowing offshore.

FISHING

As elsewhere in the region, spring and fall are the best times for fishing. Flounder, gray and speckled trout, mullet, mackerel, and other fish can be caught from one of the piers on the islands, in the surf, or in one of the rivers in the area. Charter and party boats for offshore fishing are also available.

◆ **Island Tackle.** Sells tackle, books charters. *Beach Dr., Ocean Isle Beach, NC 28469; tel. 910-579-6116. Open daily.*

◆ **Capt. Jim's Marina.** Several party boats and charter boats are based here. *Box 4900, Calabash, NC 28467; tel. 910-579-3660. Operates daily, weather permitting, mid-Feb.-Dec. Located at the water front in Calabash.*

◆ **Capt. Fred Davis.** A 25-foot boat offers full- or half-day offshore charters. *Ocean Isle Beach, NC 28469; tel. 910-579-5744. Operates daily, weather permitting. Docked at Sheffields Seafood.*

BOATING

◆ **Mace's Boat Rentals.** Rents fishing and pontoon boats. *115 Ferry Rd., Holden Beach, NC 28462; tel. 910-842-7171. Open daily.*

◆ **Ocean Isle Marina.** Rents fishing boats, Waverunners, and pontoon boats. *43 Causeway Dr., Ocean Isle Beach, NC 28469; tel. 910-579-0848. Open daily.*

BICYCLING

◆ **Julie's Bike Rentals.** Rentals. *2 Main St., Sunset Beach, NC 28469; tel. 910-579-1211. Open daily Mar.-Nov.; hours vary in off-season.*

GOLF

The Brunswick County coastal area has at least 20 golf courses, with more on the way. Though not of championship caliber, most offer pleasant play at affordable rates (greens fees are usually $50 or less). For those with an even more serious golf addiction, Myrtle Beach is less than an hour away (*see* Chapter 10).

◆ **Brick Landing Plantation.** This popular par-72, 6,473-yard course, designed by H. M. Brazil, plays along the Atlantic and the Intracoastal Waterway. *Hwy. 179, Ocean Isle Beach, NC 28469; tel. 910-754-5545, 800-438-3006. Open daily. Admission. From U.S. Hwy. 17, go 4 mi. to Hwy. 179, then 6 mi. to the Brick Landing Plantation.*

◆ **Lockwood Golf Links.** William Byrd course playing 6,836 yards at par 72, built in 1988. *19 Clubhouse Dr., S.W. Holden Beach, NC 28462; tel. 910-842-5666. Open daily. Admission. From U.S. Hwy. 17, take Hwy. 130 south 9 mi., then follow signs to the course.*

◆ **Marsh Harbour.** An early Larry Young design playing 6,690 yards, par 71. *201 Marsh Harbour Rd., Calabash, NC 28467; tel. 910-579-3161. Open daily. Admission. From U.S. Hwy. 17, take Hwy. 179 north. Go 1 mi., then turn right on Marsh Harbour Rd.*

◆ **Sea Trail Plantation & Golf Resort.** Three 18-hole championship courses, one by Dan Maples, one by Willard Byrd, and one by Rees Jones. *211 Clubhouse Rd., Sunset Beach, NC 28468; tel. 910-287-1100, 800-624-6601. Open daily. Admission. From U.S. Hwy. 17 at Shallotte, take Hwy. 904. Follow signs to Sea Trail. Ask at the gate for directions to the golf courses.*

TENNIS

Public courts are located on Third Street on Ocean Isle and at Shallotte Township Park on U.S. Highway 17 Business just south of Shallotte. The Sea Trail Plantation & Golf Resort at Sunset Beach has two lighted courts open only to resort guests.

TOURIST INFORMATION

◆ **South Brunswick Chamber of Commerce.** *U.S. Hwy. 17 Business, Shallotte, NC 28459; tel. 910-754-6644, 800-426-6644. Open Mon.-Fri. 9-5.*

CHAPTER 10

Myrtle Beach

Beauty	C
Swimming	B+
Sand	B
Hotels/Inns/B&Bs	B+
House rentals	C
Restaurants	B
Nightlife	A+
Attractions	B
Shopping	A
Sports	A
Nature	C-

For generations of kids in the Carolinas, Myrtle Beach was where you went to celebrate your graduation from high school. You borrowed your dad's '62 Chevy and left the morning after graduation ceremonies. You had a wild week of beach music, sunburn, and shag dancing (that slo-mo jitterbug invented in this area). If you were lucky, you found a summer romance, sparked by raging hormones and Budweiser.

Later in the summer, Myrtle Beach was where Dad and Mom went with the younger kids, for a few days of fried seafood, a little fishing, and a lot of time on the wide sandy beaches.

Today, although the old Myrtle Beach lingers on (the Pavilion, a traditional beachside amusement park, still lays on the cheap thrills, and aging baby boomers come back to shag again the way they did in the last summer of their youth), there's a dynamic new Myrtle Beach rising out of the sand and surf. With aggressive public relations, national advertising, a healthy dose of golf, and a vision of the area as a year-round resort destination, tourism officials and big-time developers have created a new vacation center that rivals anything Florida offers.

More people now visit Myrtle Beach each year than Hawaii. The area draws an estimated 12 million tourists, more than any

HOW TO GET THERE

◆ By car, Myrtle Beach is about 1 1/2 hr. south of Wilmington, 2 hr. north of Charleston, 3 hr. east of Columbia, and 4 hr. southeast of Charlotte. From Wilmington, take U.S. Hwy. 17 south. From Charleston, take U.S. Hwy. 17 north. From I-95, take U.S. Hwy. 501; the exit is about 18 mi. north of Florence.

◆ During the summer, expect heavy traffic and possible lengthy delays on both U.S. Hwys. 17 and 501. Once at Myrtle Beach, if possible avoid U.S. Hwy. 17 Business (also known as N. and S. Kings Hwy.); U.S. Hwy. 17 Bypass, which parallels U.S. Hwy. 17 Business to the west, has fewer stop lights and better traffic flow.

◆ By air, Myrtle Beach Jetport has commuter service and limited jet service.

◆ Amtrak has service to Charleston (98 mi.) and Florence (65 mi.).

other East Coast destination except Orlando and Disneyworld. On summer days, the year-round population of less than 40,000 often swells to 400,000 plus. More bus tours come here than to any other destination in the country except Branson, Missouri, and Washington, D.C. The bus tourists gawk at entertainment and shopping complexes that are so big they have their own visitors centers. With as many as 20 live theaters expected to be open by the year 2000, Myrtle Beach could soon pass Branson and Nashville as the country music center of America. There are more than 80 golf courses in the area, and boosters say this is one of the world's top golf destinations. It certainly merits its nickname: "Golf Coast." And even if you're one of those who feel that regular golf is just "a good walk ruined," you might enjoy what Myrtle Beach has to offer as the miniature golf capital of America.

Myrtle Beach is the largest tourist attraction in South Carolina, and before long it may account for more than half the state's tourist revenue. The area indeed offers a lot for the visitor: miles of beaches, most water sports, golf, tennis, shopping. But the growth and success have come at a price. Traffic along the main north-south arteries approaches gridlock at times during the summer. Often, the main route from the west, U.S. Highway 501, is also a traffic nightmare. The crime rate has soared. In good weather, the beaches are packed.

And quantity does not necessarily equal quality. Many of the more than 1,500 restaurants in the area serve all-you-can-eat buffets to crowds of undiscriminating diners. Some of the hundreds of hotels and condo towers—"Miami-ized" high-rises towering beside older independent motels—need refurbishing. There's not a five-star hotel in the region, and (some would say) few if any four-star places.

If you go to Myrtle Beach, be aware of the pluses and minuses. It's a high-energy destination with plenty to keep the entire family occupied. But it's not a place to relax. The savvy visitor will avoid the hectic, traffic-jammed period from Memorial Day to Labor Day and come instead in the early spring or fall, when most of the entertainment, dining, and shopping are still going full blast but with fewer lines and crowds and when temperatures are lower. Even the winter is an option. A few motels, restaurants, and theaters close in December and January. But lodging prices are slashed, often by 75 percent or more from peak rates, and aside from the occasional cold snap, the weather is fine for golf and beach walking. Myrtle Beach in winter is a bit like the Myrtle Beach of old.

The Grand Strand, as the entire region is called, is a 60-mile length of coast stretching from the North Carolina border, down through North Myrtle Beach to Myrtle Beach—both a part of Horry County (pronounced *OH-ree*)—and then south to Georgetown County. The Strand is usually thought of as being divided into three areas:

♦ **The North Strand:** This northern end of Horry County consists of several beach communities, including Cherry Grove, Ocean Drive, Crescent Beach, and Windy Hill, which together make up the municipality of North Myrtle Beach. Not technically a part of North Myrtle Beach is Atlantic Beach. Just south of Atlantic Beach, in the Lake Arrowhead area to the north of Myrtle Beach (but with Myrtle Beach addresses), is an upscale area where the Kingston (a Radisson resort) and the Hilton are located.

♦ **Myrtle Beach:** This is the heart of the Grand Strand. It's where most of the accommodations and restaurants are clustered. Just south of Myrtle Beach are Surfside Beach and Garden City Beach. The southern part of Garden City is in Georgetown County. These areas have mostly beach houses and low- and mid-rise condos instead of high-rise development.

♦ **The South Strand:** This less intensively developed part of the Strand, all in Georgetown County, is covered in the next chapter (*see* Chapter 11).

BEACHES

The Myrtle Beach area has some of the nicest beaches in South Carolina—mostly wide, sandy, and nicely swimmable. Unfortunately, developers discovered this long ago and put up hundreds of hotels, motels, time-shares, and condos along the beach front. Today, the Myrtle Beach area is one of the most highly developed beach resorts along the Eastern seaboard.

Because the beaches are so highly developed and often crowded, many county and municipality regulations govern beach use; check locally for details.

Water temperatures along the Grand Strand beaches usually average in the 50s from December to March, rising to the 70s by May and to the low 80s by mid-June and staying swimmable until October. You'll want to be in the water a lot: Summer air temperature highs hit the 80s in May and stay there through September, and the thermometer registers 90 degrees or above on about 65 days of the year.

Ocean Boulevard is the main beach-front street. Except for a few breaks, such as at Atlantic Beach, it stretches from Cherry Grove in the north to Garden City Beach in the south. As you drive along the boulevard, unless you are familiar with the area or follow a map closely, it probably will not be clear where one beach community ends and another starts. Like most beaches in the region, the Grand Strand is mostly one long stretch of sand, with no real division between one beach and another. As in the rest of this book, we've included only the better beaches.

NORTH STRAND BEACHES

This area has some of the widest beaches in the state, with hard-packed sand and excellent swimming. The North Strand is not as developed as Myrtle Beach, but it is moving in that direction fast. Beach houses, low- and mid-rise condos, and motels line most sections of beach. The areas of

Beauty	C
Swimming	B+
Sand	B
Amenities	B-

North Myrtle Beach closer to Myrtle Beach have grown rapidly in recent years, exploding with shopping centers, malls, restaurants, and live music theaters. North Myrtle Beach is popular with high school and college students at Easter break and during the summer, although strict enforcement of drinking laws is moving some of this action farther south (to Cancún, for instance).

This section includes a strip of excellent wide and sandy beach at the gated Kingston Plantation, a Radisson resort, but access is reserved for resort guests (*see* "Hotels/Inns/B&Bs").

Swimming: Excellent. The wave action is usually gentle. Most beaches have lifeguards on duty from around Memorial Day to Labor Day—look for lifeguard stations.

Sand: Most North Strand beaches are very wide at low tide. The sand is light gray to tan and hard packed. It's excellent for jogging and walking.

Amenities: Restaurants and shops are always nearby, either on Ocean Boulevard or U.S. Highway 17. Public rest rooms and changing areas are limited, although there are rest rooms and showers on First Avenue South at Ocean Drive Beach.

Sports: Swimming is the thing, but most water sports are available. Surfing is usually poor and is legal only before 9 and after 4 mid-May to mid-September, except near Cherry Grove Beach pier and at 13th, 28th, and 38th avenues south, where it's permitted anytime.

Parking: Free parking is available in small lots and at neighborhood access areas at many points along the beaches, but in summer, spaces are always at a premium.

Cherry Grove Beach

The beach here is wide and sandy, with light-tan sand. This stretch of North Myrtle Beach has mostly low-rise condos and houses along the beach front, but to the south, you can see skyscrapers in the distance. Free parking is available in small lots along Ocean Boulevard. *From U.S. Hwy. 17, take Sea Mountain Hwy. (State Rd. 9) east to Ocean Blvd.*

Windy Hill Beach

Lots of high-rise condos line the beach front here. Everywhere you look there are condos, condos, condos. The beach is unusually narrow at high tide, only 10 or 20 feet. Free parking is available in small lots along Ocean Boulevard—look for the white posts with blue letters marking the lots. *From U.S. Hwy. 17, take S. 46th Ave. (or other east-west avenues) east to Ocean Blvd.*

MYRTLE BEACH

Myrtle Beach can be divided into four areas: the north end above about North 52nd Avenue, which has many of the better hotels, motels, and condo towers and pleasant though busy beaches; the upscale residential area from about

Beauty	C+
Swimming	B+
Sand	B+
Amenities	B

North 32nd to North 52nd avenues, which has attractive beaches, fewer people, and no hotels; the heart of Myrtle Beach, near the Pavilion Amusement Park, from around North 1st to North 32nd avenues, which has many of the older accommodations and some of the most crowded beaches; and the south end of Myrtle Beach, below the Pavilion area, which has narrower beaches and a mix of older and newer accommodations. *From U.S. Hwy. 17 Bypass, take U.S. Hwy. 50 (or N. 10th, N. 21st, N. 29th, N. 38th, N. 48th, N. 52nd, or N. 76th Aves.) east to U.S. Hwy. 17 Business. Then take any of the east-west avenues a short distance to Ocean Blvd., which parallels the beach. The beach runs from around S. 29th Ave. to around N. 82nd Ave. The Pavilion is at Ocean Blvd. and N. 9th Ave.*

Swimming: Good to excellent, especially at the north end of the beach, which is usually less crowded than around the Pavilion. Typically, the wave energy is low, making gentle surf. The water is fairly shallow, especially at the north end. Lifeguard on duty from May to Labor Day.

Sand: About ten miles of tan, well-packed sand.

Amenities: Restaurants, bars, and shops are next door to the beach on Ocean Boulevard. There are no public rest rooms, but by law, hotel rest rooms must be open to the public. Myrtle Beach has 15 handicapped-access points for the beach, and free wheelchairs (not motorized) are available—ask at lifeguard stations.

Sports: In summer, around the Pavilion area you'll have a hard time finding a place to park your beach towel, much less engage in sports on the beach. Biking, surfing, and motorboating are verboten.

Parking: Myrtle Beach has done a good job of trying to maintain parking at beach access points, but demand overwhelms supply. You may have better luck north of the Pavilion area.

SOUTH MYRTLE BEACH BEACHES

The energy level drops as bit as you go south of Myrtle Beach proper. However, the beach front here is still heavily developed, with many mid- and low-rise buildings, and even the state park lacks the serenity of most other parks in the region.

Beauty	C+
Swimming	B
Sand	C+
Amenities	B

Swimming: Good to excellent. Lifeguard on duty in summer.
Sand: Light tan.
Amenities: Few, except at Myrtle Beach State Park.
Sports: The usual water sports. Pool swimming and fishing at Myrtle Beach State Park.
Parking: Free parking is available at lots along Ocean Boulevard and at several large lots at Myrtle Beach State Park (daily entry fee).

Myrtle Beach State Park

Expecting a lush subtropical park with a beautiful beach? You won't find it here. The beach front is short, and your eye catches views of condo towers in the distance. Still, this is better than the close-up views of concrete you'll have on many parts of Myrtle Beach. Amenities include rest rooms, picnic tables, a snack bar, nature trails, and even a swimming pool. You can fish and camp here. There are more than 200 parking spaces, but they go quickly in summer. Daily entry fee to the park. *Just south of Myrtle Beach off U.S. Hwy. 17 Business.*

Garden City Beach

The north end of Garden City Beach is unpromising, but as you drive south on Ocean Boulevard (it becomes Waccamaw Drive), the beach and the beach-front community become more attractive, with single-family homes and nicer condos. Free parking is available at many points in small lots along Ocean Boulevard/Waccamaw Drive. *From U.S. Hwy. 17 Business, take Atlantic Ave. east to Waccamaw Dr.*

HOTELS/INNS/B&BS

The Myrtle Beach area has more than 50,000 rooms, far more than any other destination in the Carolinas or Georgia. The vast majority of these accommodations are on Ocean Boulevard.

◆ **Kingston Plantation, A Radisson Resort** (very expensive). This is the best of all the large, full-service hotels. The resort consists of a 20-story all-suites hotel, two condo towers with one- to three-bedroom units, and a number of two- and three-bedroom condo villas located on 145 acres. The ocean-front deluxe suites (around $279 from Memorial Day to Labor Day but inexpensive to moderate off-season) in the hotel may be your best bet. They're nicely decorated in light tropical colors and are extremely spacious; each has two new TVs, three phones, and a kitchenette. The gorgeous views of the ocean will make you think you're in Aruba rather than South Carolina. The beach here is excellent and, because it's private, is less crowded than those closer to downtown Myrtle Beach. An elaborate health and fitness club, seven pools, nine outdoor tennis courts, room service, and casual and fine dining restaurants on site. *9800 Lake Dr., Myrtle Beach, SC 29572; tel. 803-449-0006, 800-333-3333; fax 803-497-1017. At the north end of Myrtle Beach, close to but not technically in N. Myrtle Beach. From the south, 1/2 mi. north of the U.S. Hwy. 17/U.S. Hwy. 17 Business merge, turn right at the first light (Lake Arrowhead Rd.). Turn left at the first light (Kings Rd.) and go 3/8 mi. From the north, 5 1/2 mi. south of the U.S. Hwy. 17/State Rd. 9 merge, turn left after Briarcliff Mall onto Kings Rd. and go 3/4 mi.*

◆ **Ocean Forest Villa Resort** (very expensive). If you want low-rise lodging with more room for the family, this is a good choice, although the prices in summer are high for what you get (rates are inexpensive in winter, moderate in spring and fall). Each unit in this three-story, 150-unit complex has two bedrooms, two baths, and a complete kitchen. Free tennis. Two pools. Guest privileges available at five other area resorts operated by the same company. *5601 N. Ocean Blvd., Myrtle Beach, SC 29577; tel. 803-449-9661, 800-845-0347; fax 803-449-9207. Across the street from the beach, about 4 mi. north of U.S. Hwy. 501.*

◆ **Patricia Suites North** (expensive). New in spring 1995, the Patricia is an all-suites 16-story high-rise on a nice stretch of beach. Each of the 194 attractively decorated suites has a separate bedroom, two TVs, a balcony, and a kitchen with a full-size refrigerator, range, and microwave. Most units have a nice ocean view. Two pools. *6804 N. Ocean Blvd., Myrtle Beach, SC 29572; tel. 803-449-4833, 800-255-4763; fax 803-449-8192. On the beach about 5 1/2 mi. north of U.S. Hwy. 501.*

◆ **Sea Island Inn** (expensive). Five-story hotel with 112 rooms, all with ocean views. This well-run spot gets a lot of repeat business, and many guests opt for the meal plan (jackets required for men at dinner). Some rooms could use a bit of refurbishing, but you'll be comfortable here. Two pools, one heated. Golf and other package plans available. *6000 N. Ocean Blvd., Myrtle Beach, SC 29577; tel. 803-449-6406, 800-548-0767; fax 803-449-4102. On the beach, about 5 mi. north of U.S. Hwy. 501.*

◆ **Hampton Inn Northwood** (moderate). New in late 1995, this 122-room motel offers the usual Hampton Inn features: good value, free local phone calls, and super-clean rooms. All have small refrigerators and microwaves. Suites (expensive) have VCRs, and some have whirlpools. Rates include a deluxe continental breakfast. Heated indoor pool. *U.S. Hwy. 17 Business and 76th Ave. N., Myrtle Beach, SC 29577; tel. 803-497-0077, 800-543-4286; fax 803-497-8845. About 4 blocks from the beach. From the junction of U.S. Hwy. 17 Bypass and U.S. Hwy. 501, go north 6 mi. on the Bypass. Turn right onto 76th Ave. and go 1 mi. or take U.S. Hwy. 17 Business to 76th Ave.*

◆ **Serendipity** (moderate). Although it bills itself as a bed-and-breakfast inn, Serendipity is more a motel—but an interesting one. The outside of the two-story building affects a Spanish mission style; inside, each of the 14 rooms and suites is decorated in a different theme: English, Japanese, Chinese. In the warmer months, flowers are on display everywhere. A neat, clean, friendly, family-run spot. Heated outdoor pool. Continental breakfast included. About three blocks to the beach. *407 71st Ave. N., Myrtle Beach, SC 29572; tel. 803-449-5268, 800-762-3229. Closed Nov.-Jan. About 5 mi. north of U.S. Hwy. 501, on a quiet street between U.S. Hwy. 17 Business and Ocean Blvd.*

HOUSE RENTALS

The Myrtle Beach area is oriented more toward hotels and high-rise condos than single-family house rentals. Most rentals are south of Myrtle Beach at Garden City and Surfside beaches or in North Myrtle Beach. The high season for rentals is mid-June to mid-August, with rates nearly as high in the weeks before and after (exact dates vary by rental company). Expect to pay $1,500 to $3,600 per week for a nice three- to five-bedroom ocean-front house in the high season, with rates dropping considerably off season and for anything not directly on the water. Ocean-front rental condos are less, usually under $1,000 a week in high season.

◆ **Advantage Vacations.** Mostly condos in Myrtle Beach and North Myrtle Beach. *Box 7809, Myrtle Beach, SC 29577; tel. 803-449-1983, 800-685-1777. Open daily.*

◆ **Elliott Realty.** Condos and homes, mostly in North Myrtle Beach. *401 Sea Mountain Hwy., N. Myrtle Beach, SC 29582; tel. 803-249-4106, 800-525-0225. Open daily.*

◆ **Pendegrass Realty.** Rents mainly in the Garden City Beach/Surfside Beach area. *212 Atlantic Ave., Garden City Beach, SC 29576; tel. 803-651-2270, 800-695-7287. Open Mon.-Sat.*

Restaurants

Myrtle Beach has more than 1,500 restaurants. Many of the dining spots emphasize quantity over quality, and all-you-can-eat buffets at modest prices are everywhere. There's a stretch of U.S. Highway 17 just north of the Myrtle Beach city limits known as Restaurant Row. Two large shopping and entertainment complexes, Broadway at the Beach and Barefoot Landing (*see* "Shopping") also have lots of restaurants.

◆ **Thoroughbreds** (expensive). Prime rib, hearty steaks, and veal dishes are the things to order at this deluxe, traditional dinner house with plenty of booths and a racetrack clubhouse decor. Start with the onion soup au gratin or the garlicky escargot and Brie. Excellent service. *9706 U.S. Hwy. 17, Myrtle Beach, SC 29572; tel. 803-497-2636. Open for dinner daily. On the east side of U.S. Hwy. 17, on Restaurant Row, between Magnolia Plaza and the Galleria.*

◆ **Collectors Cafe** (moderate). You'd never believe Myrtle Beach has a place like this: a hip café with local art displayed everywhere. Collectors Cafe specializes in Mediterranean-style dishes and gourmet coffees. The menu changes seasonally, but signature dishes include veal sirloin with pasta and medallions of beef topped with crabmeat, roasted peppers, and Parmesan cheese. *7726 N. Kings Hwy. (U.S. Hwy. 17 N.), Myrtle Beach, SC 29572; tel. 803-449-9370. Open Mon.-Sat. for dinner. In a small shopping center on the east side of U.S. Hwy. 17 near 79th Ave. N.*

◆ **Latif's** (moderate). Delightful café and bakery in an airy, bright setting. Light sandwiches and salads for lunch, more filling dishes, such as salmon, at dinner. Desserts fresh from the bakery are a specialty here. *503 61st Ave. N., Myrtle Beach, SC 29577; tel.*

803-449-1716. Open Mon.-Sat. for lunch and dinner and Sun. for brunch. Bakery open daily 8-4. Closed about 3 weeks in Jan. About 5 mi. north of U.S. Hwy. 501, 1 block west of U.S. Hwy. 17 Business.

◆ **Sea Captain's House** (moderate). Immensely popular, with lines even in the dead of winter, Sea Captain's has among the best views of any restaurant on the Grand Strand. The atmosphere in this rambling oceanside wood-shaked house is comfortable, never stuffy, and you can see the water from most tables. The food is excellent too, with traditional items like fried shrimp and oysters and lighter dishes, such as a salad of shrimp marinated in olive oil with capers. *3002 N. Ocean Blvd., Myrtle Beach, SC 29577; tel. 803-448-8082. Open for breakfast, lunch, and dinner daily. About 1 1/2 mi. north of U.S. Hwy. 501.*

NIGHTLIFE

Myrtle Beach and its environs have more nightlife than most of the rest of South Carolina put together. The biggest attractions are the country music theaters, large live-music houses where many of the biggest stars play.

Anyone raised in the South knows about the shag. Although aficionados may argue over exactly where and when shag dancing started, many believe it originated on Ocean Drive in North Myrtle Beach in the 1950s, and most agree that today Myrtle Beach is the shag capital of the world. Shagging is a slow, shuffling dance—"jitterbugging on Valium," according to humorist Lewis Grizzard. It's danced to 1950s and '60s beach music: tunes by the Drifters, the Temptations, and the Four Tops. To be really with it, you need to wear a Gant madras shirt and Bass Weejuns.

◆ **Alabama Theater.** The country music group Alabama plays here about a dozen times a year, while other big names fill in other dates. An Opryland staged show combining country music, rock, dancing, and comedy is featured. *4750 U.S. Hwy. 17 S., N. Myrtle Beach, SC 29582; tel. 803-272-1111, 800-342-2262. Show dates vary. At Barefoot Landing.*

◆ **Atlantis Nightlife.** Three clubs in one: one featuring live entertainment, one Top 40, and one a dance club with the floor built over a 4,000-gallon aquarium. *U.S. Hwy. 501, Myrtle Beach, SC 29577; tel. 803-448-4200. Open daily.*

◆ **Carolina Opry.** First and still one of the best country music the-aters. *8901-A U.S. Hwy. 17 Business, Myrtle Beach, SC 29572; tel. 803-238-8888, 800-843-6779. Shows Mon.-Sat. Mar.-Oct. and Dec. and Tue.-Sat. Feb. and Nov. Closed Jan. At the junction of U.S. Hwy. 17 Bypass and U.S. Hwy. 17 Business.*

◆ **Dixie Stampede.** Big, family-oriented dinner theater developed by the Dolly Parton/Dollywood folks. *8901-B U.S. Hwy. 17 Business, Myrtle Beach, SC 29577; tel. 803-497-9700, 800-433-4401. Open for dinner shows Mon.-Sat. Mar.-Apr. and daily May-Dec. At the junction of U.S. Hwy. 17 Bypass and U.S. Hwy. 17 Business.*

◆ **Legends.** See—live and on stage—Elvis, Michael Jackson, the Blues Brothers, Madonna, and John Lennon. They're all imper-sonators, of course, but good ones. A fun show. *301 U.S. Hwy. 17 Business, Surfside Beach, SC 29575; tel. 803-238-7827, 800-960-7469. Open Mon.-Sat. late Feb.-Dec.; call for a schedule. About 8 mi. south of Myrtle Beach at Surfside Beach.*

◆ **Medieval Times.** Have dinner while watching knights on horseback joust and stage sword fights in a ring near your table. *2904 Fantasy Way, Myrtle Beach, SC 29577; tel. 803-236-8080, 800-436-4386. Open nightly for dinner shows May-Oct.,Wed. and Fri.-Sat. Feb., Tue.-Sat. Mar. and Nov.-Dec., and Mon.-Sat. Apr. Closed Jan. At Fantasy Harbour.*

◆ **Palace Theater.** This is one of four planned theaters at the glitzy new Broadway at the Beach complex. Superstars such as Bill Cosby headline here. *U.S. Hwy 17 Bypass at 21st Ave N., Box 3467, Myrtle Beach, SC 29578; tel. 803-444-3200, 800-819-2282. Show dates vary. At Broadway at the Beach.*

◆ **Studebaker's.** This bar is one of the many places where you can shag. DJs spin 'em, and the "Studeboppers" dance to the music. *2000 N. Kings Hwy., Myrtle Beach, SC 29577; tel. 803-448-9747, 803-626-3855. Open nightly Mar.-Oct. and Wed.-Sat. Nov.-Feb.*

ATTRACTIONS

Entertainment and shopping complexes such as Fantasy Harbour, Outlet Park, Broadway at the Beach, and Barefoot Landing are attractions in themselves, with visitors arriving by the busload.

◆ **Myrtle Waves.** About 20 acres of water rides. Admission. *3000 10th Ave. N., Myrtle Beach, SC 29577; tel. 803-448-1026. Open* *daily 10-7 Jun.-Aug. and 10-5 May and Sep. Closed Oct.-Apr. Admission. Off U.S. Hwy. 17 Bypass.*

◆ **Pavilion Amusement Park.** Old-time beach-town amusement park, with a Ferris wheel, roller coaster, merry-go-round, cotton candy. Admission. *Ocean Blvd. and 9th Ave. N., Myrtle Beach, SC 29577; tel. 803-448-6456. Open daily Memorial Day-Labor Day and weekends Mar.-May and Sep.-Oct. Admission.*

SHOPPING

◆ **Barefoot Landing.** More than 80 boutiques and outlet shops, plus restaurants and theaters. There's also Myrtle Beach's version of ecotourism—Alligator Adventure, with exhibits of albino alligators, king cobras, and other exotic wildlife. *4898 U.S. Hwy. 17, N. Myrtle Beach, SC 29582; tel. 803-272-8349, 800-272-2320. Open daily.*

◆ **Broadway at the Beach.** New in 1995 and anchored by a pyramid-shaped Hard Rock Cafe and the Palace Theater, Broadway at the Beach appears headed to become Myrtle Beach's hottest and glitziest entertainment and shopping complex. *U.S. Hwy. 17 Bypass, Myrtle Beach, SC 29577; tel. 803-444-3200, 800-819-2282. Open daily. Between 21st and 29th Sts.*

◆ **Outlet Park at Waccamaw/Fantasy Harbour.** With 125 outlet stores in three malls, Outlet Park claims to be the largest outlet shopping center on the East Coast. Adjoining it is Fantasy Harbour, an entertainment complex with a number of different theaters (*see* "Nightlife"). *U.S. Hwy. 501 at the Waterway, Myrtle Beach, SC 29577; tel. 803-236-7902, 803-236-1400, 800-444-8258. Stores open daily. About 5 mi. west of Myrtle Beach.*

◆ **Eagles Beachwear.** This chain of stores, lit at night in gaudy neon, sells beach gear and cheap gifts. Pure Myrtle Beach. Outlets every few blocks along U.S. Highway 17 Business. *301 S. Kings Hwy., U.S. Hwy. 17 Business, Myrtle Beach, SC 29577; tel. 803-448-2160. Open daily. About 20 other area locations.*

BEST FOOD SHOPS

◆ **Harris Teeter.** In addition to groceries, fresh produce, and seafood, it has a good selection of wines, beer, and soft drinks. *North Village Shopping Center, N. Myrtle Beach, SC 29577; tel.*

803-272-8225. Open daily 24 hr. Other locations around the area.
SANDWICHES: ◆ **River City Cafe.** *404 21st. Ave. N., Myrtle Beach, SC 29577; tel. 803-448-1990. Open daily.*
BAKERY: ◆ **Latif's.** *503 61st Ave. N., Myrtle Beach, SC 29577; tel. 803-449-1716. Open daily 8-4. Closed about 3 weeks in Jan. About 5 mi. north of U.S. Hwy. 501, 1 block west of U.S. Hwy. 17 Business.*
ICE CREAM: ◆ **Painter's Home-Made Ice Cream.** *5706 S. Kings Hwy. (U.S. Hwy. 17), Myrtle Beach, SC 29577; tel. 803-238-2724. Open daily. Also 2 other area locations.*
BEVERAGES: ◆ **Owens Discount Beverages.** Liquor, beer, wine. *8000 N. Kings Hwy., Myrtle Beach, SC 29572; tel. 803-449-6833. Open Mon.-Sat.*

SPORTS
FISHING
Serious anglers probably will go a bit north or south, rather than to Myrtle Beach itself, but fishing can be fairly good either offshore or from the piers. The fishing piers are at Myrtle Beach State Park, Cherry Grove, Surfside, and Garden City, and there are two piers in Myrtle Beach.
◆ **Hurricane Fishing Fleet.** Half- and full-day trolling and Gulf Stream fishing on a variety of boats. *Vereen's Marina, U.S. Hwy. 17 at 11th Ave. N., N. Myrtle Beach, SC 29582; tel. 803-249-4575. Operates daily, weather permitting.*
◆ **Myrtle Beach State Park Pier.** Has a bait-and-tackle shop. *U.S. Hwy. 17, Myrtle Beach, SC 29577; tel. 803-238-5326. Open daily. Admission.*

BOATING
◆ **Downwind Sails.** Sailboat rentals, lessons. *2915 S. Ocean Blvd., Myrtle Beach, SC 29577; tel. 803-448-7245. Open daily Apr.-Oct.*
◆ **Hurricane Fleet.** Its 3 1/2-hour cruise offers an easy way to see porpoises and other marine life. *Vereen's Marina, U.S. Hwy. 17 at 11th Ave. N., N. Myrtle Beach, SC 29582; tel. 803-249-3571. Operates daily, weather permitting.*

BICYCLING
You take your life in your hands if you try biking on Myrtle

Beach's crowded streets. Bicycles are banned from the beaches of Myrtle Beach but are permitted on North Myrtle Beach. Unusual three-wheelers—the rider reclines and steers with his or her feet—are rented on the beach.

◆ **Bicycles-n-Gear.** Rentals. *515A Hwy. 501, Myrtle Beach, SC 29577; tel. 803-626-2453. Open daily.*

GOLF

The Myrtle Beach area now boasts more than 80 golf courses, making it one of the top golf destinations in the world and earning it the nicknames "Golf Coast of America" and "America's Seaside Golf Capital." The majority of the courses (unlike at many other golf destinations) are public or semiprivate, so visitors can play most of them. Visitors center racks are stuffed with brochures on golf resorts and golf packages, and most hotels routinely offer golf packages (for information, call Golf Holiday at 803-448-5942 or 800-845-4653). Many of the courses are clustered along U.S. Highway 17 Bypass and along U.S. Highway 501 toward Conway. Here are some of the best.

◆ **Dunes Golf & Beach Club.** This par-72 Robert Trent Jones, Sr., course is one of the most popular on the Grand Strand. It was named the best course in South Carolina in 1995 by *Golf Digest.* It plays a hefty 7,165 yards from the champ tees. Although it's a private course, reciprocity is available with many clubs and facilities. *9000 N. Ocean Blvd., Myrtle Beach, SC 29572; tel. 803-449-5914. Open daily. Admission. From U.S. Hwy. 17 Business south, take Hwy. 73. Make the first left onto Club Dr., continue until you reach Ocean Blvd., and turn left.*

◆ **Heather Glen Golf Links.** Three 9-hole courses played as 18-hole combinations. Rated one of the top 50 public courses in the country by *Golf Digest. U.S. Hwy 17 N., Little River, SC 29566; tel. 803-249-9000. Open daily. Admission. From Myrtle Beach, take U.S. Hwy. 17 north.*

◆ **Legends.** This club has three 18-hole courses with three different styles of play. The 6,785-yard, par-71 Heathland Course, designed by Tom Doak, is a British links course with no trees. The 6,799-yard, par-72 Pete Dye-designed Moorland Course rewards accuracy. The Parkland Course, newest of the three, is wilder, with tree-lined fairways and massive greens. It plays to 7,170 yards at par 72. *1500 Legends Dr., Myrtle Beach, SC 29578; tel. 803-236-9318. Open daily. Admission. Take U.S. Hwy. 501 west and turn left on Legends Dr., following the signs.*

◆ **Myrtle Beach National.** Three courses—King's North, Southcreek, and West—all with the Arnold Palmer touch. The King's North Course, completely redesigned by Palmer in 1995, is the best. *4900 National Dr., Myrtle Beach, SC 29577; tel. 803-448-2308, 800-344-5590. Open daily. Admission. From Myrtle Beach, take U.S. Hwy. 501 about 8 mi.*

◆ **Wild Wing Plantation.** Four good courses, two by Willard Byrd, one by Larry Nelson, and one by Rees Jones. *1000 Wild Wing Blvd., Conway, SC 29526; tel. 803-347-1900. Open daily. Admission. About halfway between Myrtle Beach and Conway off U.S. Hwy. 501.*

TENNIS

There are about 15 free public outdoor courts around Myrtle Beach, including 6 in a complex at U.S. Highway 17 and 19th Avenue South. Among the better private facilities (open to visitors by advance reservation) are the following.

◆ **Kingston Plantation Sport and Health Club.** Nine clay and Har-Tru courts. *9760 Kings Rd., Myrtle Beach, SC 29572; tel. 803-497-2444. Open daily. Admission.*

◆ **Prestwick Health & Tennis Club.** Eleven clay courts, one stadium court, and two hard-surface courts with lights. *1375 McMaster Dr., Myrtle Beach, SC 29575; tel. 803-828-1000. Open daily. Admission.*

TOURIST INFORMATION

◆ **Myrtle Beach Chamber of Commerce.** The Myrtle Beach chamber has several offices around the area, but the Official Grand Strand Welcome Center is on U.S. Highway 501 in Conway (open daily 8:30 to 5). When calling the main office, ask for the current *Myrtle Beach Stay & Play Vacation Guide*, a 300-plus-page guide to hotels and attractions. *1200 N. Oak St., Box 2115, Myrtle Beach, SC 29578; tel. 803-626-7444, 800-356-3016. Open Mon.-Fri. 8:30-5 and Sat. 9-5 in season and Sat. 9-12 the rest of the year. The 800 number has a voice-mail system that allows you to leave a request for tourist information.*

CHAPTER 11

Southern Grand Strand

Beauty	**B**
Swimming	**B+**
Sand	**B+**
Hotels/Inns/B&Bs	**B**
House rentals	**A**
Restaurants	**B**
Nightlife	**C-**
Attractions	**B**
Shopping	**B**
Sports	**B**
Nature	**B**

ooking for excellent beaches? Want easy access to loads of entertainment and nightlife but would rather not be right in the middle of it? Appreciate good restau-

rants and don't mind paying a little more for a fine dinner? Want plenty of golf, tennis, fishing, and other sports? Enjoy exploring historical towns and old plantations and don't mind a few ghosts (most reputedly friendly) on the side? Demand a

131

choice in lodging, from rental homes to B&Bs?

Then you may find Georgetown County to your liking. This part of the South Carolina coast is variously known as the South Strand, the southern part of the Grand Strand, Waccamaw Neck, and Georgetown, or (by the local tourism folks) Georgetown and the Tidelands. The area, as covered in this chapter, is a long, narrow band of land set between the Intracoastal Waterway on the west and the Atlantic Ocean on the east and stretching from around Murrells Inlet in the north to the town of Georgetown in the south, a total distance of almost 30 miles. U.S. Highway 17 is the north-south land artery, bridging two very different areas: booming, bustling Myrtle Beach, next door to the north, and the Low Country of rural Charleston County and the historic city of Charleston to the south.

The heart of beach country here is the center of the strip of land along the coast: Huntington Beach, Litchfield Beach, Pawleys Island, and private gated communities to the south of Pawleys.

Huntington Beach is at Huntington Beach State Park, a 2,500-acre state park with a three-mile stretch of undeveloped beach. This beach, wide and sandy, was rated No. 1 in South Carolina by Dr. Stephen Leatherman, the beach consultant to

HOW TO GET THERE

◆ Murrells Inlet, at the north end of Georgetown County, is about 13 mi. (or a 1/2-hr. drive) south of downtown Myrtle Beach, a little more than 2 hr. south of Wilmington, and about 1 1/2 hr. north of Charleston.

◆ From Wilmington and Myrtle Beach, take U.S. Hwy. 17 south; from Charleston, take U.S. Hwy. 17 north. From I-95, at the Manning exit take U.S. Hwy. 521 east to Georgetown.

◆ By air, Myrtle Beach Jetport has commuter service and limited jet service, but Charleston is the airport of choice. Charleston also has Amtrak service.

this guidebook series. This may be the only beach you'll ever visit with its own castle. In the early 1930s, wealthy railroad heir Archer Huntington and his wife, Anna Hyatt Huntington, a noted sculptor, constructed a 30-room mansion on the beach. Because of the Huntingtons' love of Spanish architecture, they built the house (without benefit of an architect) after the style of Moorish castles along the Mediterranean Sea. Atalaya (Spanish for "watchtower"), so named because of a four-story water tower in the courtyard, is now only an unfurnished shell, but the remarkable castle is open for self-guided tours.

To the south of Huntington Beach is Litchfield Beach. It is best known for its giant resort complex, now called the Litchfield Beach & Golf Resort, but many still refer to it by its former name, Litchfield-by-the-Sea. Litchfield also has private homes and many condominiums.

A bit farther south of Litchfield is Pawleys Island. Pawleys is indeed an island, about three and a half miles long, but the mainland along U.S. Highway 17 is also called Pawleys Island. (In fact, the Litchfield Beach & Golf Resort has a Pawleys Island address.) The island is one of the oldest beach resorts in America. In the 18th and 19th centuries, wealthy rice planters built houses here, where they lived from May to November in an attempt to escape malaria and yellow fever. The oldest home on the island, Pawley House, dates back about two and a half centuries. A number of other old cottages, dating from the mid 19th century, still stand in a small historic district on the south end of the island. For many years, Pawleys was famous in the region for its self-proclaimed slogan, "Arrogantly Shabby." Because of hurricanes and rising property values, however, many of the shabby homes have been replaced by upscale beach houses.

Equally unshabby are the luxury homes at several private developments near Pawleys Island, including Pawleys Plantation and Litchfield Plantation. DeBordieu, a private development south of Pawleys Island (the original, local name was Debidue Beach), is being sold in an unlikely partnership venture with the University of South Carolina, which has plans to set aside a large tract for a coastal research center and a habitat for wildlife.

Two other areas on the coast, Murrells Inlet and the town of Georgetown, are a different kettle of seafood. Murrells Inlet is a small village at the north end of Georgetown County known for the number—if not necessarily the haute cuisine—of its seafood restaurants. It's also the offshore fishing center for the Grand Strand. Its most famous resident is tough-guy novelist Mickey Spillane.

Anchoring the south end of the region, on the southwest side of the Sampit River, is Georgetown. A steel mill and an odoriferous paper plant create a gritty first impression, but the historic district by the Sampit River is charming, with pre-Revolutionary War houses, attractive shops, and a nice collection of bed-and-breakfasts. Georgetown was once one of the jewels of the Carolina coast, a port city where wealthy rice planters and merchants built lovely homes.

By some accounts, Georgetown has more ghosts per capita than any place in America. About 100 ghostly apparitions have been spotted here. One specter, the ghost of a little girl drowned in Winyah Bay, is said to haunt the unmanned North Island lighthouse, across the bay from Georgetown.

High season here runs approximately from Memorial Day to Labor Day, but spring and fall offer comfortable weather for golf and other sports, as well as sightseeing in the historic district and other areas.

BEACHES
HUNTINGTON BEACH STATE PARK

The drive into this state park gives a hint as to why this is a special place. You cross a short causeway with alligators sunning on islands in the lagoon and a plethora of birds to add to your life list. Then you arrive at the beach: Ahead is

Beauty	B+
Swimming	A-
Sand	B+
Amenities	A

a broad, beautiful expanse of sand leading to the gently breaking ocean. To your right, on the beach, are the remains of Atalaya, a logic-defying Moorish-style castle, once the winter home and studio of the sculptor Anna Hyatt Huntington and her husband. You can hike on nature trails, picnic, or just veg on the beach. Huntington is the least-disturbed, best-preserved beach

on South Carolina's Grand Strand. *About 3 mi. south of Murrells Inlet. Watch for signs on the east side of U.S. Hwy. 17.*
Swimming: Excellent, in clean water. Wave energy is moderate, so this is a good area for children. Lifeguard on duty in summer.
Sand: The beach is wide and sandy, with light-gray to nearly white sand. There are few dunes—just a broad expanse of beach.
Amenities: Rest rooms, showers, park store, snack bar, picnic tables.
Sports: Swimming, surf fishing, shelling.
Parking: There are more than 200 parking spaces near Atalaya and another 125 at the north end of the park ($3 per vehicle park admission, except in winter).

LITCHFIELD BEACH

Development at Litchfield Beach has made it less appealing than some of Georgetown County's other beaches. Even so, it's not bad, with mostly wide, sandy beaches with a gentle slope just right for sunning and swimming. The

Beauty	B-
Swimming	B
Sand	B
Amenities	C-

homes here are generally more downscale than those on Pawleys Island, and there are more condos lining the beach.
From U.S. Hwy. 17, take Litchfield Dr. east.
Swimming: Very good. No lifeguard.
Sand: Light gray to near white.
Amenities: This is a residential beach—don't expect much in the way of amenities for day visitors.
Sports: Swimming, surf fishing.
Parking: A 100-car free parking lot is across from the Litchfield Inn on Norris Road at Sundial Drive. For other parking along the beach front, look for tan-colored beach access markers.

PAWLEYS ISLAND BEACH

Pawleys has a lazy, old-time feel, which is not unusual for an island that's one of the oldest resorts in the United States. The three-and-a-half-mile beach front is pleasant, if not exceptional. The old cottages along the beach in the island's

Beauty	B
Swimming	B+
Sand	B
Amenities	C-

small historic district are absolutely wonderful—if there were nothing else here, they alone would be reason enough for a visit. *From U.S. Hwy. 17, turn east on N. Causeway Rd. or S. Causeway Rd. and follow to Pawleys Dr., which parallels the beach.*
Swimming: Excellent. No lifeguard.
Sand: The beach here has a gentle slope. The sand is light gray to near white. The beach is fairly narrow at high tide. There are groins at the south end of the beach.
Amenities: This is a residential beach, and day-trippers are discouraged, so there are few amenities.
Sports: Swimming, surf fishing.
Parking: At several points along Pawleys Drive, the road bordering the beach, there are small neighborhood parking lots, each with about a dozen free parking spaces.

HOTELS/INNS/B&BS

For B&Bs, stay in the historic district of Georgetown. Near the historic district, along U.S. Highway 17, there are also several modest motels, and a Hampton Inn is set to open in mid-1996.

◆ **Litchfield Plantation Inn** (very expensive). If you've always imagined waking up in a luxurious suite in a beautiful 250-year-old Low Country plantation mansion, this is the place for you. At the end of a long driveway framed by moss-draped live oaks, the plantation inn sits on landscaped grounds next to a marsh. Each of the inn's four suites is large and lovely. The Ballroom Suite on the second floor, with a whirlpool bath, veranda, and king-size bed, is extraordinary. The inn is in the private Litchfield Plantation real-estate development, and the management company also offers accommodations in a large guesthouse and in several luxury cottages (expensive); these are very nice, but you should book one of the suites at the plantation inn, which is more interesting and romantic. Free tennis, pool. Guests also have use of a private beach club on Pawleys Island. Don't confuse this place with the motellike Litchfield Inn. *216 U.S. Hwy. 17 S., Box 290, Pawleys Island, SC 29585; tel. 803-237-9121, 800-869-1410. When checking in during regular office hours, stop at the guest center on U.S. Hwy. 17; after hours, stop at the guarded gate to the development. From U.S. Hwy. 17, take Waverly Rd. west about 1*

3/4 mi. Make a right on Kings River Rd. and go 3/4 mi. to the guarded entrance gate to the Litchfield Plantation development, on the left.

◆ **Litchfield Beach & Golf Resort** (expensive). Huge resort complex with an all-suite hotel, one- to three-bedroom beach-front condos, condo villas, restaurants, shops, several pools, tennis center with 17 courts, and three golf courses. The resort and its real-estate developments sprawl over several thousand acres and include a long stretch of very good beach. The best accommodations here are the two- and three-bedroom units in the high-rise condo towers (very expensive), which are near the beach and have terrific swimming pools; the ocean-view units are the choicest. Rooms in the 96-suite hotel tower could use some refurbishing, and the hotel is a considerable walk, or a shuttle ride, from the beach. *U.S. Hwy. 17 S., Drawer 320, Pawleys Island, SC 29585; tel. 803-237-3000, 800-845-1897; fax 803-237-3282.*

◆ **1790 House B&B** (moderate). One of the most attractive B&Bs in South Carolina, this 200-year-old house, built in a West Indies style when rice was king in the Low Country, has five rooms decorated to the hilt. Gabrielle's Library, with a working gas fireplace and a Victorian iron and brass bed, and the Rice Planter's Suite, at a huge 500 square feet, are favorites. A detached cottage out back (expensive) is a romantic hideaway with a Windsor bed and a whirlpool tub. Gourmet breakfast, cable TV in all rooms, and complimentary sherry, beer, and soft drinks. *630 Highmarket St., Georgetown, SC 29440; tel. 803-546-4821, 800-890-7432. In the historic district, about 3 blocks from the water front.*

◆ **King's Inn at Georgetown B&B** (moderate). Seven rooms in a Federal-style 1825 home. The house is listed on the National Historic Register. Each room is decorated differently with antiques and reproductions. The Blue Room (expensive), with a French Provincial canopied king-size bed and Oriental rugs, is a top choice here. Rooms have private baths. There's a small lap pool. Full breakfast, afternoon tea and sherry, and terry bath robes. *230 Broad St., Georgetown, SC 29940; tel. 803-527-6937, 800-251-8805. In the historic district, about 3 blocks from the water front.*

◆ **Brookwood Inn** (inexpensive). This small independent motel nestled under some oaks will remind you of the way the South Carolina coast used to be. It's not fancy, but the rooms are clean, and it's an excellent value. The top choice is a suite with a king-size bed and a whirlpool bath in a small detached building. *U.S. Hwy. 17 Business, Box 544, Murrells Inlet, SC 29576; tel. 803-651-2550.*

HOUSE RENTALS

Most vacationers rent a house or a condo villa. Pawleys Island has primarily single family homes, while Litchfield offers both homes and condos in larger buildings. DeBordieu is a private, ocean-front community south of Pawleys Island that offers rentals, with access to miles of beach and golf on a private course. The priciest rental season is early June to late August, with May and September rates often a third less. The rest of the year, houses go for half the peak summer rates or less. For an ocean-front four- or five-bedroom home in summer, you'll pay $2,000 to $3,000 or more per week. One block from the ocean, the rental rates are much lower, often under $1,500. Two- and three-bedroom condos usually go for less than $1,000 a week. Book in January for the best selection.

◆ **DeBordieu.** Rents homes in the private DeBordieu community, which has an excellent beach. *129 Luvan Blvd., Georgetown, SC 29440; tel. 803-546-4176. Open daily.*

◆ **Dune Realty.** Rents homes on Pawleys Island and in Litchfield Beach. *13236 U.S. Hwy. 17 N., Pawleys Island, SC 29585; tel. 803-237-4473, 800-779-3947. Open Mon.-Sat.*

◆ **Pawleys Island Realty.** Rents homes on Pawleys Island and in Litchfield Beach. *Box 306, Pawleys Island, SC 29585; tel. 803-237-4257, 800-937-7352. Open Mon.-Sat.*

RESTAURANTS

Here you'll find quietly sophisticated dining at a fairly stiff price. Murrells Inlet, at the north end of Georgetown County, is a special case: Like Calabash, North Carolina (*see* Chapter 9), it's a small fishing village that has become known as a place to go for fresh and inexpensive seafood dinners.

Most restaurants in Georgetown County close on Sundays, because alcohol can't be served then.

◆ **Frank's** (expensive). This is the most popular restaurant in the area, with reservations difficult to get in summer. Frank's has an open grill and the comfortable, almost clubby atmosphere of an upscale steak house. The menu, however, is broader than that of a steak house, with veal, fish, chicken, and other dishes. You won't find innovative cooking here, but everything is done just right and the service is excellent. Try the rack of lamb or the steak *au poivre*, both with seasoned mashed potatoes. Out Back at Frank's serves lighter fare at lunch. *U.S. Hwy. 17, Pawleys Island, SC 29585; tel. 803-237-3030. Open Mon.-Sat. for dinner. Out Back at Frank's (tel. 803-237-1777) is open Mon.-Sat. for lunch. At the traffic light at Pawleys Island.*

◆ **Community House** (moderate). It's a nice surprise to find such a good Northern Italian restaurant near the beach. This one's in an old schoolhouse, with a bright and pleasant atmosphere. Chef-owner David Bardari serves delicious pasta, veal, and seafood. *10555 Ocean Hwy. (U.S. Hwy. 17), Pawleys Island, SC 29585; tel. 803-237-8353. Open daily for dinner. At the traffic light at Pawleys Island.*

◆ **Rice Paddy** (moderate). The best restaurant in Georgetown, it has no view and is tucked away in a small commercial center. But once you taste the Low Country cuisine here, you'll know why it's busy all the time. Signature dishes include pan-fried quail with grits, baked snapper stuffed with spinach and shrimp, and lump crab cakes. *408 Duke St., Georgetown, SC 29440; tel. 803-546-2021. Open Tue.-Fri. for lunch and dinner and Sat. for dinner. Closed several weeks in January. In the historic district.*

◆ **Island Cafe and Deli** (inexpensive). Good spot for sandwiches at lunch or light entrées at dinner. Casual café atmosphere. Try the Clubby Checker (a club sandwich with roast beef and turkey) from the deli. Wednesday dinners feature a 1 1/4-pound Maine lobster for $10.95. *Island Shops, U.S. Hwy. 17 S., Pawleys Island, SC 29595; tel. 803-237-9527. Open daily for lunch and dinner.*

◆ **Russell's Seafood Grill** (inexpensive). Although there are many choices in Murrells Inlet, Russell's is special because it's like the old-time Murrells Inlet restaurants that made the little village famous. The atmosphere is nautical without being hokey, and locals drop in for a beer at the bar or a basket of fried "creek shrimp" (tasty small local shrimp). *U.S. Hwy. 17 Business, Murrells Inlet, SC 29576; tel. 803-651-0553. Open Mon.-Sat. for lunch and dinner. On the west side of U.S. Hwy. 17 Business.*

NIGHTLIFE

You'll find a few bars in Murrells Inlet, but for serious entertainment and late-night action, head north to Myrtle Beach (*see* Chapter 10).

ATTRACTIONS

◆ **Brookgreen Gardens.** Considered the finest public sculpture garden in the United States, Brookgreen has more than 560 works of art by more than 240 artists, displayed in a beautiful setting on 300 acres of formal and natural gardens. It was owned by railroad heir Archer Huntington and his sculptor-wife, Anna Hyatt Huntington. This National Historic Landmark also has a wildlife area with deer, alligators, and two aviaries. *1931 Brookgreen Dr., Murrells Inlet, SC 29576; tel. 803-237-4218, 800-849-1931. Admission. Open daily for self-guided tours 9:30-4:45.*

◆ **Georgetown Historic District.** Georgetown was founded in 1729. A number of pre-Revolutionary War homes still stand in the historic district, which is about 24 square blocks in size. You can stroll the district on your own. It's eminently walkable—especially in spring and fall, when the weather's not too hot. Get a historic district map from the Chamber of Commerce (*see* "Tourist Information"). You can take a 55-minute tram tour (Georgetown Tour Co., tel. 803-546-6827) or a guided walking tour. Nell Morris Cribb, a Georgetown native who is quite knowledgeable about local history (including the ghosts), conducts walking tours (tel. 803-546-3975).

◆ **Hopsewee Plantation.** The small house, built of black cypress from 1735 to 1740 and excellently preserved, is one of the oldest standing plantation homes in the region. *494 Hopsewee Rd. (U.S. Hwy. 17 S.), Georgetown, SC 29440; tel. 803-546-7891. House open Tue.-Fri. 10-4 Mar.-Oct.; grounds open daily. Admission. About 12 mi. south of Georgetown.*

◆ **Kaminski House.** The appeal of this pre-Revolutionary War house/museum is its collection of fine antiques, including many objects crafted in Charleston. *1003 Front St., Georgetown, SC 29440; tel. 803-546-7706. Guided tours on the hour Mon.-Sat. 10-4 and Sun. 1-4. Admission. On the west end of the historic district.*

◆ **Plantation Tours.** Tours of area plantations, churches, and historical homes that are not usually open to the public are held annually, usually on two days in March or April. Ask the Georgetown Chamber of Commerce (*see* "Tourist Information") for dates and schedules, or contact the sponsor of the tour: *Prince George Winyah Episcopal Church, 300 Broad and Highmarket Sts., Box 674, Georgetown, SC 29442; tel. 803-546-4375. Admission.*

SHOPPING

Front Street on the Sampit River in the historic district of Georgetown has many quaint small shops and galleries. Along U.S. Highway 17 near Pawleys Island and Litchfield Beach are two shopping areas of interest to the visitor: the Hammock Shops and the Island Shops.

◆ **Mark Twain Store.** Small bookshop with sizable collection of local-interest books. *723 Front St., Georgetown, SC 29440; tel. 803-546-8212. Open Mon.-Sat. and occasionally on Sun.*

◆ **Original Hammock Shop.** Pawleys Island-style rope hammocks, which have been made in the area for more than 100 years, are woven without knots for comfort (they cost about $100). *U.S. Hwy. 17, Box 201, Pawleys Island, SC 29595; tel. 803-237-9122, 800-332-3490. Open daily. In the Hammock Shops shopping complex.*

BEST FOOD SHOPS

◆ **Harris Teeter.** Besides groceries, produce, and baked goods, it carries wine, beer, and soft drinks. *Litchfield Landing, U.S. Hwy. 17, Pawleys Island, SC 29585; tel. 803-237-8456. Open daily.*

SANDWICHES: ◆ **Daniel's.** *713 Front St., Georgetown, SC 29940; tel. 803-546-4377. Open Mon.-Sat. On the water front in the historic district.*

SEAFOOD: ◆ **Independent Seafood Co.** *1 Cannon St., Georgetown, SC 29940; tel. 803-546-6642. Open Mon.-Sat.*

BAKERY: ◆ **Kudzu Bakery.** *714 Front St., Georgetown, SC 29940; tel. 803-546-1847. Open Mon.-Sat.*

ICE CREAM: ◆ **Pawleys Island Ice Cream Parlor.** *U.S. Hwy. 17, Pawleys Island, SC 29585; tel. 803-237-8867. Open daily.*

BEVERAGES: ◆ **SeaBreeze Liquors & Fine Wines.** *4317 Litchfield Landing, U.S. Hwy. 17, Pawleys Island, SC 29585; tel. 803-237-1292. Open Mon.-Sat. Next to the Harris Teeter.*

SPORTS
FISHING

Capt. Dick's Marina (*see* "Boating") at Murrells Inlet is the center for offshore fishing. There's also inshore and surf fishing, crabbing, and seining for shrimp. In the cooler months, you can collect oysters and clams at low tide.

BOATING

◆ **Capt. Dick's Marina.** Full-service marina rents slips, sells bait, and offers fish cleaning. Also rents boats with outboard motors for fishing, crabbing, or sightseeing. *U.S. Hwy. 17 Business, Murrells Inlet, SC 29576. Open daily.*

BICYCLING

◆ **Island Bikes.** Rentals. *10080 Ocean Hwy. (U.S. Hwy. 17), Pawleys Island, SC 29585; tel. 803-237-1918, 800-450-9636. Open daily.*

GOLF

The South Strand offers excellent and plentiful golf on courses that in many cases have been carved out of old rice plantations. For additional choices, head to Myrtle Beach (*see* Chapter 10).

◆ **Blackmoor Club.** Gary Player designed this 6,614-yard, par-72 public course in 1990. *Hwy. 707, Murrells Inlet, SC 29576; tel. 803-650-5555. Open daily. Admission. From U.S. Hwy. 17, take Hwy. 707 west 3 1/2 mi. The course is on the left.*

◆ **Litchfield Beach & Golf Resort.** This large resort offers three good courses, all open to the public. The 6,677-yard, par-72 River Club, designed by Tom Jackson, is very difficult. The Litchfield Country Club, built in 1966, was designed by Willard Byrd and plays to 6,752 yards at par 72. The third course, Willbrook Plantation, also par 72 at 6,674 yards from the champ tees, was designed by Dan Maples. *U.S. Hwy. 17, Drawer 320, Pawleys Island, SC 29585; tel. 803-237-3000, 800-845-1897. Open daily. Admission. Resort check-in is on the east side of U.S. Hwy. 17 at Pawleys Island.*

◆ **Pawleys Plantation.** A Jack Nicklaus design, this 7,026-yard, par-72 course is private, but play is available to those renting a villa here or by reciprocal agreement with other private clubs. *U.S.*

142

Hwy. 17, Pawleys Island, SC 29585; tel. 803-237-1736. Open daily. Admission. Entrance on east side of U.S. Hwy. 17 at Pawleys Island.

TENNIS

◆ **Litchfield Beach & Golf Resort.** The Litchfield Racquet Club (open to the public) has been named one of the 50 best tennis resorts in the United States by *Tennis* magazine. It has 17 Har-Tru courts, 3 of which are lighted, and 2 indoor courts. *U.S. Hwy. 17, Drawer 320, Pawleys Island, SC 29585; tel. 803-237-3411, 800-845-1897. Open daily. Admission. Resort check-in is on the east side of U.S. Hwy. 17 at Pawleys Island.*

NATURE

◆ **Bellefield Nature Center.** Part of the Belle W. Baruch Foundation, which owns a 17,500-acre wildlife preserve and conducts marine research, the center has a museum with nature exhibits, displays, and small terrariums and aquariums. *Hobcaw Barony, Georgetown, SC 29440; tel. 803-546-4623. Open Mon.-Fri. 10-5 and Sat. 1-5. On the east side of U.S. Hwy. 17, about 1 1/2 mi. north of Georgetown.*

◆ **Huntington Beach State Park.** Besides an excellent beach, this 2,500-acre park also offers excellent bird- and alligator-watching areas. *U.S. Hwy. 17, Murrells Inlet, SC 29576; tel. 803-237-4440. Open daily 6-10 Apr.-Sep. and 6-6 Oct.-Mar. Admission is $3 per person ($1.50 for children 6-12), except in winter.*

◆ **Tom Yawkey Wildlife Preserve.** This 20,000-acre preserve, owned by the state, consists of three islands rich in wildlife. Access to much of the area is by boat only, and all of the preserve is closed to the public. The Yawkey Wildlife Center, a field lab and research facility, conducts three-hour field trips to South and Cat islands once a week. These free trips are limited to 14 people and are usually booked two to four months in advance. *Yawkey Wildlife Center, Rte. 2, Box 181, Georgetown, SC 29440; tel. 803-546-6814.*

TOURIST INFORMATION

◆ **Georgetown County Chamber of Commerce.** *102 Broad St., Box 1776, Georgetown, SC 29442; tel. 803-546-8436, 800-777-7705. Open Mon.-Sat. 9-5 and Sun. 10-2.*

CHAPTER 12

Charleston

Beauty	B
Swimming	B
Sand	B-
Hotels/Inns/B&Bs	A
House rentals	A-
Restaurants	A
Nightlife	A
Attractions	A
Shopping	A
Sports	B
Nature	B-

A visit to Charleston offers the appealing combination of good beaches and one of America's most interesting and historic cities. As in San Francisco, it's easy to lose your heart to this charming and sophisticated town. The area offers so much to do, see, and enjoy that it is routinely named one of the top visitor destinations in America, garnering among other honors the No. 5 ranking in *Condé Nast Traveler* magazine's 1995 readers' poll of favorite U.S. vacation cities.

Alas, Charleston's sandy beaches and its eminently walkable downtown historic districts are separated by miles of suburban sprawl and, in some cases, bitter urban poverty. The city's popularity, too, has meant high demand and high prices for lodging in its historic inns and luxury hotels. Aside from these two lamentable realities, Charleston is a nearly ideal destination for travelers seeking a variety of activities and attractions by the sea—pleasant beaches and plentiful water sports, historic sites galore in a 325-year-old city, terrific dining with a distinctive regional cuisine, a lively arts scene, and good golf, fishing, and other sports, all in a subtropical climate where camellias, azaleas, and magnolias grow almost like weeds.

By American standards, Charleston is an old city. It was founded in 1670 as Charles Town, named for Britain's King Charles II. By the early 1700s the city had become one of the leading Colonial ports. After the British left in 1783, the city was renamed Charleston. From then until the Civil War, Charleston's fortunes grew. Many Low Country planters

HOW TO GET THERE

◆ **Charleston is midway between Savannah, GA, and Myrtle Beach (about 2 hr. by car). From Savannah, take I-95 about 45 mi., then U.S. Hwy. 17 north at Point South. Go about 58 mi. on U.S. Hwy. 17 north to Charleston. From Myrtle Beach, take U.S. Hwy. 17 south, about 98 mi.**

◆ **From Columbia, Charleston is 120 mi. (2 1/4 hr.) southeast on I-26.**

◆ **Charleston International Airport, about 12 mi. northwest of the downtown historic district, has jet service on five carriers, plus commuter service. The city also has Amtrak service.**

amassed immense wealth, which they then used to build and furnish elaborate homes in Charleston. That period ended with the secession of South Carolina from the Union and the April 1861 occupation, by Confederate forces, of Fort Sumter in Charleston Harbor. Union forces blockaded the city for three years and finally drove out the Confederate defenders, but most of Charleston was spared the destruction of some other Southern cities, such as Atlanta. Reconstruction was a difficult time for Charleston, and it wasn't until well into the 20th century that the city began to enjoy an economic rebound as part of the Sunbelt South.

What's high season in Charleston? It depends. If you're staying at the beach, high season is early May to September, when the ocean is warm enough for comfortable swimming. In town, prime time is the spring, roughly March through early May, and again in the fall, September to mid-November: These periods offer the most pleasant weather, with high temperatures in the 60s to 70s and lows in the 40s and 50s. There are tours of otherwise private homes during these periods: The Festival of Houses and Gardens is held mid-March to mid-April, and the Candlelight Tours of Houses and Gardens is held late September to October. The two weeks after Memorial Day are very busy in Charleston because of Spoleto Festival U.S.A., the international festival celebrating the arts, and its companion festival, Piccolo Spoleto, which focuses on local and southeastern arts and music. Summer is hot and very humid, with air temperatures reaching the 90s and humidity 90 percent on some days.

BEACHES

Charleston's three main Atlantic beaches are east and south of the city. Each offers a somewhat different atmosphere, although all are relatively low-key. Folly Beach, to the south, is a traditional beach destination for area residents, and an attractive county park offers some of the best swimming in the area. George Gershwin lived at Folly when he wrote *Porgy and Bess*, which is set in Charleston. Sullivan's Island (sometimes written as Sullivans Island, as apostrophes were in short supply when this and other islands along the coast were named) and the Isle of Palms, to the east, are residential areas with public beach access. Wild Dunes, Charleston's largest resort, is on the Isle of Palms. At all beaches, erosion has been a significant problem.

ISLE OF PALMS

The Isle of Palms, about 11 miles from the downtown historic district, is a newer community than Folly Beach or Sullivan's Island, dating from just after World War II. It's also a bit flashier and has some of the area's most upmarket beach

Beauty	**B-**
Swimming	**B**
Sand	**B**
Amenities	**C+**

homes. The beach here—seven miles along the Atlantic—is pleasant rather than breathtaking, and continued beach erosion means that in places the beach is very narrow, especially at high tide.

This is primarily a residential area, with some commercial development along the major road through the island, Palm Boulevard, and a concentration of beach shops, bars, and restaurants on Ocean Boulevard, just off Palm Boulevard at an area called Front Beach.

While young people hang out at the Ocean Boulevard commercial area and beach, most activities start and end at homes on the island. There is beach access on paths next to houses, about every block or two off Palm Boulevard, Ocean Boulevard, or one of the avenues that cross these streets. Wild Dunes Resort, at the island's eastern end, is a private, gated community, and only residents and rental guests may enter the beach at the resort (although once you're on the beach, you can visit any part of it, including Wild Dunes).

Because of the length of the beach—and the fact that there are no large hotels or massive high-rise developments, except at Front Beach at the Ocean Boulevard commercial area—the beach is usually not jammed with people, even in peak summer periods. *From the downtown historic district, take U.S. Hwy. 17 north to U.S. Hwy. 17 Business. Turn onto Hwy. 703 at the Coleman Blvd. exit. Stay on Hwy. 703 across Sullivan's Island to the Isle of Palms. There's a sharp left turn shortly after you enter Sullivan's Island. (Hwy. 703 is called Jasper Blvd. on Sullivan's Island and Palm Blvd. on the Isle of Palms.) Alternatively, take U.S. Hwy.*

17/U.S. Hwy. 701 north to the Isle of Palms Connector (Hwy. 517). Follow the Connector 3.9 mi. to its intersection with Palm Blvd. To reach the Ocean Blvd./Front Beach area, cross Palm Blvd. and go straight about 1 block to Ocean Blvd. Limited on-street parking is available here. To reach Wild Dunes, turn left on Palm Blvd.

Swimming: In summer, the warm waters offer good swimming. No lifeguard.

Sand: The beaches here have light-gray to tan sand, with gentle slopes. Beach erosion is a continuous problem.

Amenities: Because the Isle of Palms is a residential area, there are not a lot of amenities. The Ocean Boulevard area has rest rooms and plenty of places to get a meal or a drink.

Sports: In addition to the usual water sports on the beach, the Isle of Palms has a recreation area at 24th to 28th avenues, with baseball, soccer, and football fields, tennis and basketball courts, and playgrounds. Surfing can be good here, especially during periods of tropical storm activity in the Atlantic, although The Washout at Folly Beach is better known as a surfing beach.

Parking: Limited parking on Ocean Boulevard at Front Beach and on the street at the many beach access points. However, most visitors rent a house and walk to the beach.

SULLIVAN'S ISLAND

Sullivan's Island, about nine miles east of Charleston's downtown historic district, is one of the oldest beach communities in the South: Charlestonians began building summer cottages and year-round homes here in the early 19th century.

Beauty	B-
Swimming	B
Sand	B-
Amenities	C

One of its most famous residents was Edgar Allan Poe, who researched "The Gold Bug," a tale of buried pirate treasure, on the island. Today, the island is a middle-class, family-oriented residential area, with little commercial development on the beach. It has almost no hotels and only a few restaurants and bars on Middle Street. As on the Isle of Palms, the beach here is pleasant but not spectacular, with homes, some of them dating to the 19th century, along the beach front. The beach is usually not crowded.

Fort Moultrie, an important Revolutionary War site and

part of the Fort Sumter National Monument park, stands with its lighthouse at the southwest end of Sullivan's Island. *From the downtown historic district, take U.S. Hwy. 17 north to U.S. Hwy. 17 Business. Turn onto Hwy. 703 at the Coleman Blvd. exit. Stay on Hwy. 703 to Sullivan's Island—there's a left turn shortly after you enter Sullivan's Island. (Hwy. 703 is called Jasper Blvd. here.) Alternatively, take U.S. Hwy. 17/U.S. Hwy. 701 north to the Isle of Palms Connector (Hwy. 517). Follow the Connector 3.9 mi. to its intersection with Palm Blvd. (Hwy. 703). Turn right and go about 2 mi. to Sullivan's Island.* Swimming: The swimming is good. No lifeguard.
Sand: The beach is gently sloping, with light-gray to tan sand.
Amenities: Very limited.
Sports: Swimming is the main activity. A small park on Middle Street has a couple of tennis courts and other sports facilities.
Parking: Limited parking along residential streets.

FOLLY BEACH

About 12 miles from the downtown historic district, Folly is an old beach community. A popular spot for Big Bands to play until the late 1940s, it went into something of a decline after World War II, but today it has emerged as a com-

Beauty	B-
Swimming	B
Sand	B
Amenities	B

fortable blend of unpretentious old beach homes and some new development. Parts of Folly will remind you of small towns on the Florida Panhandle, with screened porches and quiet streets shaded by cedar, cherry laurel, and palmetto (the name *Folly* comes from an Old English word for an area with dense foliage).

Folly Beach stretches more than six miles along the Atlantic on Folly Island. At the southwestern tip of the island is Folly Beach County Park, an attractive park with some of the best beaches and swimming in the Charleston area (admission: $3 per vehicle). On the Folly River side of the park, there are beautiful views of the marsh.

The center of the island has a little commercial development, a handful of motels and guesthouses, a few restaurants and shops, and a fishing pier. The beach here is less attractive than at the park because of development. The northeastern end of the island is purely residential, and the beach is very eroded. At the northeasternmost end of the island, the section known locally as The Washout (aptly named because the churning sea washes out the sand, leaving rough beach surface and unpredictable currents), is poor for swimming but popular for surfing.

If you ask people in South Carolina about Folly Beach, they may tell you that it's not as nice as Isle of Palms and Sullivan's Island. But with the heavy residential and tourist pressures on these areas, Folly—with its laid-back, unpolished style—is looking better and better. Add to that the attractive natural setting of Folly Beach County Park and you may decide that you like Folly best of all. *From Charleston's historic district, take Hwy. 30 across the Ashley River to James Island and the junction with Hwy. 171, about 4 mi. Turn south on Hwy. 171 (also known as Folly Rd. as it approaches Folly Island) and drive about 9 mi. Folly Rd. ends at a stoplight at its intersection with Ashley Ave. To get to the fishing pier, go straight on Center St.—parking is to the left of the Holiday Inn. To get to Folly Beach County Park, turn right and follow Ashley Ave. to its end at Folly Beach County Park. Park in the paved lots inside the park. For The Washout or the northeast end of the island, turn left instead of right off Folly Rd. onto Ashley Ave. Arctic Ave., 1 block over toward the ocean, is a narrow one-way street that parallels the Atlantic on the northeast end of the island. Limited parking is available at the many neighborhood beach access points along the streets adjoining the beach.*

Swimming: Swimming is good at the Folly Beach County Park and in the center of the island. Erosion makes swimming less inviting the farther northeast you go. Water temperatures reach the 80s June to September. Lifeguard on duty at the park only from May through August and on weekends in September.

Sand: Light gray to tan. The beach is wide and sandy at low tide, with a gentle slope. There are low dunes in places but no trees or other shade on the beach.

Amenities: At Folly Beach County Park there are attractive changing rooms and a snack bar.

Sports: Surfing is popular year-round at The Washout, on the northeast end of the island. Fishing and crabbing are fair to good at the 1,000-foot Folly Pier, next to the Holiday Inn.

Parking: There's parking (adequate except on summer weekends) at Folly Beach County Park, limited parking (fee) at the Folly Pier, and free parking at points along the roads next to the beach (Arctic and Ashley avenues).

HOTELS/INNS/B&BS

Charleston has more interesting hotels and charming inns than any other city in South Carolina, and most of them are fully booked in spring and fall. For B&Bs, you may want to use a reservation service, such as Historic Charleston Bed and Breakfast (60 Broad St., Charleston, SC 29401; tel. 803-722-6066). Many hotels are on Meeting Street, one of the two main north-south streets on the peninsula. The lower Meeting Street numbers are at the Battery near Charleston Harbor, and by the time you get to the 375 range, you're near the upper edge of the safe, walkable part of the downtown area.

Accommodations on or near the beach, where high season is early May to September, are limited to a few motels and one large resort.

◆ **Charleston Place, An Orient-Express Hotel** (very expensive). This is the one for you if you're looking for a luxurious, modern hotel with all the full-service trimmings, well-located in the historic district. The best rooms are on the top two floors: They have extra amenities, such an included breakfast and an open bar. For the best views of the historic district, ask for one of the rooms facing east. Elegant public rooms, indoor pool, gym, sauna, and steam room. *130 Market St., Charleston, SC 29401; tel. 803-722-4900, 800-611-5545; fax 803-722-4074. In the heart of the downtown historic district.*

◆ **Two Meeting Street Inn** (very expensive). This is one of the most popular B&Bs in the entire state, and with good reason. The house is an architectural delight, with curved bays, wraparound porches, English oak paneling, winding staircases, and Tiffany stained-glass windows. The location is unbeatable, right on the Battery overlooking White Point Park, with moss-draped live oaks shading the house, and Charleston Harbor in the distance. The best of the nine rooms are on the second of the three floors: These rooms have 12-foot ceilings, canopy beds, and private baths. No credit cards. Children over 12 only. *2 Meeting*

St., Charleston, SC 29401; tel. 803-723-7322. In the historic district.

◆ **Wild Dunes Resort** (very expensive). The area's largest resort has two excellent golf courses (*see* "Golf") and a nationally ranked tennis program (*see* "Tennis"), as well as a long stretch of beach. At this private, gated community, accommodations are in condo villas; there are also rental houses (*see* "House Rentals"). Most lodgings are in clusters of two- to five-story villas, some ocean front, some with golf-course or other views. Rates vary significantly from villa to villa and seasonally and don't include fees for sports and recreational activities. The resort has on-site restaurants, a fitness center, marina, shops, a rec center, bike and Rollerblade rentals, children's programs, and a number of swimming pools. *5757 Palm Blvd., Isle of Palms, SC 29451; tel. 803-886-6000, 800-845-8880; fax 803-886-2916. At the eastern tip of Isle of Palms. Follow Palm Blvd. to the entrance (watch for signs).*

◆ **Charleston on the Beach** (expensive). This Holiday Inn is your best hotel choice—in fact, one of your few choices—at Folly Beach. A coral-colored nine-story high-rise, it is directly on the beach, next to the fishing pier. Although the hotel claims a complete remodeling was done in 1994-95, carpets and other furnishings in some of the 132 rooms look as if they were skipped. All rooms face the ocean and have small balconies. Those on the higher floors have the best views. Ocean-front bar with pool. *1 Center St., Folly Beach, SC 29439; tel. 803-588-6464, 800-290-0001; fax 803-588-2500. At the junction of Hwy. 171 (Folly Rd.) and Center St.*

◆ **Kings Courtyard Inn** (expensive). A group of buildings dating from 1853 have been renovated and converted into a pleasant 41-room inn. By far the best digs in the three-story hotel are the four two-room suites with fireplaces and king-size four-poster canopy beds (very expensive). A continental breakfast is delivered to your room, and afternoon sherry is served in the lobby. Tiny pool. Excellent location. *198 King St., Charleston, SC 29401; tel. 803-723-7000, 800-845-6119; fax 803-720-2608. In the heart of the downtown historic district.*

◆ **Hampton Inn Historic District** (moderate). This is one of the nicest Hampton Inns you'll ever stay in, and it's an excellent value. The 171 guest rooms in this five-story motor hotel are attractively decorated in a style to suit the historic surroundings, and the lobby, with its shiny wood floors, looks more like the entrance to an upscale hotel than a budget/value inn. Nice courtyard, pool. The only downside is that it's at the north edge of the historic district, adjacent to the visitors center but a long walk, or shuttle ride, from most points of interest. *345 Meeting St., Charleston, SC 29403; tel. 803-723-4000, 800-426-7866; fax 803-722-3725.*

HOUSE RENTALS

Most Charleston visitors whose primary interest is the beach rent a house. In high season (roughly Memorial Day to Labor Day on Sullivan's Island and Isle of Palms) expect to pay from $1,000 to $4,000 weekly for a beach-front house and $750 to $2,500 for one that's a block or two from the beach. Off-season, prices drop by up to half, with the greatest discounts being November through early March. Houses at Folly Beach, many of them older and less fancy than those on other beaches, are less expensive; here, most ocean-front homes go for less than $1,500 a week in summer and less than $1,000 the rest of the year.

◆ **Dunes Properties.** Rentals on the Isle of Palms, including Wild Dunes and Sullivan's Island. *Ocean Park Plaza, 1400 Palm Blvd., Isle of Palms, SC 29451; tel. 803-886-5600, 800-476-8444; fax 803-886-6537. Open daily.*

◆ **Fred P. Holland Realty.** Rentals at Folly Beach. *50 Center St., Folly Beach, SC 29438; tel. 803-588-2325, 803-588-9237; fax 803-588-2562. Open Mon.-Sat.*

RESTAURANTS

Charleston is the New Orleans of the Atlantic coast in terms of food. Charleston she-crab soup is world famous. It's a heavenly combination of she-crab, crab roe (or sometimes egg yolk), milk, cream, butter, seasonings, and dry sherry.

Charleston restaurants are spread all around the area, but most of the city's best are in the downtown historic district. There is also a group of popular seafood restaurants on Shem Creek, off Highway 703 as you enter Sullivan's Island.

◆ **Louis's Charleston Grill** (expensive). Chef Louis Osteen has gotten raves for his creative interpretations of Low Country cooking. He uses as many local ingredients as possible. The menu changes frequently, but go for the sautéed red snapper, the grilled swordfish with risotto, or one of the veal dishes—if they're available when you visit. Clubby atmosphere, with mahogany-paneled walls and leather seats. *224 King St., Charleston, SC 29401; tel. 803-577-4522. Open daily for dinner. At the Charleston Place Hotel in the heart of the historic district.*

◆ **Carolina's** (moderate). Hip in crisp black-and-white decor, Carolina's is where you go to be seen . . . and to eat well. The Low Country meets the Far East here, with dishes such as beef tenderloin tips or quail with Thai crepe. Spicy Jamaican and Cajun dishes are on the menu too. *10 Exchange St., Charleston, SC 29401; tel. 803-724-3800. Open daily for dinner. Near the Battery in the historic district, just off E. Bay St.*

◆ **Magnolias** (moderate). "Uptown American cuisine with a down South flavor" is how Magnolias describes itself. The restaurant is in an early-19th-century warehouse, but there's nothing old-fashioned about it. Magnolias has a contemporary bistro feel and stays jumping until late in the evening. Even the meatloaf here is delicious and unusual: It's veal with crispy onions, and, darlin', it is *good.* Feeling very southern? Try the smoked double pork loin chop with herb butter, collard greens, and buttermilk mashed potatoes. Magnolias is our choice for the place to go if you have only one meal in Charleston. The tables by the window on Bay Street are the best in the house. *185 E. Bay St., Charleston, SC 29401; tel. 803-577-7771. Open daily for lunch and dinner. In the heart of the historic district.*

◆ **Shem Creek Bar & Grill** (moderate). Owner John Avinger runs this usually packed place with an emphasis on grilled, not fried, seafood. Try any of the grilled fish specials or the grilled shrimp with red rice. There's a noisy raw bar and a dockside bar that gets the boating crowd in warm weather. *508 Mill St., Mt. Pleasant, SC 29464; tel. 803-884-8102. Open daily for lunch and dinner. From Charleston, take U.S. Hwy. 17 north to U.S. Hwy. 17 Business and exit at Coleman Blvd. Make the first left after crossing the bridge over Shem Creek.*

◆ **Anchor Line** (inexpensive). This is hardly more than a shack by the road on Oak Island Creek. It doesn't merit a special trip, but if you're at Folly Beach, eat where the locals and the delivery drivers do—for ultrafresh, mostly fried seafood at low prices. Everything's just off the boats except the clam strips and crab cakes. Salty, low-budget atmosphere. *Hwy. 171, Folly Beach, SC 29438; tel. 803-795-7518. Open Mon.-Sat. for lunch and dinner. On your right at Oak Island as you approach Folly Beach.*

NIGHTLIFE

You can have a good time in Charleston—at the sophisticated late-night bistros and clubs downtown or with loud music and plain drink at a beachside bar. There are several music clubs in the Old City Market area in the downtown historic district, with other venues spread around the city. Nightlife on the Isle of Palms is concentrated in the Ocean Boulevard area at Front Beach.

◆ **A. W. Shucks.** This rambling, casual restaurant also has a popular bar area with taped music. *State Street Market, Charleston, SC 29401; tel. 803-723-1151. Open daily. In the Old City Market area in the downtown historic district.*

◆ **Best Friend Lounge, Mills House Hotel.** Good spot for cocktails and talk. *115 Meeting St., Charleston, SC 29401; tel. 803-577-2400. Open daily. In the heart of the downtown historic district.*

◆ **Windjammer.** This is one of the oldest rock-and-roll beach clubs around Charleston, although the present site is in a new, post-Hurricane Hugo building on the beach. Live bands on weekends. *1008 Ocean Blvd., Isle of Palms, SC 29451; tel. 803-886-8596. Open daily. Admission for live bands. On Front Beach.*

ATTRACTIONS

Charleston has myriad attractions. Space permits listing only the highlights; abundant further information is available at the terrific Charleston Visitors Center (*see* "Tourist Information"). To really appreciate Charleston, you must walk its streets. The downtown historic district occupies a large area with 2,000 historic homes and buildings on the southeastern tip of the Charleston peninsula. The main part of the historic district is roughly bounded by Calhoun Street on the north, the Cooper River on the east, the Battery on the south, and Legare Street on the west. For ease of exploration, divide the historic district into two parts: the Battery and the area south of Broad Street (SOB, as Charlestonians say) and the area north of Broad (NOB).

◆ **Charleston Historic District: Battery/SOB.** A Battery/SOB walking tour takes from two to four hours or longer, depending on your pace and which if any buildings you visit. Some of the homes and public buildings are open to the public; others are private. A helpful booklet, *The Complete Walking Tour* ($3.95), covers the entire historic district and is sold at local bookstores. The Charleston Visitors Center also provides information and maps on walking tours. Recommended highlights include the following: Charleston Harbor; White Point Gardens; Calhoun Mansion, a Victorian hotel that is now a museum; Edmonston-Alston House, a Greek-Revival home that's now also a museum; Cabbage Row, a former tenement building that was the inspiration for Catfish Row in *Porgy and Bess*; Old Exchange and Provost Dungeon, where American patriots were imprisoned during the Revolutionary War; Heyward-Washington House, where George Washington slept in 1791; and St. Michael's Episcopal Church, the oldest church in Charleston, begun in 1752.

◆ **Charleston Historic District: NOB.** A north of Broad (NOB) walking tour takes two to four hours, depending on your pace. The visitors center provides information and maps on walking tours (*see* the previous listing). Among the highlights are: Dock Street Theatre, one of America's first playhouses, built in 1735; French Huguenot Church; Old Slave Mart, where slaves were sold outdoors until 1856; Old Powder Magazine, the oldest public building in Charleston, built in 1712; Old City Market, at North and South Market streets, a group of low buildings that were once produce and fish markets and are now mostly shops and restaurants; and Joseph Manigault House, an Adams-style house from 1803.

◆ **Charleston Historic District Guided Tours.** Many different tour companies offer guided tours of Charleston. Ask at the visitors center for information. Among the possible tours are one-hour horse- or mule-drawn carriage tours, offered by the Charleston Carriage Company (tel. 803-577-0042), the Old South Carriage Company (tel. 803-723-9712), and others; bus tours by Doin' the Charleston Tours (tel. 803-763-1233) and others; and special-interest walking tours by Charleston Strolls (tel. 803-766-

2080), Original Charleston Walks (tel. 803-577-3800), and others. Some walking tours concentrate on churches, some on haunted houses, some on architecture, and others on Confederate history and a variety of other topics. Tour guides in Charleston are licensed and must pass a test on the history of the city. *Admission.*

◆ **Charleston Museum.** This is Charleston's attic for history, nature, art, and science. *360 Meeting St., Charleston, SC 29401; tel. 803-722-2996. Open Mon.-Sat. 9-5 and Sun. 1-5. Admission. Across Meeting St. from the visitors center.*

◆ **Fort Sumter National Monument.** The first shot of the Civil War was fired on April 12, 1861, against Union troops in Fort Sumter by Confederate forces. Boat tours, which include a harbor tour and visit to the fort, leave from Patriots Point (*see* the Patriots Point Naval and Maritime Museum listing, below) and from the Charleston City Marina. Fort Moultrie, with its lighthouse, on Sullivan's Island, is also part of the national monument. *Fort Sumter Tours, Charleston, SC 29401; tel. 803-722-1691. Open daily. Tour hours vary. Admission.*

◆ **Magnolia Plantation and Gardens.** The 50-acre formal garden, begun in the late 17th century, is the draw here. There are more than 900 varieties of camellias and 250 types of azaleas. The plantation house was built during Reconstruction. The separate Audubon Swamp Garden has 60 acres of swamp accessible on boardwalks and dikes. *Ashley River Rd., Hwy. 61, Charleston, SC 29414; tel. 803-571-1266. Open daily 8-5:30 spring-summer; reduced hours the rest of the year—call for schedule. Admission. Take U.S. Hwy. 17 south to Hwy. 61, then drive about 10 mi.*

◆ **Middleton Place.** Begun in 1741, the landscaped gardens at Middleton Place offer incredibly beautiful walks. Middle House was built in 1755; only one wing remains. *Ashley River Rd., Hwy. 61, Charleston, SC 29414; tel. 803-556-6020. Gardens open daily 9-5; house open Tue.-Sun. 10-4:30 and Mon. 1:30-4:30. Admission. Take U.S. Hwy. 17 south to Hwy. 61, then drive about 14 mi.*

◆ **Patriots Point Naval and Maritime Museum.** The "Fighting Lady," the U.S.S. *Yorktown*, an aircraft carrier that served in World War II and the Vietnam War, is permanently docked here. A nuclear merchant ship, a Navy submarine and destroyer, and a Coast Guard cutter can also be toured. *40 Patriots Point Rd., Mt. Pleasant, SC 29464; tel. 803-884-2727. Open daily 9-6. Admission. From Charleston, take U.S. Hwy. 17 north to U.S. Hwy. 17 Business and exit at Coleman Blvd. Watch for signs on the right.*

SHOPPING

Charleston really shines for the visiting shopper in its downtown historic district, where all of the following shops can be found. Antiques shops and art galleries are especially plentiful.

◆ **Art Thomas Gallery.** Well-known contemporary-art gallery. *2 Queen St., Charleston, SC 29401; tel. 803-577-0534. Open Tue.-Sun.*

◆ **Chapter Two Bookstore.** Many books of local interest. *199 E. Bay St., Charleston, SC 29401; tel. 803-722-4238. Open daily.*

◆ **Charleston Place.** Collection of upscale shops, including Polo/Ralph Lauren, Laura Ashley, Talbots, and Gucci. *130 Market St., Charleston, SC 29401; tel. 803-722-4900. Open daily.*

◆ **Civil War and Maritime Shop.** Original and reproduction artifacts from the Civil War era. *239 King St., Charleston, SC 29401; tel. 803-577-8896. Open daily.*

◆ **Geo. C. Birlant Co.** Antiques. *191 King St., Charleston, SC 29401; tel. 803-722-3842; fax 803-722-3846. Open Mon.-Sat.*

BEST FOOD SHOPS

For the best selection, you'll need to drive from the beach areas to North Charleston, Mount Pleasant, or other suburban areas around Charleston.

◆ **Harris Teeter.** Besides groceries, sells wine, beer, and soft drinks. *Village Pointe Shopping Center, Mt. Pleasant, SC 29464; tel. 803-881-1983. Open daily. Off U.S. Hwy. 17—convenient to the Isle of Palms and Sullivan's Island.*

SANDWICHES: ◆ **Lite Affair Cafe.** Unusual offerings, such as a roast beef and artichoke sandwich. *30 Cumberland St., Charleston, SC 29401; tel. 803-722-0023. Open daily. In the historic district.*

SEAFOOD: ◆ **Mt. Pleasant Seafood.** *Shem Creek, Mt. Pleasant, SC 29464; tel. 803-884-4122. Open daily. Convenient to the Isle of*

Palms and Sullivan's Island beaches.

FRESH PRODUCE: ◆ **Harris Teeter.** *Village Pointe Shopping Center, Mt. Pleasant, SC 29464; tel. 803-881-1983. Open daily. Off U.S. Hwy. 17—convenient to Isle of Palms and Sullivan's Island beaches.*

ICE CREAM: ◆ **Pier Ice Cream.** *1400 Palm Blvd., Charleston, SC 29451; tel. 803-886-5985. Open daily.*

BEVERAGES: ◆ **Isle of Palms Liquor Store.** *1501 Palm Blvd., Isle of Palms, SC 29451; tel. 803-886-6569. Open Mon.-Sat.*

WINE: ◆ **Clyde Burris Liquor Store.** Wines and liquors; also has a store in Mount Pleasant. *415 Meeting St., Charleston, SC 29403; tel. 803-723-0077. Open Mon.-Sat.*

SPORTS
FISHING

◆ **Captain Ivan's Island Charters.** Offshore charters. *Ripley Light Marina, Ashley Pointe Dr., Charleston, SC 29401; tel. 803-762-2020. Operates daily, weather permitting.*

◆ *Carolina Clipper.* Party boat offers half-day trips, with beginners welcome. Rods, reels, tackle, and bait provided. *U.S. Hwy. 17 Business, Shem Creek, Mt. Pleasant, SC 29464; tel. 803-884-2992. Operates daily, weather permitting.*

BOATING

Life on the water is part of what Charleston is about. The area has more than a dozen marinas.

◆ **Charleston City Marina.** One of the largest local marinas, it has transient dockage, charters. *17 Lockwood Dr., Charleston, SC 29401; tel. 803-723-5098. Open daily.*

◆ **City Water Sports.** Offers parasailing and sightseeing and environmental trips; rents Jet Skis and other equipment. *Charleston City Marina, 17 Lockwood Dr., Charleston, SC 29401; tel. 803-853-4386. Open daily.*

◆ **Ripley Light Marina.** Transient dockage, rentals, charters. *56 Ashley Pointe Dr., Charleston, SC 29407; tel. 803-766-2100. Open daily.*

SURFING

◆ **Ocean Sports Surf Shop.** *23 Center St., Folly Beach, SC 29438; tel. 803-588-9175. Open daily.*

BICYCLING

◆ **The Bicycle Shoppe.** Rentals. *280 Meeting St., Charleston, SC 29401; tel. 803-722-8168. Open daily.*

GOLF

◆ **Wild Dunes Resort.** Guests of this private resort get preferential tee times and greens fees, although nonguests are also welcome (reserving a tee time grants you access at the gate). The Wild Dunes Harbor Course, a 6,446-yard, par-70 Tom Fazio design, plays tougher than you might expect, with water on 17 holes and six par-threes along the Intracoastal Waterway. The Wild Dunes Links Course, built in 1980 to a Tom Fazio design and rebuilt to USGA specifications following Hurricane Hugo, is a 6,722-yard, par-72 course ranked in the world's top 100 by *Golf Digest. 5757 Palm Blvd., Isle of Palms, SC 29451; tel. 803-886-6000, 800-845-8880. Open daily. Admission. At the eastern tip of Isle of Palms. Follow Palm Blvd. to the entrance to Wild Dunes.*

◆ **Dunes West Golf Club.** This Arthur Hills-designed 6,871-yard, par-72 course has been highly ranked by two golf magazines. *3535 Wando Plantation Way, Mt. Pleasant, SC 29464; tel. 803-856-9000. Open daily. Admission. From Charleston, take U.S. Hwy. 17 north to Hwy. 41. Go west 3 1/2 mi. on Hwy. 41 to Dunes West.*

TENNIS

◆ **Wild Dunes Tennis Center.** Ranked among the top ten resort tennis centers in the United States by *Tennis Magazine*, Wild Dunes has 17 clay and 2 hard courts, and 6 are lighted. Those who are not guests at the Wild Dunes Resort need to obtain an ID card (fee) from Wild Dunes. Guests get preferential court times and reduced fees for play. *Wild Dunes Resort, 5757 Palm Blvd., Isle of Palms, SC 29451; tel. 803-866-6000, 800-845-8880. Open daily. Admission. At the eastern tip of Isle of Palms.*

NATURE

◆ **Bull Island.** A 20-minute passenger ferry takes you to Bull Island, part of Cape Romain refuge (*see* listing below). You can hike 16 miles of trails and dirt roads and enjoy a long stretch of undeveloped beach. Take drinking water, food, and plenty of insect repellent. There are rest rooms and picnic facilities but no accommodations. Coastal Expeditions, a U.S. Fish and Wildlife Service concessionaire, operates the ferry and kayak trips; ferries depart from Moores Landing. *Coastal Expeditions, 514B Mill St., Mt. Pleasant, SC 29464; tel. 803-881-4582. Call for ferry schedule. Admission. Moores Landing is about 21 mi. from Charleston. Take U.S. Hwy. 17 north 16 mi. and turn right onto Sewee Rd. Follow signs for Moores Landing. Go 3 mi. and follow additional signs.*

◆ **Cape Romain National Wildlife Refuge.** Stretching 22 miles along the coast of South Carolina, Cape Romain offers the intrepid visitor the chance to see birds and animals in a natural setting. More than 260 bird species, 12 types of amphibians, 24 reptile species, and 36 varieties of mammals have been recorded in the refuge. Most of the refuge is accessible only by boat. A new visitors center, the Sewee Environmental and Education Center, operated jointly by the Cape Romain Refuge and the Francis Marion National Forest, is scheduled to open in the fall of 1996 on U.S. Highway 17 about 18 miles north of Charleston. *5801 U.S. Hwy. 17 N., Awendaw, SC 29429; tel. 803-928-3368. Refuge open daily sunrise-sunset; office open Mon.-Fri. 8:30-5. To get to the existing office from Charleston, take U.S. Hwy. 17 north about 20 mi. Watch for sign on the right.*

◆ **Francis Marion National Forest.** About a quarter of a million acres of coastal flatlands and black swamp adjoin the Cape Romain refuge north of Charleston. Camping, fishing, and hiking are available, and a new visitors center is planned (*see* the Cape Romain National Wildlife Refuge listing, above). *U.S. Forest Service, Wambaw Ranger District, 1015 Pinckney St., McClellanville, SC 29458; tel. 803-887-3257. National forest open 24 hr. daily; ranger station open Mon.-Fri. 8-4:30. From Charleston, take U.S. Hwy. 17 north about 18 mi. Watch for National Forest signs.*

TOURIST INFORMATION

◆ **Charleston Visitors Center.** One of the truly great visitors centers in the country. Movie on Charleston (admission). *375 Meeting St., Charleston, SC 29403; tel. 803-853-8000. Open daily 8:30-5:30 Mar.-Oct. and 8:30-5 the rest of the year. From I-26, take Meeting St. exit. The center is across from the Charleston Museum.*

CHAPTER 13

Kiawah & Seabrook Islands

Beauty	B+
Swimming	B+
Sand	B
Hotels/Inns/B&Bs	C-
House rentals	B
Restaurants	B-
Nightlife	C-
Attractions	C-
Shopping	C-
Sports	A
Nature	B-

iawah and Seabrook are semitropical private islands about 45 minutes by car south of Charleston. Although located within about a mile of each other, the two developments differ considerably.

The larger of the two, Kiawah (*KEE-ah-wah*)—named after the Kiawah Indians, who inhabited the area until the 1600s—is a 10,000-acre island with about 5,000 homes and condominiums. It features five championship golf courses, two nationally known tennis centers, a small shopping village, several restaurants, and the only hotel in the area. Despite the number of homes on the island and the intensive development that has been taking place

HOW TO GET THERE

◆ Kiawah and Seabrook islands are about 22 mi. southwest of Charleston. From Charleston, take U.S. Hwy. 17 south to Main Rd. (Rte. 20). Turn left onto Main Rd. and follow it for about 6 mi. It becomes Bohicket Rd. at the intersection with SC Hwy. 700. Continue on Bohicket about 10 1/2 mi., following signs to Kiawah and Seabrook. As you near the islands, bear left on Kiawah Island Pkwy. and follow it about 1 mi. to the Kiawah security gate. For Seabrook, bear right instead of left and stay on Bohicket Rd. past the Bohicket Marina, to the Seabrook check-in and entrance gate. (Both Kiawah and Seabrook are private. Seabrook generally allows only owners, guests, and those renting on the island to enter. Kiawah is more lenient: You can get a permit, available from the guard at the gate, to visit the island to shop, dine, or play golf or tennis.)

◆ The islands are about 100 mi. (nearly 2 hr.) northeast of Savannah. From Savannah, take I-95 north to U.S. Hwy 17 north; at Main Rd. (Rte. 20), turn right and follow directions above.

◆ Charleston International Airport, served by jet and commuter airlines, is about 28 mi. from Kiawah-Seabrook. Charleston also has Amtrak service.

since the early 1970s (about 85 percent of the land earmarked for use has already been developed), the island has plenty of green space, thanks to an intelligent master plan. The island's 10 miles of beaches on the Atlantic, 45 miles of frontage on lagoons, marshes, and estuaries, and expanses of maritime forest with miles of nature trails provide a setting of much natural beauty. Kiawah is home to more than 150 species of birds and about 50 species of mammals and reptiles, including white-tailed deer, sea turtles, and alligators.

Some view Seabrook as a smaller, more middle-class version of Kiawah. Heavy on condos and villas—about 800 of the 1,300 residential units on the island are condos—rather than super-luxury private homes, it occupies about 2,200 acres, with two golf courses, about three miles of beach, and one tennis center. Some public areas (Seabrook's club facilities are owned in an equity arrangement by members rather than a developer) could stand an infusion of money and TLC. Such things are relative, however. While some of Kiawah's ocean-front lots go for $1 million or more (sans house) and top-of-the-market homes can sell in the $2 million range, Seabrook has plenty of homes priced at half a million or more. So Seabrook, once part of a plantation owned by the wealthy William Seabrook, is today hardly a poor man's playground, even compared with its ritzier next-door neighbor. If anything, Seabrook may be more private than Kiawah. Day-trippers generally are not allowed on Seabrook, whereas if you're staying on Seabrook you can get a pass to parts of Kiawah for shopping or dining.

Golf provides a major reason for visiting either island. Along with Myrtle Beach, Charleston, and Hilton Head, Kiawah-Seabrook is one of South Carolina's four top golf destinations, with Kiawah in particular known nationally. The 1991 Ryder Cup was played on its treacherous, windy Ocean Course, where grown men have been known to throw down their clubs and run screaming in frustration (it has been called the toughest resort golf course in America by one golf magazine). Besides Kiawah's five courses and Seabrook's two, an eighth course, Oak Point, is near the entrance gates to both islands.

Tennis buffs also flock here. Kiawah's program routinely

ranks among the top tennis resorts in the United States.

Both islands are essentially residential. Neither offers the high-energy beach resort activities you expect at Myrtle Beach or even Hilton Head. A Kiawah Island real-estate salesperson bragged that there wasn't a video game room on the island—a plus, she said, for family life. Both islands are oriented to low-key family activities—swimming, beachcombing, fishing, clamming, crabbing, oyster raking, biking, tennis, and other outdoor sports—and both have extensive kids programs in the summer.

With the exception of the one inn on Kiawah, vacations here involve renting a condominium or private home, with April through Labor Day being the period of highest demand for rentals. Golf is played year-round, with the heaviest play March through October. Even in January and February, temperatures at midday usually get into the high 50s and low 60s.

BEACHES

Because Kiawah and Seabrook are private, the beaches are open only to owners and those who are renting property on the island (or, in the case of Kiawah, staying at the Inn at Kiawah). Seabrook generally permits access only to property owners and renters; Kiawah allows visitors to come on the island to visit restaurants or shops but not to swim. However, Beachwalker Park, on Kiawah's west end, is open to the public seasonally.

Ocean swimming is possible from April to October, with water temperatures usually in the low 80s June to September.

KIAWAH ISLAND BEACH

Kiawah Island commands some ten miles of Atlantic beach. Although along the length of the beach there is some variance in width (generally it is narrow at high tide but up to 100 yards wide at low tide) and although there are names

Beauty	A
Swimming	B+
Sand	B
Amenities	C+

for different stretches (West Beach, East Beach, Royal Beach, and Osprey Beach), this is really one long beach rather than a series of small beaches broken by coves.

Where you get onto the beach depends on where you are

staying on Kiawah's 15 square miles. For most visitors, the main access points are at West and East beaches, because these are close to the inn and to clusters of rental villas and cottages. West and East beaches have more than a dozen designated access points. You will be given a map at check-in.

Once you're actually on the beach at Kiawah, you can walk or bike along any part of it, including the area belonging to Kiawah's gate within a gate: a private community at the east end of the island. This private residential area has a beach club and an excellent beach area, but it is not open to those staying at the rental villas or the inn (except if you walk along the beach to get to it, as all beaches in the region are public up to the high-water mark). If you are staying within this second security gate, there are additional beach access points along Royal and Osprey beaches. The Beach Club here has a beautiful beach, with first-rate amenities at the clubhouse, but it's available only to those who are members or guests of the private Kiawah Island Club. *To get to West Beach Village and the Kiawah Island Inn and villas, make the first right, Kiawah Beach Rd., after the main security checkpoint. To get to East Beach Village, follow Kiawah Island Pkwy. and turn right on Sea Forest Dr. To get to the private Beach Club (members and guests only), follow Kiawah Island Pkwy. to the second security checkpoint. Turn right on Governor's Dr. and follow to Ocean Marsh Rd. Turn right and follow Ocean Marsh Rd. a short distance to the Beach Club and beach access point.*

Swimming: Good, especially in summer's warm waters. Wave action is generally moderate, and the beaches have a gentle slope. No lifeguard.

Sand: The sand is grayish-white and mostly hard-packed. Along much of the beach, there are very low dunes. Because of Kiawah's east-west orientation, the island has not had the erosion problems of some other coastal areas.

Amenities: Since most visitors stay in rental homes or condos, there are few amenities, except near the East and West beach areas, where you'll find restaurants, bars, a food court, playgrounds, and other amenities. Those few with privileges at the private Beach Club have access to a full-fledged club including food and beverage service.

Sports: Besides the usual water sports on the beach, guests on the island have access to a 21-acre park that includes a basketball court, soccer field, 25-meter pool, and other sports facilities.

Parking: Those staying at rental houses and villas have parking there. There is limited parking—the lot is often full—at the Straw Market shops near the inn, and very limited parking at some other access points. Most Kiawah guests not staying directly on the beach bike or walk to it, usually in a few minutes.

BEACHWALKER PARK

On the west end of Kiawah Island lies Beachwalker, a 30-acre park with a small, 300-foot beach maintained by Charleston County. You reach the park via a boardwalk through oaks and palmettos and over low dunes. This is the

Beauty	**B+**
Swimming	**B**
Sand	**B**
Amenities	**B**

only beach in the Kiawah-Seabrook area that is open to the public. The park is closed November to March. *Turn right on Beachwalker Dr., just before you get to the main security checkpoint for Kiawah Island, and follow about 2/3 mi. to the park.*

Swimming: Good, especially during the warmer months. Lifeguard on duty daily Memorial Day to Labor Day and on weekends in late spring and early fall.

Sand: An attractive beach with grayish-white sand.

Amenities: Snack bar, rest rooms, outdoor showers, beach umbrella rentals, picnic area.

Sports: Swimming, surf fishing.

Parking: The 150 spaces here go fast in the summer—arrive early ($3 parking fee).

SEABROOK ISLAND BEACH

Seabrook has more than three miles of beach, mostly on the Atlantic and at the mouth of the North Edisto River. Beach access is for owners and renters only at this private, gated resort. Overall, Seabrook's beach is not quite as nice as

Beauty	**B-**
Swimming	**B**
Sand	**B**
Amenities	**C+**

Kiawah's: It is not as long, some areas have suffered erosion from storm surges, and condo and villa development along the beach is more intrusive than on Kiawah.

The main beach area on Seabrook is North Beach, on the Atlantic, but there is beach access at more than half a dozen spots along the ocean and river. Where you enter the beach depends in part on where you're staying, since most guests walk or bike to the beach from their rental units. *To get to the Beach Club from the security checkpoint at the entrance to Seabrook, follow Seabrook Island Rd. past Pelican Watch and Beach Club villas. Look for signs for the Beach Club. To get to North Beach, continue on Seabrook Island Rd. past the Beach Club to Oyster Catcher Court. Turn right on Oyster Catcher and continue to the small parking area for North Beach.*

Swimming: Good from April to October. Wave action is moderate, and the beaches have a gentle slope. Because the Edisto River mouth is wide here, where it meets the ocean, there is little difference between ocean-front and river-front beach areas. No lifeguard.

Sand: Grayish-white sand. Though fairly narrow at high tide, the beach becomes wide and expansive at low tide.

Amenities: Seabrook's guests stay in homes or villas, so the island does not have the type of facilities available at day beaches. A Beach Club (open to members, guests, and those renting on the island) offers a snack bar, swimming pool, rest rooms, and other facilities. However, the beach access at the club is not good, and there is beach erosion.

Sports: Fishing, crabbing, sailing, and even horseback riding. A kids program in summer offers organized nature programs and other activities on the water. Bikes, Rollerblades, and other equipment are available for rent at the Beach Club.

Parking: For the Beach Club, park in the large lot across Seabrook Island Road from the Club. There is limited parking at North Beach. Most guests walk or bike to the beach from their rental villas or houses.

HOTELS/INNS/B&BS

The Kiawah-Seabrook area has just one true hotel, the Kiawah Island Inn. A second full-service hotel on Kiawah is in the planning stages. The alternative for short-term stays is a condo rental (*see* "House Rentals"). These offer everything a hotel does except room service (there may also be an extra charge for maid service).

◆ **Kiawah Island Inn** (very expensive). The inn is located in the middle of things on Kiawah, at West Beach Village, close to the beach, restaurants, and shopping. According to hotel management, the 150 rooms are scheduled to be refurbished in early 1996, and they're ready for it. Although the rooms are bright and airy, they verge on the motellike, and some of the furnishings have seen better days—not perhaps what you'd expect when you're paying up to $250 a night. Most rooms have ocean views, but they're several hundred feet from the water, not directly on it. Rates include one hour of tennis per day. *12 Kiawah Beach Dr., Kiawah Island, SC 29455; tel. 803-768-2121, 800-654-2924; fax 803-768-9339.*

HOUSE RENTALS

You can rent condos or homes from either the resort operator (Kiawah Island Resort and Seabrook Island Resort) or independent real-estate companies in the area. Rentals from independent firms are usually cheaper, but the selection is smaller and you may not have access to resort amenities such as swimming pools. Also, the resorts give priority tennis court and golf tee times, with somewhat lower rates, to those renting through them.

If you want something bigger and more luxurious than a condo, both Seabrook and Kiawah have luxury homes for rent. On Kiawah, large four- and five-bedroom homes on the beach go for $3,500 to $5,000 or more a week during the peak periods (March to mid-April, a heavy golfing time, and mid-June to mid-August, prime time for beaches). However, the majority of homes on Kiawah rent for less than $2,000 a week, and prices drop by a third or more off-season. Some homes can be rented on a daily basis, especially off-season. House rentals on Seabrook are generally cheaper than on Kiawah, with most less than $2,000.

◆ **Kiawah Island Resort** (very expensive). Several hundred one- to four-bedroom condo villas are offered at Kiawah, on a daily or weekly basis. Most are in low- and mid-rise condo buildings in the East Beach Village, West Beach Village, and Night

Heron areas of the island. All units are attractively designed and are furnished in individual styles. The resort also rents luxury houses. Golf and tennis packages available. *12 Kiawah Beach Rd., Kiawah Island, SC 29455; tel. 803-768-2121, 800-654-2924; fax 803-768-9339. Open daily.*

◆ **Seabrook Island Resort Villas** (very expensive). One-, two-, and three-bedroom villas with kitchens in low-rise condo apartment buildings are available for daily and weekly rentals. Since most are individually owned, furnishings and decor vary, but you can expect attractive digs. The most expensive season is late March to mid-August, with sizable reductions at other times (especially November through March, when prices fall to the moderate range). Check out the bewildering variety of golf, tennis, family, and honeymoon packages. The resort also rents luxury houses. *1002 Landfall Way, Seabrook Island, SC 29455; tel. 803-768-1000, 800-845-2475; fax 803-768-4922. Open daily.*

◆ **Beachwalker Rentals.** Kiawah Island rentals. *3690 Bohicket Rd., Suite 4-D, Johns Island, SC 29455; tel. 803-768-1777, 800-334-6308. Open Mon.-Sat. spring-fall and Mon.-Fri. in winter.*

◆ **Ravenel Associates.** Kiawah and Seabrook rentals. *Ravenel Center, Kiawah Island, SC 29445; tel. 803-768-2300, 800-247-5050. Open daily.*

RESTAURANTS

Kiawah and Seabrook's upmarket residents and visitors expect a high standard in restaurants, and you can eat well here—although Charleston, 45 minutes away, remains the destination of choice for a really top meal (*see* Chapter 12). From May to late September, Kiawah holds an outdoor oyster roast and barbecue about once a week—upon arrival, ask for details.

◆ **Gilligan's** (moderate). It's about 17 miles from Seabrook and Kiawah, but locals say Gilligan's is worth the half-hour drive because it has some of the best seafood on the south side of Charleston. Steamed clams, roast oysters, and boiled shrimp are popular. Casual atmosphere. *160 Main Rd., Johns Island, SC 29455; tel. 803-766-2244. Open daily for lunch and dinner. About 17 mi. from Kiawah-Seabrook, just south of the intersection of Main Rd. and U.S. Hwy. 17.*

◆ **Indigo** (moderate). This bistro, operated by the Kiawah Island Resort, adds a South Carolina twist to pastas and French and Caribbean dishes. Good selection of wines by the glass and bottle. The setting is intimate, even romantic. *Town Center, Kiawah Island, SC 29455; tel. 803-768-2121. Open daily for dinner.*

◆ **Rosebank Farms Cafe** (moderate). New in 1995, this family-run café gets many of its vegetables from its own farms. Fresh seafood is featured—a natural for this casual water-front spot on Bohicket Marina—but almost everything is good, from the blue-plate lunch specials like barbecued pork with hopping john (rice and peas) to the dinner specialties, such as the barbecued catfish with whipped turnips and fried okra or the grilled trout with red-pepper-pecan mole, leeks, and a side order of grits or fried green tomatoes. *Bohicket Marina Village, Seabrook Island, SC 29455; tel. 803-768-1807. Open daily for lunch and dinner.*

◆ **Sweetgrass Cafe** (moderate). Billing itself as a "Low Country bistro," Sweetgrass is popular for a casual lunch, with tables outside going fast on nice days. Try the roasted corn chowder with shrimp and the veal meatloaf. *Straw Market, Kiawah Island, SC 29455; tel. 803-768-0500. Open daily for lunch and Wed.-Sat. for dinner.*

NIGHTLIFE

For serious nightlife, head to Charleston (*see* Chapter 12).

◆ **Sunset Lounge at Privateer Restaurant.** Live music some nights in season. *Bohicket Marina, Seabrook Island, SC 29455; tel. 803-768-1290. Open daily.*

◆ **Topsider Lounge.** Live music on Thursdays, Fridays, and Saturdays in summer. *Kiawah Island Inn, 12 Kiawah Beach Dr., Kiawah Island, SC 29455; tel. 803-768-2121. Open daily.*

ATTRACTIONS

Within an easy drive of Kiawah and Seabrook are a number of antebellum plantation homes and all the historic sights of Charleston (*see* Chapter 12).

◆ **Charleston Tea Plantation.** It's the only working tea plantation in the United States, and though private, it gives free tours. *6617 Maybank Hwy. (Hwy. 700), Wadmalaw Island, SC 29487; tel. 803-559-0383. Tours first Sat. of each month May-Oct.; first tour starts at*

10 a.m., last tour at 1:30. Admission. From Kiawah-Seabrook, take Bohicket Rd. to the intersection of Hwy. 700. Turn left and follow Hwy. 700 about 10 mi. Look for signs.

SHOPPING

Don't expect quantity, but you'll find some quality. The main shopping areas are the Straw Market, a small shopping center on Kiawah, and the Island Center Plaza on Bohicket Road about four miles from Kiawah. Charleston's suburban malls and historic-district shops are 45 minutes away (*see* Chapter 12).

◆ **Berlin's.** Branch of a venerable and well-known downtown Charleston clothing retailer. *Straw Market, Kiawah Island Resort, Kiawah Island, SC 29455; tel. 803-768-2000. Open daily.*

◆ **Indigo Books.** Small, but with a good selection of regional books. *Island Center Plaza, Bohicket Rd., Johns Island, SC 29455; tel. 803-768-2255; fax 803-768-3200. Open Mon.-Sat. Drive about 4 mi. toward Charleston from Kiawah.*

BEST FOOD SHOPS

◆ **Piggly Wiggly.** Small grocery with beer and soft drinks. *Island Center Plaza, Bohicket Rd., Johns Island, SC 29455; tel. 803-768-4721. Open daily.*

SANDWICHES: ◆ **Fiddleheads.** Subs, pizza, deli items. *Bohicket Rd., Johns Island, SC 29455; tel. 803-768-4356. Open Mon.-Sat.*

FRESH PRODUCE: ◆ **Rosebank Farms.** Grows its own vegetables and operates a roadside stand on Bohicket Road. *3953 Betsy Kerrison Pkwy., Johns Island, SC 29455; tel. 803-768-9139. Open daily in season.*

BEVERAGES: ◆ **Island Spirits.** Liquor and wine. *Island Center Plaza, Bohicket Rd., Johns Island, SC 29455; tel. 803-768-9751. Open Mon.-Sat. Drive about 4 mi. toward Charleston from Kiawah; near the Piggly Wiggly.*

SPORTS
FISHING

There are man-made reefs offshore, and the tidal creeks and rivers offer good fishing in spring and fall. Kids will enjoy crabbing, clamming, and netting shrimp.

◆ **Bohicket Boat Rentals & Yacht Charters.** Inshore and offshore charters. *1880 Andell Bluff Blvd., Johns Island, SC 29455; tel. 803-768-7294. Open daily, weather permitting.*

BOATING

◆ **Bohicket Boat Rentals & Yacht Charters.** Rents small boats and offers sailboat and powerboat charters to barrier islands and marshes. *1880 Andell Bluff Blvd., Johns Island, SC 29455; tel. 803-768-7294. Open daily.*

BICYCLING

◆ **West Beach Bike Shop.** Rentals. *Kiawah Island Resort, Kiawah Island, SC 29455; tel. 803-768-6005. Open daily.*

GOLF

Golf is taken seriously here. Kiawah has five courses, four of them open to the public, although resort guests get priority on tee times. The newest, the River Course, opened in late 1995 and is for members only (it is not normally open to Kiawah Resort guests). Three of the Kiawah courses, Osprey Point, Turtle Point, and Ocean Course, have been listed in the top 75 resort courses in the United States by *Golf Digest*. Seabrook has two courses, both open only to owners and guests at Seabrook.

◆ **Crooked Oaks.** Robert Trent Jones, Sr., designed this 6,832-yard, par-72 course. Small greens, well-elevated and bunkered, with forgiving, flat fairways. *Seabrook Island Resort, Seabrook Island, SC 29455; tel. 803-768-2529. Open daily. Admission.*

◆ **Oak Plantation.** An 18-hole, 6,759-yard, par-72 public course. *4255 Bohicket Rd., Johns Island, SC 29455; tel. 803-768-7431. Open daily. Admission. About 1 mi. from the entrance to Kiawah.*

◆ **Ocean Course.** Pete Dye created this 18-hole, par-72, 7,371-yard course with ocean views from every hole. Host of the 1991 Ryder Cup matches, it is windy, unforgiving, and one of the most frustrating and difficult courses you'll ever play. *Kiawah Island Resort, Kiawah Island, SC 29455; tel. 803-768-7272. Open daily. Admission.*

◆ **Osprey Point.** Designed by Tom Fazio, this par-72, 18-hole course plays to 6,678 yards. It doesn't have the sea views of the Ocean Course, but it does have four lakes and water on 15 holes. *Kiawah Island Resort, Kiawah Island, SC*

29455; tel. 803-768-2121. Open daily. Admission.

◆ **Turtle Point.** Designed by Jack Nicklaus, this 18-hole, par-72 course plays to 6,914 from the gold tees. *Kiawah Island Resort, Kiawah Island, SC 29455; tel. 803-768-2121. Open daily. Admission.*

TENNIS

◆ **Kiawah Island Resort.** The program at Kiawah has garnered a rating of No. 3 in the United States by *Tennis* magazine. The West Beach Tennis Club has 14 clay courts and 2 lighted hard courts. The East Beach Tennis Club has 9 clay and 3 hard courts, with 1 lighted. *Kiawah Island Resort, Kiawah Island, SC 29455; tel. 803-768-2121. Open daily. Admission.*

◆ **Seabrook Island Resort.** Thirteen clay courts, open only to those staying at Seabrook. *1002 Landfall Way, Seabrook Island, SC 29455; tel. 803-768-7543. Open daily. Admission.*

HORSEBACK RIDING

◆ **Seabrook Equestrian Center.** You need not be a guest at Seabrook to rent horses for trail or beach rides here. *1002 Landfall Way, Seabrook Island, SC 29455; tel. 803-768-7541. Open daily. Near the entrance gate to Seabrook Island Resort.*

NATURE

◆ **Kiawah Island Resort Nature Programs.** Kiawah Island Resort offers nature tours and interpretative programs on the flora and fauna of the undeveloped part of the island. Marsh canoeing, island walks, birding trips, and ocean seining trips are available. *Kiawah Island Resort, Kiawah Island, SC 29455; tel. 803-768-6001. Schedule varies; call for information. Admission.*

TOURIST INFORMATION

Both islands are private, so you need to contact the resorts for information.

◆ **Kiawah Island Resort.** *12 Kiawah Beach Dr., Kiawah Island, SC 29455; tel. 803-768-2121, 800-654-2924; fax 803-768-9339. Open daily 24 hr.*

◆ **Seabrook Island Resort.** *1002 Landfall Way, Seabrook Island, SC 29455; tel. 803-768-1000, 800-845-2475; fax 803-768-4922. Open daily 24 hr.*

CHAPTER 14

Edisto Island

Beauty	B-
Swimming	B
Sand	B-
Hotels/Inns/B&Bs	C-
House rentals	B+
Restaurants	B-
Nightlife	D
Attractions	C+
Shopping	C-
Sports	C
Nature	B

Y ou don't get to Edisto Island by accident. It's off the beaten path. You have to want to come here, and not everyone does. The high-energy crowd goes farther south to Hilton Head; the antiques-and-gourmet bunch stays in Charleston. Most Edistonians, and those visitors who consider Edisto a little piece of unpretentious paradise, like it just fine that way.

The drive through Edisto Island to the small town

of Edisto Beach along state Highway 174 provides a hint of what to expect from this out-of-the-way part of the South Carolina coast: You see few cars on the lovely two-lane road, with its overhanging canopy of live oaks draped in Spanish moss. Here and there you find a country store or an antique shop but no large shopping centers. You pass old churches and cemeteries full of history and, rumor has it, even a ghost or two.

If you turn off Highway 174 onto one of the small rural byways, you may occasionally come to a private road leading to an antebellum plantation, in some cases still in the same family as when the plantation grew indigo, rice, or cotton.

The most profitable crop of all, grown throughout the 19th century and into the early 20th, was Sea Island cotton. A local mud, called Pluf mud, taken from the creeks and used as fertilizer, was thought to give the cotton its prized soft feel, with characteristically fine long and silky fibers. In 1914, the boll weevil, an insect that eats the cotton plant, invaded the cotton fields, and by the early 1920s, cotton production here—and throughout the South—had shrunk to almost nothing. Only in recent years, with the introduction of weevil-resistant strains, has cotton begun to stage a comeback. At the time of the Civil War, there were about 10,000 slaves on Edisto Island's plantations alone. Today, the entire permanent population of the

HOW TO GET THERE

◆ Edisto Island is about a 1-hr. drive south of Charleston or a 2-hr. drive north of Savannah. From Charleston, take U.S. Hwy. 17 south about 20 mi. Turn left on SC Hwy. 174 and follow it about 22 mi. to Edisto Beach. From Savannah, take I-95 north about 47 mi. to U.S. Hwy. 17 at Point South. Follow Hwy. 17 north about 37 mi. Turn right on SC Hwy. 174 and follow it about 22 mi. to Edisto Beach.

◆ Both Charleston and Savannah have jet and commuter air service as well as Amtrak service.

island, African-American and white, is less than 2,000.

Back on Highway 174, you soon arrive at the town of Edisto Beach (and its eponymous beach). The beach is a strip of turf shaped like a hockey stick and fronting on the Atlantic Ocean and the South Edisto River, at the southern tip of Edisto Island. This is a beach community the way they used to be. The "main drag," Palmetto Boulevard, isn't jammed with traffic even on busy summer weekends. The street is lined with mostly unassuming older beach cottages. The handful of restaurants and shops are equally unambitious. There is at present not a single motel on the beach, and other than rentals, few choices for short-term stays. Many visitors have been coming back here for years, if not generations, staying in the same house. Edisto is quiet, a bit old-fashioned, oriented to family life and such outdoor activities as shelling, fishing, shrimping, and swimming.

About the only off-key note to Edisto's charmingly retro tune is the hulking Fairfield Ocean Ridge, a time-share and golf development at the island's southern tip. Although it was welcomed by some island businesspeople for the money it brings to the area, this gated resort is viewed by others as being out of place in Edisto's small-town atmosphere.

High season runs from Easter to just after Labor Day. However, for sightseeing and other active pursuits away from the water, summertime is simply too hot and humid for many visitors.

A note on addresses: Edisto Beach and Edisto Island share the same zipcode. Some businesses in the town of Edisto Beach use the Edisto Beach address; others, on the same street, list themselves as being on Edisto Island, not Edisto Beach. In the listings in this chapter, we've used the addresses as given by the businesses themselves—either Edisto Island or Edisto Beach.

BEACHES
EDISTO ISLAND BEACHES

It's one long beach that runs about five miles from the southern point of the island at the South Edisto River and St. Helena Sound, northeast along the Atlantic Ocean parallel to Palmetto Boulevard (Highway 174). The beach,

Beauty	B
Swimming	B
Sand	B-
Amenities	B-

residential in nature in the little town of Edisto Beach, continues on into Edisto Beach State Park, where it is undeveloped. The best and most-attractive part is at Edisto Beach State Park. The park, at the northeast end of town, is convenient to restaurants and shops. The part of Edisto Beach in town, though pleasant, has cottages all along the beach front, and concrete groins, designed to help control beach erosion, jut out into the water at a number of points on the beach. From May through October, Edisto is a nesting ground for loggerhead turtles. They should not be disturbed in any way. During the nesting season, dogs on the beach must be on a leash.

Swimming: Although the beach slope is fairly steep at many points, and the water is sometimes murky, swimming is pretty good. The wave action is gentle to moderate. The calmest spot on the beach is at the southern end, where the Atlantic meets the South Edisto River and St. Helena Sound. The water is usually warm enough for swimming from late April to September or early October. No lifeguard; undertows and rip currents are always possible.

Sand: The beach is moderately wide. The sand is tan, with lots of shells. In fact, Edisto is one of the best shelling beaches in South Carolina. This is also a good area for finding prehistoric fossils such as shark's teeth: One of the best fossil areas is at the north end of the beach in Edisto State Park.

Amenities: Edisto State Park has several rest rooms, a gift shop, a snack bar, and plenty of picnic tables. There are no changing rooms or other amenities along Palmetto Boulevard, since most people who go to the beach here are renting a cottage on or near the beach and can simply walk or bike to it.

Sports: Surf fishing—for spot-tail bass, sea trout, drum, and whiting—can be productive in spring and fall, both at the state park and elsewhere along Edisto Beach. Crabbing is popular year-round. You may also want to buy a seine net and try your hand at netting shrimp.

Parking: Parking, some of it shaded, is available in the state park. Except on summer weekends, when spaces may fill early, parking is usually adequate. In town, there's street parking along the beach, and in some cases there's parking for a few cars in small lots next to the beach at designated access points.

Edisto Beach State Park

This is a 1,255-acre state park with a mile and a half of frontage on the Atlantic, picnic areas, campgrounds, nature trails, a few vacation cabins, and plenty of natural beauty. Even in busy summer periods, you won't find big crowds here (or anywhere in Edisto for that matter). There are fewer people the farther north you go on the park's beach.

Backing the beach are low, natural dunes and maritime forest, with walking paths and nature trails shaded by tall palmettos (cabbage palms) and live oaks. In places, attempts at beach "nourishment" have been made: Piles of sand have been brought in to make low sand dunes. *The main park entrance to the beach area and campground is on Hwy. 174 near the Pavilion parking area at the point where Hwy. 174 turns sharply to the southwest. Another entrance, to the marsh side of the park, cabins, and primitive campground, is to the north of the main entrance on Hwy. 174. Watch for signs.*

Edisto (Town) Beach

There are a number of access points to Edisto Beach along Palmetto Boulevard—about one per block. This is a residential area, with cottages directly on the beach on the south side of Palmetto Boulevard as well as for several streets back from it. If you're renting one of these, you can walk to the beach. There are no amenities and no lifeguard on duty.

The beach here is somewhat less attractive than at the state park, because of the cottages right on the beach and the concrete groins (built in an effort to reduce washing) that jut out into the water every few hundred yards. At low tide, you can go around these groins, but to walk down the beach at high tide you'll have to climb over them. Families with small children may prefer to be farther south on the beach, around the 2000 to 3000 blocks of Palmetto Boulevard, since the wave action is gentler here, on and near the Edisto River and St. Helena Sound. *Drive along Palmetto Blvd. and watch for beach access point signs. Parking at these areas is very limited—rarely for more than 3 or 4 cars.*

OTHER BEACHES

More-remote areas, such as Edingsville Beach (just north of Edisto Beach but separated from it by marsh) and Otter Island, offer unpeopled stretches of sand and great shelling, but access is by private boat only (*see* "Boating" for information on rentals and guided tours of these beaches).

HOTELS/INNS/B&BS

Edisto is primarily a rental-cottage beach area, and accommodations by the night are very limited.

◆ **Fairfield Ocean Ridge** (expensive). One- and two-bedroom villas and some larger units are available, either on a daily (two-night minimum) or a weekly rental basis, in this gated time-share resort on 300 acres at the south end of Edisto Island. Guests have access to a full-size and a kiddie swimming pool, a rec center, and a beach cabana. The resort has an 18-hole golf course (*see* "Golf") and four tennis courts (*see* "Tennis"). Some units can be rented (*see* "House Rentals"). *1 King Cotton Rd., Edisto Island, SC 29438; tel. 803-869-2561, 800-845-8500.*

◆ **Cassina Point Plantation** (moderate). An extraordinary place to stay. The four guest rooms on the second floor, with fireplaces and ten-and-a-half-foot ceilings, are furnished with antiques and family heirlooms. Rooms have half baths en suite and share two full baths. Guests of this restored 1847 plantation have use of two public rooms on the first floor plus a basement rec room (complete with graffiti by Union soldiers who once occupied the plantation). The house is on 145 acres, adjacent to a salt marsh and on the North Edisto River, with pecan trees, a horse barn, and riding trails. Kayak and canoe rentals are available to guests and the public. No credit cards. *Box 535, Edisto Island, SC 29438; tel. 803-869-2535. Open Wed.-Sun. Mar.-Dec. From Hwy. 174, turn east on Indigo Hill Rd. and go 1 1/3 mi. Turn left on Clark Rd. Just after pavement ends, turn right and go through cypress fence for 1/2 mi. on a dirt road. Turn left at small sign and drive 1/2 mi. to house.*

◆ **Edisto Beach State Park** (inexpensive). Five two-bedroom cabins are in a quiet wooded area overlooking the marsh and Scott Creek. Though not fancy, the cabins are beautifully situated and offer excellent value for families. They are fully furnished, with heat and air-conditioning. Rentals, often booked many months in advance, are weekly, from Monday to Monday. Nightly or weekend rentals are possible off-season, depending on availability. *8377 State Cabin Rd., Edisto Island, SC 29438; tel. 803-869-2756. The main park entrance and cabin check-in is on Hwy. 174 near the Pavilion parking area, at the point where Hwy. 174 turns sharply to the southwest.*

HOUSE RENTALS

Rentals in established residential areas on Edisto Island are mostly older wood beach cottages built for comfort, not to impress the neighbors. In season—Easter to Labor Day—they range in price from $400 to $2,000 per week, with proximity to the beach being a major factor in the rental rate. Away from the beach, most rentals are less than $1,000. Off-season rates drop by a third to half. Time-share condos and villas at Fairfield Ocean Ridge, most some distance from the beach, go for about $300 to $800 a week in season, slightly less off-season.

◆ **Edisto Sales and Rentals Realty.** *1405 Palmetto Blvd., Edisto Island, SC 29438; tel. 803-869-2527, 800-868-5398. Open daily Jan.-Nov. and Mon.-Sat. in Dec.*

RESTAURANTS

Edisto doesn't have a lot of restaurants, but one, the Old Post Office, is regionally renowned, and several offer good, fresh seafood at honest prices. In this small town, restaurants may close on whim or change hours without notice in the off-season. Even the town's only fast-food chain restaurant, Burger King, closes from October to March.

◆ **Old Post Office Restaurant** (moderate). Without a doubt the best restaurant in the area, and one that would be highly success-ful even in Charleston or Savannah. The building housing the restaurant dates from 1825, but the interior is modern. The sig-nature dish is shrimp and speckled grits: boiled shrimp with mousseline sauce on whole-grain, organically grown grits. If available, try Firecracker Flounder (fried flounder with tomato-pepper sauce) or Veal Edistonian (veal with pecans and shrimp in a mousseline sauce). Menu changes monthly. *442 Hwy. 174, Edisto*

Island, SC 29438; tel. 803-869-2339. Open Tue.-Sat. for dinner year-round and Mon.-Sat. Jun.-Aug. Usually closed 2 weeks in Jan.

◆ **Pavilion Restaurant** (moderate). Casual seafood place with views of the Atlantic. Good fried and broiled seafood and blue-plate specials. Prime rib is a Sunday dinner special. *102 Palmetto Blvd., Hwy. 174, Edisto Beach, SC 29438; tel. 803-869-3061. Open for lunch and dinner daily Apr.-Sep., Wed.-Mon. Oct.-early Dec., and Thu.-Sun. late Dec.-Mar. Closed most of Dec.*

◆ **Gracie Mansion Cafe** (inexpensive). It looks nothing like its namesake in New York, but it does serve good New York-style pizza and a nice selection of sandwiches and pasta. This former Subway location is now a cheerful café with striped tablecloths. *145 Jungle Rd., Edisto Beach, SC 29438; tel. 803-869-4300. Open Fri.-Wed. for breakfast, lunch, and dinner. Usually closed Jan.*

NIGHTLIFE

Nightlife on Edisto is watching the sea oats grow. For bright lights and music, head to Charleston (*see* Chapter 12).

◆ **Coot's Lounge.** Live music some nights in summer. *102 Palmetto Blvd., Edisto Beach, SC 29438; tel. 803-869-3063. Open daily at 5. At the Pavilion Restaurant.*

ATTRACTIONS

Edisto is known for its old churches, several of which are in love-ly settings on Highway 174. You can visit them on a self-guided driving tour or take a guided tour (*see* the Plantation Tour listing, below). Of special note are the following two churches:

◆ **Edisto Island Presbyterian Church.** Founded in 1685, with the pre-sent building dating to 1830. The pink Legare mausoleum at the back of the cemetery is said to be haunted by the ghost of a young girl who, the story goes, was inadvertently buried alive in it. *2164 Hwy. 174, Edisto Island, SC 29438; tel. 803-869-2326. Grounds and cemetery open daily; church usually locked except during services.*

◆ **Trinity Episcopal Church.** Founded in 1774, with the present sanctuary dating from 1880. *1589 Hwy. 174, Edisto Island, SC 29438; tel. 803-869-3568. Grounds and cemetery open daily; church usually locked except during services.*

◆ **Edisto Museum.** This tiny museum dedicated to the history of

Edisto, open only briefly each week, is worth a visit if you happen to be in the area during open hours. *Hwy. 174 and Chisholm Rd., Edisto Island, SC 29438; tel. 803-869-1954. Open Tue., Thu., and Sat. 1-4.*

◆ **Plantation Tour.** Until the Civil War, Edisto had a thriving plantation economy. Oak Island, built in 1828, and Chisholm House, built around 1815, are two notable homes that are still standing. One of the plantations is routinely open: the Cassina Point Plantation, which now operates as a bed-and-breakfast (*see* "Hotels/Inns/B&Bs," above). The rest of the plantations are private, mostly on nonpublic roads with no trespassing allowed, and closed to visitors except on the Island Tour of Historic Plantations held annually in October. The only other way to glimpse some of the plantations is on a guided tour. *Box 34, Edisto Island, SC 29438. Contact Marie Elliott, a native Edistonian, for a 2 1/2-hr. van tour of plantations, churches, and other points of interest; tel. 803-869-1937. Operates year-round. Admission.*

SHOPPING

Shopping? Not on Edisto. For anything much more complex than a crab net or a jug of milk, head north to Charleston.

◆ **Farmers Hardware & Building Supply.** Fishing gear, crab traps, and other supplies. *796 Hwy. 174, Edisto Island, SC 29438; tel. 803-869-2160. Open Mon.-Sat.*

◆ **Store Creek Antiques.** Glassware and other collectibles. *8083 Point of Pines Rd., Edisto Island, SC 29438; tel. 803-869-3560. Open daily. Behind the Old Post Office Restaurant.*

BEST FOOD SHOPS

An indication of what to expect in food shopping on Edisto is that a top spot for ice cream cones is the BP gas station. For a wider selection of gourmet items and fancy wines, make a day-trip to Charleston (*see* Chapter 12).

◆ **Food Pride.** New grocery opened in late 1995—small but bright and clean. Beer, wine, and soft drinks. *487 Hwy. 174, Edisto Island, SC 29438; tel. 803-869-1144. Open daily.*

◆ **Geechee Gourmet.** Small gourmet shop. Fresh breads, Ben & Jerry's ice cream, organic speckled grits. *143 Jungle Rd., Edisto Beach, SC 29438; tel. 803-869-1000. Open daily.*

SANDWICHES: ◆ **Cafe Edisto.** Restaurant offers take-out. *102 Hwy. 174, Edisto Beach, SC 29438; tel. 803-869-0808. Open Tue.-Sun.*

SEAFOOD: ◆ **Joe Wannamaker.** Call the "Clam Man" for fresh seafood: He'll deliver (he doesn't have a store), and he can even cook it for you. *Edisto Island, SC 29438; tel. 803-869-1509. Operates daily.*

ICE CREAM: ◆ **BP Service Station.** *101 Hwy. 174, Edisto Beach, SC 29438; tel. 803-869-3134. Open daily.*

BEVERAGES: ◆ **Sea Spirits ABC Store.** Liquor and wine; no beer. *Hwy. 174 and Jungle Rd., Edisto Beach, SC 29438; tel. 803-869-1822. Open Mon.-Sat.*

SPORTS

Edisto is oriented to outdoor activities, but most of them, such as shelling, crabbing, and fishing, are of the do-it-yourself variety, rather than organized resort activities. Fairfield Ocean Ridge, the time-share complex, offers the only golf and tennis on the island.

FISHING

Edisto Island's nutrient-rich marshes and tidal creeks provide wonderful fishing in the spring and fall. Offshore fishing also can be good. Crabbing is fun, especially for kids; it's excellent at the Live Oak boat landing and at Bay Point, both on Big Bay Creek northeast of Fairfield Ocean Ridge. Shrimping with a cast net is also popular. There's a special 60-day season, from September to November, when shrimp baiting (catching shrimp with a baited net) is allowed. A permit for this is required—$25 for South Carolina residents, $500 for nonresidents.

◆ **Captain Ron Elliott's Beachcombing, River Tours & Inshore Fishing Trips.** Native Edistonian Ron Elliott gets high marks from locals for his knowledge and his skill at finding fish. Also offers shelling and in-shore fishing tours. *Box 34, Edisto Island, SC 29438; tel. 803-869-1937. Operates daily, weather permitting.*

BOATING

◆ **Edisto Marina.** Small-boat rentals, parasailing, and fishing charters are available at this marina on Big Bay Creek. *3702 Dock Site Rd., Edisto Beach, SC 29438; tel. 803-869-3504. Open daily.*

◆ **Edisto Water Sports & Tackle.** Tours of the ACE Basin, inshore and offshore fishing charters, parasailing, and boat, water bike, and Jet Ski rentals. *Hwy. 174, Edisto Beach, SC 29438; tel. 803-869-0663. Open daily in season; reduced hours the rest of the year.*

BICYCLING

◆ **Edisto Essentials.** Rentals. *495 Hwy. 174, Edisto Beach, SC 29438; tel. 803-869-0951. Open daily.*

GOLF

◆ **Fairfield Ocean Ridge.** This 18-hole course designed by Tom Jackson is the only one on Edisto. It plays to 6,400 yards, with creeks, lagoons, and other water traps on 14 of the holes. *1 King Cotton Rd., Edisto Island, SC 29438; tel. 803-869-2561. Open daily. Admission. Ask at Fairfield gate for pass and directions to golf course.*

TENNIS

◆ **Fairfield Ocean Ridge.** Four grass-tex courts, two equipped for night play. *1 King Cotton Rd., Edisto Island, SC 29438; tel. 803-869-2561. Open daily. Admission. Ask at Fairfield gate for pass and directions to tennis courts.*

NATURE

Edisto Beach State Park (*see* "Beaches") offers convenient access to beach, tidal creeks, and marsh areas. For those with more time and a boat, the ACE Basin is an area of great natural beauty.

◆ **ACE Basin.** This 350,000-acre estuarine area, named for the rivers that bound it (the Ashepoo, Combahee, and Edisto), is home to more than 100 other bird species. Sea turtles, otters, and other wildlife roam the saltwater marshes and rivers. Guides take visitors into the ACE by boat (*see* "Fishing" and "Boating," above, for guided tours and boat rentals). The headquarters are at Grove Plantation, a private plantation home. *Grove Plantation, Jehossee Island Rd., Edisto Island, SC 29438; tel. 803-889-3084. Open daily.*

TOURIST INFORMATION

◆ **Edisto Chamber of Commerce.** Leave your name on the answering machine and eventually you may get some information. *Box 206, Edisto Island, SC 29438; tel. 803-869-3867.*

CHAPTER 15

Hunting & Fripp Islands

Beauty	B+
Swimming	C+
Sand	B-
Hotels/Inns/B&Bs	B
House rentals	B-
Restaurants	B
Nightlife	C-
Attractions	B
Shopping	B-
Sports	B
Nature	B

*T*ake one of the nicest beach-front state parks in the region, add a historic seaside town, throw in an exotic local culture and plenty of southern history, and you've got the recipe for a delightful and varied vacation. In fact, the Hunting Island, Fripp Island, and Beaufort area has such appeal that it has been the setting for several movies, including *The Great Santini*, *The Big Chill*, *Forrest Gump*, and *Something to Talk*

About. Despite its appeal, the area sees much less tourism than nearby Hilton Head to the south or Charleston to the north, so you never feel you're part of a tour-bus group.

Hunting Island State Park is one of the few South Carolina barrier islands that today is still much as it was before Europeans arrived in America. The lush subtropical island was never fully settled or farmed, as were many other islands in the area. It was used as a hunting reserve (hence the name), and access was by boat only until the 1940s. Today, the park is a joy to visit. Its 5,000 acres include four miles of beaches, an interpretive center where you're welcomed by 'gators in the swamp (and helpful state park staff, too), 15 cabins, a 200-site campground, and a lighthouse.

The island is home to many creatures besides human beachgo-

HOW TO GET THERE

◆ Beaufort is about 70 mi. from downtown Charleston, with Hunting Island another 16 mi. From Charleston, take U.S. Hwy. 17 south about 52 mi.; turn left on U.S. Hwy. 21 at Gardens Corner and follow it about 18 mi. to Beaufort.

◆ From Savannah, it's about 45 mi. to Beaufort and another 16 mi. to Hunting Island. Take U.S. Hwy. 17 Alt. north to SC Hwy. 170 and follow that to Beaufort. Alternatively, from Savannah take I-95 to Exit 8. Take Hwy. 88 (look for signs to Beaufort) to SC Hwy. 170 and follow it to Beaufort.

◆ From Beaufort, take U.S. Hwy. 21 to Hunting Island and Fripp Island.

◆ For jet and commuter service, fly into either the Charleston or Savannah airports.

◆ Both Charleston and Savannah also have Amtrak service.

ers. Loggerhead turtles nest here in the summer. Hunting Island's 3,000 acres of salt marsh provide a fertile environment for many types of birds, including the great blue heron, the white heron, the marsh hen, and the osprey. Bottle-nosed dolphins can be seen swimming in the salt marsh at high tide and off the beaches in the Atlantic.

Next to Hunting Island, and very different from it, is Fripp Island. Fripp is a gated private resort community, one of the oldest planned resorts on the southeast coast, with more than 200 houses and condos for rent. Its beaches are open only to property owners, renters, and guests. The resort also offers two golf courses, tennis, fishing, beach and pool swimming, and a children's program. Though developed, it has areas of natural beauty (part of the 1994 Disney movie version of *The Jungle Book* was filmed here).

About 16 miles (an easy 25-minute drive) from Hunting Island is the delightful and historic town of Beaufort (*BYEW-fort*, with the first syllable pronounced like the first syllable in *beautiful*, as opposed to the North Carolina coastal town of the same name, which is pronounced *BO-ford*). While it has no beaches of its own, Beaufort offers much—in the way of lodging, dining, attractions, and just plain charm—to round out your beach vacation in this area.

Beaufort is South Carolina's second-oldest town, after Charleston. It was chartered in 1711 as Beaufort Town. The farming of indigo, rice, and, later, the prized Sea Island cotton brought great wealth to the coastal planters, who used some of their money to build fine homes here. Despite being a center of secessionary fervor, the town was spared destruction in the Civil War. Today, Beaufort claims to have more antebellum homes per block than any other southern town, and the entire downtown area is a National Historic Landmark District.

Beaufort has been made famous by the novels of Pat Conroy, who grew up here, in the historic district. *The Prince of Tides* and *The Great Santini*, two of his novels, have been made into movies and filmed in Beaufort.

Nearby St. Helena Island (often pronounced *Sint HEL-e-na*) is a focus for Gullah, the unique culture that developed on the

Sea Islands of South Carolina and Georgia among those brought as slaves from West Africa to work on the plantations. Many freed slaves stayed on the islands after emancipation, developing and enhancing a way of life that, until recently, was isolated from the rest of the South and indeed the world. On St. Helena Island, Penn Center, founded in 1862, was the first school for freed slaves in America. The African-American Sea Islanders spoke, and in many cases still do, their own language: Gullah, or Sea Island Creole.

High season on Hunting and Fripp islands is the summer, mid-May to early September. Water temperatures then are in the high 70s and low 80s, ideal for swimming. Spring and fall are also popular on these islands; they are the best times for fishing and outdoor sports, since air temperatures are more bearable than in summer. Temperatures in July and August, especially away from the water, hit the 90s, with high humidity. Spring and fall are also the best for appreciating the historical sights and old homes of Beaufort.

BEACHES
HUNTING ISLAND STATE PARK BEACH

Like most barrier islands along the South Carolina coast, Hunting Island fights an everlasting but very natural war against erosion. Beach erosion at Hunting is among the most severe in the state, averaging ten feet per year.

Beauty	B+
Swimming	C+
Sand	B-
Amenities	B+

You'll see remnants of trees standing in the surf: These were once in the inland maritime forest.

Nevertheless, Hunting Island's four miles of beach are lovely. As a state park, it is undeveloped, except for a few cabins, the campground, and picnic shelters. Hunting is one of the "boneyard" beaches, so named because of driftwood on the beach. Close to the beach at many points are large palmetto palms and other maritime trees offering pleasant shade.

Although it is one long beach on the Atlantic, Hunting Island is divided into North Beach and South Beach. North, which is close to the lighthouse, the picnic area, and the camping area, is generally wider than South, which is where most of the park cabins are located.

Since Hunting Island is somewhat off the beaten path, the beach here is usually quiet and uncrowded. Off-season, except for a few campers and picnickers, you'll have most of the beach to yourself. *From Beaufort, take U.S. Hwy. 21 about 16 mi. The park entrance is on the left before you reach the bridge to Fripp Island (watch for signs). Once in the park, follow signs (several park roads are one-ways) and park in designated areas. The main parking lots are in the center of the island, near the picnic area.*

Swimming: Pretty good from May to September. The gentle waves and shallow water make this a nice area for children. Beach erosion can make a big difference from one summer to the next, however. Ask locally about beach conditions. Lifeguard on duty from about Memorial Day to Labor Day.

Sand: The beach has a gentle slope and light gray to tan sand. There are some primary dunes subject to erosion. At places, the beach is more than 100 yards wide at low tide, but it's mostly narrow at high tide. Shelling is fairly good here, with clam shells, Atlantic cockles, and angelwings the most common.

Amenities: The state park offers extensive picnic facilities, along with a number of rest rooms and changing rooms. There's a snack bar near the lighthouse and a small general store at the campground. Most of the amenities are located at or near North Beach.

Sports: Surf and pier fishing, crabbing, and clamming.

Parking: The park has adequate, shaded parking. A $3-per-car daily admission fee covers parking.

FRIPP ISLAND BEACH

Fripp Island is a private, gated resort community. The three miles of beaches and most recreation facilities are open to you only if you are staying on the island. As at Hunting Island, much of the beach front suffers from moderate to

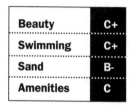

Beauty	C+
Swimming	C+
Sand	B-
Amenities	C

severe erosion. Large boulders have been put in place in some areas as a seawall or revetment. At points, especially at the south end of the island, there is no beach at high tide, although the beach at low tide is 200 or more feet wide. The north end has suffered less from recent erosion.

Development at Fripp has been controlled and tasteful, but the presence of ocean-front homes means that the beach isn't as attractively natural as Hunting Island. Since development at Fripp has been low density, there are no crowds on this private island, although the areas at the Beach Club and Ocean Point are busy in summer.

Access to the beach is at the Beach Club, which is at the middle of the Atlantic beach front; at the Ocean Point complex at the north end of the island; and at various points along residential areas of Tarpon Boulevard, Dolphin Road, and Marlin Drive. Those renting beach-front homes have direct access to the beach over boardwalks or paths. *From Beaufort, take U.S. Hwy. 21. Fripp Island is about 18 mi. from downtown Beaufort, at the end of U.S. Hwy. 21. Check in at the security gate after crossing the bridge over Fripp Inlet. The resort will provide a map that shows beach access points. Park in designated areas.*

Swimming: Swimming is fairly good from May to September. Wave action is usually moderate. No lifeguard.

Sand: Light gray to tan. The beach slope is gentle to moderate.

Amenities: The Beach Club, open to resort guests, has a restaurant and lounge that are open year-round and a beachside bar that's open seasonally, plus a beach house with rest rooms. The Ocean Point complex has a seasonal café and rest rooms.

Sports: The Beach Club offers a swimming pool, croquet courts, shuffleboard, a playground, and a basketball court. The Ocean Point complex has a sand volleyball court, a pool, and a children's playground. In addition, there's surf fishing, crabbing, and clamming on the island.

Parking: Parking at the Beach Club and Ocean Point complexes is adequate. For beach entry at other points, residents and renters walk or bike to the beach.

HOTELS/INNS/B&BS

Beaufort has a nice variety of small inns and B&Bs in the downtown historic district. Outside the historic district in Beaufort there are several chain and independent motels. Between

Beaufort and Hunting Island there is one small independent motel, at Frogmore on St. Helena Island.

◆ **Beaufort Inn** (expensive). A stunning total renovation turned a 1907-vintage building into the most upscale inn in Beaufort. This three-story inn is beautifully, even extravagantly furnished in antiques and reproductions, and—surprise!—there's even an elevator. Several of the 13 rooms have fireplaces; two have whirlpool baths. The Palmetto Plantation Suite (very expensive) is the most-requested room: It has a fireplace, a king-size bed, and a wet bar. When Julia Roberts was here filming *Something to Talk About*, she stayed in the Oak Grove Plantation Room; it has a small veranda and a king-size canopy bed. Full breakfast. Excellent restaurant and full-service bar. Children over seven only. *809 Port Republic St., Beaufort, SC 29902; tel. 803-521-9000; fax 803-521-9500. Located 1 block from the Beaufort water front, in the historic district.*

◆ **Rhett House Inn** (expensive). This elegant B&B in the former mansion of a southern aristocrat is furnished with English and American antiques. Beautiful wraparound porches are inviting for a lazy afternoon read. Barbra Streisand stayed here when she was scouting locations for *The Prince of Tides*. Full breakfast and use of bicycles included. The inn can provide beach chairs and towels and a gourmet lunch for a trip to the beach. Rhett House Restaurant open to the public. *1009 Craven St., Beaufort, SC 29902; tel. 803-524-9030; fax 803-524-1310. 1 block from the Beaufort water front, in the historic district.*

◆ **Best Western Sea Island Inn** (moderate). Attractive, recently renovated 43-room motel has a terrific location near downtown shops and historic sights. On Beaufort Bay (but no views). Tasteful rooms. Pool in an attractive courtyard. If you want a motel rather than a B&B or an old inn, this is the best choice in Beaufort. *1015 Bay St., Beaufort, SC 29902; tel. 803-522-2090, 800-528-1234; fax 803-521-4858. Beaufort historic district.*

◆ **TwoSuns Inn** (moderate). Five-room B&B in a 1917 Neo-classical Revival house, directly on Beaufort Bay. Rooms are decorated in Victorian and country motifs. Co-owner Ron is the founding president of the South Carolina B&B Association and gives workshops on operating a B&B—so he knows his business. Great for a casual, unstuffy B&B experience. Breakfast and afternoon "tea and toddy hour." *1705 Bay St., Beaufort, SC 29902; tel. 803-522-1122, 800-532-4244; fax 803-522-1122. In the Beaufort historic district, about 8 blocks from the main restaurant area.*

◆ **Royal Frogmore Inn** (inexpensive). At about $40 for a double, this independent motel is an excellent value. Small, basic but clean rooms. Closest motel to Hunting Island, and near Penn Center. Fills up during Marine Corps graduation ceremonies. *U.S. Hwy. 21, St. Helena Island, SC 29920; tel. 803-838-5400; fax 803-838-7137. Midway between Beaufort and Hunting Island.*

HOUSE RENTALS

In addition to the high-end Fripp Island Resort and the attractively priced beach-front cabins at Hunting Island State Park, there are also a variety of homes and condos in several private developments nearby, including Harbor Island.

◆ **Fripp Island Resort.** During peak season (mid May to early September) expect to pay $600 to $1,200 a week for a two- or three-bedroom condo villa here, with the higher rates for units with water views. Ocean-front three- or four-bedroom luxury homes go for $2,000 to $2,500 a week in summer and half that away from the water. Rates for condos and homes drop slightly in spring and fall and by almost half in winter. Daily rates are available except in the summer. Golf packages available. *1 Tarpon Blvd., Fripp Island, SC 29920; tel. 803-838-3535, 800-845-4100. Open daily. Fripp Island is at the end of U.S. Hwy. 21.*

◆ **Harbor Island Rentals.** Three- and four-bedroom condos and luxury homes, some on a private beach. Rates similar to those at Fripp Island. *Harbor Island, 2123B Sea Island Pkwy., St. Helena Island, SC 29920; tel. 803-838-4800, 800-553-0251. Open daily. From Beaufort, take U.S. Hwy. 21. Harbor Island is on the left, before you get to Fripp Island.*

◆ **Hunting Island State Park.** The 15 cabins here (7 three-bedroom, 7 two-bedroom, and one one-bedroom, of which 9 are directly on the beach) aren't fancy, but they're a terrific value at $400 to $500 a week. Unfortunately, everybody knows this, and for summer or holiday rentals you have to book up to 11 months in advance. The cabins are completely furnished, with TVs, heat, and air-conditioning. Seven units have fireplaces. Weekly rentals Memorial Day to Labor Day; weekend and daily rentals at other times, depending on availability. *2555 Sea Island Pkwy., Hunting Island, SC 29920; tel. 803-838-2011. Open daily. From Beaufort, take U.S. Hwy 21 about 16 mi.*

RESTAURANTS

◆ **Beaufort Inn Restaurant** (expensive). Dine by candlelight at this intimate restaurant at the Beaufort Inn. The Dutch-born chef cooks Low Country seafood and other dishes with a European flair. The menu changes frequently, but if they're available, start with the jalapeño grits cakes with a shrimp and tasso sauce or the shiitake crab cakes. For your entrée, try the crispy whole flounder with strawberry and mango chutney. Best wine list in Beaufort. Breakfast menu includes eggs Benedict made with Daufuskie crab and sinfully filling raspberry pancakes with warm maple syrup. Afternoon tea. *809 Port Republic St., Beaufort, SC 29902; tel. 803-521-9000. Open daily for breakfast and dinner. Located 1 block from the Beaufort water front, in the historic district.*

◆ **Bank Waterfront Grill & Bar** (moderate). Located in what was formerly the lobby of a bank, the restaurant is a bit too cute, with its financial menu—appetizers are the "Beginning Balance" and kids' plates are "Junior Investors"—but the steaks, grilled seafood, burgers, pasta, and other unfancy fare are tasty. There's usually a crowd. *926 Bay St., Beaufort, SC 29902; tel. 803-522-8831. Open daily for lunch and dinner. In the Beaufort historic district.*

◆ **Plums Restaurant and Cafe** (moderate). Extremely popular bistro at Waterfront Park. Tables on the porch have a nice bay view. Try the baked Brie with raspberry preserves as an appetizer, then the Shrimp Santa Fe pasta. Hip, friendly, casual service. Great ice cream. *904 1/2 Bay St., Beaufort, SC 29902; tel. 803-525-1946. Open for lunch and dinner Mon.-Sat. and for brunch 10-3 Sun. In the Beaufort historic district.*

◆ **Shrimp Shack** (inexpensive). This is exactly what the name says: a shack on the marsh serving fresh local shrimp, fish, and other seafood. At this joint, you may see a new Mercedes parked next to a rusty pickup. Go to the window, place your order, and enjoy it at the plain wood tables inside or, in good weather, at the tables outside. The shrimp burger is famous—and delicious.

U.S. Hwy. 21, St. Helena, SC 29920; tel. 803-838-2962. Open Mon.-Sat. for lunch and dinner mid-Mar.-mid-Oct. and for lunch Mon.-Sat. mid-Oct.-mid-Mar.; call to verify hours during the off-season. On the left as you near Hunting/Fripp islands.

NIGHTLIFE

What action there is in downtown Beaufort is centered on the water front on Bay Street. U.S. Highway 21 and areas close to Parris Island have some bars.

◆ **Bananas.** Billed as the "fun spot on the water front," Bananas has late-night burgers, spirits, and, on weekends, live music. *910 Bay St., Beaufort, SC 29902; tel. 803-533-0910. Open daily. In the Beaufort historic district, at Waterfront Park.*

ATTRACTIONS

◆ **Beaufort Historic District.** The 304-acre Old Point historic district is the jewel of Beaufort, with more than 150 antebellum homes. It's best toured on foot or bicycle. There are also horse-drawn carriage tours and guided walking tours. Most of the tours start at the Chamber of Commerce (*see* "Tourist Information"), where you can also get maps for self-guided tours. Carriage Tours of Beaufort (tel. 803-521-1651) is one company giving horse-drawn tours; The Point (tel. 803-522-3576) gives guided tours on minibuses. Among the highlights of a historic district tour are the following, all open to the public: the Henry C. Chambers Waterfront Park, a delightful park on Beaufort Bay; John Mark Verdier House, a 1790 merchant's house now operated as a museum; and St. Helena's Episcopal Church, part of which dates from 1724. There are many note-worthy historic homes in the district, but most are privately owned and not open to the public, except during the annual Fall Tour of Homes (for information, contact the Historic Beaufort Foundation, tel. 803-524-6334) and the Spring Tour of Homes (tel. 803-524-0363). One of the best-known private homes is the Edgar Fripp House, or "Tidalholm" (1 Laurens Street), which was featured in the movie *The Big Chill.*

◆ **Beaufort Museum.** Learn about Beaufort's historic past and natural history. The museum is in the Beaufort Arsenal, which dates to 1798. *713 Craven St., Beaufort, SC 29901; tel. 803-525-7077. Open Mon.-Tue. and Thu.-Sat. 10-5. Admission.*

◆ **Hunting Island Lighthouse.** Built in 1874, the lighthouse was dismantled in 1899 and moved to its present site. Climb the tower for a good view of the island from about 12 stories up. *Hunting Island State Park, 2555 Sea Island Pkwy., Hunting Island, SC 29920; tel. 803-838-2011. Lighthouse open daily 10-4. Closed during storms. Park open daily 6-9 Apr.-Sep. and 6-6 Oct.-Mar. Admission.*

◆ **Parris Island Museum.** A wide range of displays trace the history of Parris Island, the Marine Corps, and recruit training. *War Memorial Building, Bldg. 111, Marine Corps Recruit Depot, Parris Island, SC 29905; tel. 803-525-2951. Open daily 1000-1630 hr. (10-4:30 civilian time). From Beaufort, take Bay St. to Ribaut Rd. (Hwy 802) and follow signs to the Recruit Depot main gate. Stop and ask the guard for permission to visit the museum.*

◆ **Parris Island Tour.** You might think touring a military base would be the last thing you'd want to do on a vacation, but a driving tour of the Marine Corps Recruit Depot at Parris Island is fascinating. Make your first stop the Douglas Visitors Center, to get a free booklet describing the driving tour, which includes a visit to a small historic district, the drill instructor school, a rifle range, the parade field, and the Iwo Jima monument. *Marine Corps Recruit Depot, Parris Island, SC 29905; tel. 803-525-3650. Open daily during daylight hours. From Beaufort, take Bay St. to Ribaut Rd. (Hwy. 802) and follow signs to the Recruit Depot main gate. Stop and ask the guard for permission to enter the base.*

◆ **Penn Center.** One of the most important African-American historical sites in the United States, the center was founded in 1862 as Penn School, the first school for freed American slaves, by Quaker missionaries from the North. In the early 1960s, Dr. Martin Luther King, Jr., used the center as a training and meeting facility for civil rights workers. Today the center's mission is to help preserve the Sea Island Gullah culture. The campus has 19 buildings, which may be visited on a self-guided tour. *Martin Luther King Jr. Dr., St. Helena Island, SC 29920; tel. 803-838-2432. Museum (tel. 803-838-2235) open Tue.-Fri. 11-4; campus open daily. Admission. From Beaufort, take U.S. Hwy. 21 to Frogmore on St. Helena Island. Turn right on Lands End Rd. and go about 1 mi.*

SHOPPING

Beaufort has a small but delightful shopping area on and near Bay Street, the town's "main street" near the water. Antiques and art galleries are the thing here. For more mundane needs, there are shopping centers and discount stores on U.S. Highway 21.

◆ **Bay Street Trading Co.** Good selection of regional books. Knowledgeable staff. *808 Bay St., Beaufort, SC 29902; tel. 803-524-2000. Open Mon.-Sat. In the Beaufort historic district.*

◆ **Fordham Hardware.** A real old-fashioned hardware store and a good place to get your fishing and crabbing gear. *701 Bay St., Beaufort, SC 29902; tel. 803-524-3161. Open Mon.-Sat. In the Beaufort historic district.*

◆ **Red Piano Too Art Gallery.** Fascinating collection of southern, Caribbean, African-American, and other folk art. *838 Sea Island Pkwy., St. Helena Island, SC 29920; tel. 803-838-2241. Open daily 10-5. About 7 mi. from Beaufort, at Frogmore.*

◆ **Rhett Gallery.** Large gallery with extensive collections of 19th-century prints, antique maps, nautical charts, Audubon prints, bird carvings, Civil War artifacts, Low Country paintings, and more. *901 Bay St., Beaufort, SC 29902; tel. 803-524-3339. Open Mon.-Sat. and "occasionally on Sun." In the Beaufort historic district.*

BEST FOOD SHOPS

◆ **Winn-Dixie.** Besides groceries, it sells beer, wine, and soft drinks. *Island Square Center, Beaufort, SC 29902; tel. 803-522-0930. Open daily.*

SANDWICHES: ◆ **Alvin Ord's Sandwich Shop.** *1415 Ribaut Rd., Port Royal, SC 29935; tel. 803-524-8222. Open Mon.-Sat.*

SEAFOOD: ◆ **W. J. Gay Seafood.** *2242 Boundary St., Beaufort, SC 29902; tel. 803-521-5090; fax 803-521-5088. Open daily.*

FRESH PRODUCE: In June and July, a farmer's market is held Saturday mornings in Waterfront Park in the Beaufort historic district, with fresh produce for sale.

BAKERY: ◆ **Sweet Temptations Bakery and Cafe.** *205 West St., Beaufort, SC 29902; tel. 803-524-6171. Open Mon.-Sat. In the historic district.*

ICE CREAM: ◆ **Plums Restaurant and Cafe.** *904 1/2 Bay St., Beaufort, SC 29902; tel. 803-525-1946. Open daily. In the historic district.*

BEVERAGES: ◆ **Bill's Liquor Store.** *Island Square Center, Beaufort,*

SC 29902; tel. 803-522-2022. Open Mon.-Sat.

WINE: ◆ **Bill's Liquor Store.** *Island Square Center, Beaufort, SC 29902; tel. 803-522-2022. Open Mon.-Sat.*

SPORTS
FISHING

◆ **Paradise Pier.** This 1,120-foot pier provides good fishing and crabbing. Bait and tackle available. *Hunting Island State Park, 2809 Sea Island Pkwy., Hunting Island, SC 29920; tel. 803-838-7437. Open daily Mar.-Nov., with days sometimes reduced in early spring and late fall. Admission ($4 to fish, 50 cents to stroll).*

◆ **Sea Wolf Charters.** Charters in local waters and in the Gulf Stream. *Port Royal Landing Marina, 1 Landing Dr., Port Royal, SC 29935; tel. 803-525-1174. Operates daily, weather permitting.*

BOATING

◆ **Downtown Marina.** Charters, rentals. *1010 Bay St., Beaufort, SC 29902; tel. 803-524-4422. Open daily. At Waterfront Park.*

◆ **Fripp Island Excursions.** Rents Jet Skis, skiffs, and kayaks. Also offers cruises in a small boat. *Paradise Pier, 2809 Sea Island Pkwy., Hunting Island, SC 29920; tel. 803-838-1518. Open daily.*

BICYCLING

◆ **Lowcountry Bicycles.** Rentals. *904 Port Republic St., Beaufort, SC 29902; tel. 803-524-9585. Open Mon.-Sat.*

GOLF

The area has a dozen golf courses. Half of these, however, are private, open only to members and guests. If you can't find enough golf around Beaufort, try Hilton Head (*see* Chapter 16).

◆ **Cat Island Golf Club.** An 18-hole, 6,518-yard, par-71 public course designed by George Cobb. *8 Waveland Ave., Beaufort, SC 29902; tel. 803-524-0300. Open daily. Admission. From Beaufort, take U.S. Hwy. 21 toward Fripp Island. Turn right on Meridian Rd. and go about 6 mi. to Cat Island.*

◆ **Fripp Island Resort.** Fripp has two challenging courses: the par-72, 6,590-yard Ocean Point Golf Links (tel. 803-838-1521), built in 1964 on a George Cobb design, with 15 holes on the water or with an ocean view; and the new Ocean Creek Golf Course (tel. 803-838-1576), the inaugural design of Davis Love III, a par-71, 6,600-yard "back-to-the-basics" course that opened in 1995. The lake at the 11th hole is the one seen in Disney's *Jungle Book*. Although this is a private resort, those not staying here may play on a space-available basis—call in advance for tee times and a guest pass. *1 Tarpon Blvd., Fripp Island, SC 29920; tel. 803-845-4100. Open daily. Admission. From Beaufort, take U.S. Hwy. 21 about 18 mi. to its end. Stop at security gate for a pass.*

◆ **Golf Professionals Club.** Two scenic 18-hole courses with moderate greens fees. The par-72, 6,811-yard Champions Course is more demanding than the 5,929-yard, par-72 Players Course. *93 Francis Marion Circle, Beaufort, SC 29902; tel. 803-522-9700. Open daily. Admission. From Beaufort, take Hwy. 802 to Lady's Island.*

TENNIS

Fripp Island Resort's courts are available only to resort residents and guests. Harbor Island and other private communities also have courts for residents and guests. Beaufort has public courts at the corner of Bladen and Boundary streets, near downtown.

NATURE

◆ **Hunting Island State Park.** This 5,000-acre park on an undeveloped barrier island is home to many animals, birds, and reptiles and offers lush semitropical coastal scenery. An informative interpretive center has displays and helpful staff. A 200-site campground offers tent and RV camping at the beach. *2555 Sea Island Pkwy., Hunting Island, SC 29920; tel. 803-838-2011. Park open daily 6-9 Apr.-Sep. and 6-6 Oct.-Mar. Interpretive center open Mon.-Fri. 9-5 and Sat.-Sun. 11-5. Admission.*

TOURIST INFORMATION

◆ **Greater Beaufort Chamber of Commerce.** *1006 Bay St., Box 910, Beaufort, SC 29901; tel. 803-524-3163. Open Mon.-Sat. 9:30-5:30 and Sun. 10-5.*

◆ **Hunting Island State Park.** *2555 Sea Island Pkwy., Hunting Island, SC 29920; tel. 803-838-2011. Office open Mon.-Fri. 9-5 and Sat.-Sun. 11-5.*

CHAPTER 16

Hilton Head Island

Beauty	B-
Swimming	B
Sand	B-
Hotels/Inns/B&Bs	B+
House rentals	B+
Restaurants	A-
Nightlife	B+
Attractions	C
Shopping	B+
Sports	A+
Nature	C+

*M*ore than one and a half million people visit Hilton Head each year. They come to play its 30 golf courses and 300 tennis courts, enjoy its 12 miles of sandy beaches, eat blue crabs, shrimp, or Greek *spanakopita* at its more than 200 restaurants, and shop the tony boutiques and discount factory-outlet stores.

Hilton Head is the largest island, in terms of land area, on the coast of the Carolinas and Georgia, and one of the largest on the East Coast. The island, only 15 miles north of Savannah as the seagull flies, is 12 miles long and as much as 5 miles wide, with a total area of about 42 square miles. Look at the map and you'll see that it is shaped almost exactly like a running shoe. The toe is South Beach at Sea Pines Plantation. The sole, along the Atlantic Ocean, includes Shipyard and Palmetto Dunes plantations. Its heel is Port Royal Plantation, and above that, on the ankle, is Hilton Head Plantation, both fronting on Port Royal Sound.

Hilton Head, as befits its running-shoe shape, is the polar opposite of a laid-back island. While, in theory, you can relax and do nothing here, and almost a third of Hilton Head's permanent population of 30,000 are retirees, this is an active, high-energy island. It's a shop-till-you-drop, brunch-it-and-munch-it, bike-and-hike, use-it-or-lose-it destination. Vacationers get up at six

HOW TO GET THERE

◆ Hilton Head is about 1 hr. (40 mi.) by car north of Savannah. The major north-south route to Hilton Head is I-95. From the south, take Exit 5 off I-95 at Hardeeville. Follow SC Hwy. 46 to U.S. Hwy. 278 east, which brings you directly onto Hilton Head. You're on the island when you cross the William Graves Memorial Bridge. An alternate route from Savannah is U.S. Hwy. 17A to Hwy. 46 and then to Hwy. 278.

◆ From the north, take Exit 28 off I-95 at Coosawhatchie. Follow SC Hwy. 462 to SC Hwy. 278 east.

◆ Hilton Head's airport is small and has only commuter service. Savannah, about 40 mi. away, is the closest airport with jet service; many resorts on Hilton Head offer van shuttle service (about $25 per person) from here. Savannah also has Amtrak service.

in the morning for golf, do lunch at sophisticated bistros, hit the tennis courts in the afternoon, take a dip in the pool or the ocean, and then enjoy drinks and dinner on the water.

One of the penalties for this hyperactivity is heavy traffic. The island's main artery, U.S. Highway 278, also called the William Hilton Parkway, can become a parking lot at rush hour during the summer. William Hilton, a 17th-century sea captain from Barbados who explored the island and for whom the road (and the island) is named, couldn't have imagined what his quiet island would become at 5 p.m. on a late 20th-century weekday.

Let's stop a moment and see how it got this way. Locals still express amazement that things have changed so much, so quickly. Although Hilton Head was once a thriving and wealthy center for indigo and Sea Island cotton production, the Civil War and the boll weevil took their toll. By the early 20th century the island had reverted to its sleepy past. Only 40 years ago, Hilton Head was mostly pine trees and palmettos, gators and mosquitoes. Then, in 1956, a bridge was built connecting the island to the mainland. Charles Fraser, the Yale-educated son of a Georgia lumberman who had purchased large tracts on Hilton Head, had visions of a new kind of residential and resort community and began building Sea Pines Plantation. Fraser opened the island's first hotel, golf course, and upscale shops. Soon his early success attracted other developers, and the modern Hilton Head was born.

Today, the contribution of Fraser's vision is evident, not just in Sea Pines but also in the highly controlled and, most would say, tasteful development of the island. Fraser, an early environmentalist, tried to minimize the impact of commercial development. Thus, while you can get a McDonald's hamburger or shop at a mall on Hilton Head, you won't see any big golden arches or neon signs. Signage is circumspect and low-key, lending an upscale and conservative air to the island. All development must meet rigorous zoning and architectural standards.

Another of Fraser's legacies is the dominance of private gated communities on the island, many called "plantations." Following Sea Pines, there evolved on the island 4 main developments, then 6, and now at least 11, with additional ones on the mainland nearby. There are, at last count, at least 14 security gates on Hilton Head, blocking entry to tens of thousands of acres. Thus, the majority of Hilton Head Island is not readily accessible to tourists. Some of the best golf courses, tennis centers, and beach access points are off-limits, except to owners and their guests. For visitors it's a little like going to Disney World and being locked out of many of the best attractions.

Access to the gated communities varies. Sea Pines Plantation permits visitors to enter for a small daily admission fee ($3 per car), although the pass is not valid for using the beaches or for fishing and crabbing. Palmetto Dunes, Shipyard, and some other plantations are open to those who rent homes or are staying at the hotels in the gated community. Still others, such as Hilton Head Plantation and Indigo Run, are totally private residential communities and do not permit even short-term rentals or day visitors.

The season at Hilton Head continues to expand. Once high season was the summer only. Now the spring, with its golf tournaments and pleasantly moderate weather, is about as busy as summertime. Fall, with its respite from the hot, humid coastal weather, is coming on strong for tourism. The off-season, to the extent that there is one, is December through February—and even then you can play golf and tennis, with the thermometer usually reaching the low 60s by midday.

BEACHES

Hilton Head's beaches are one of the island's greatest assets. The 12 miles of beaches and the clean water are a drawing card for swimmers, beachcombers, and sports enthusiasts. There are long strands of fine beaches from the toe of

Beauty	B-
Swimming	B
Sand	B-
Amenities	B

the island at Sea Pines Plantation to the heel at Port Royal Plantation. However, you need to know two things about the beaches that you would discover in the tourist brochures only by reading between the lines.

First, erosion is a continuing problem on parts of the Hilton Head seashore, as it is on many other barrier islands. In this case, the ocean takes sand from the center of Hilton Head Island— the sole of the shoe—and deposits it at the toe and heel. At South

Beach, the toe end of the island, the beach is actually growing rapidly as sand is washed southward. A part of the private Sea Pines Plantation, South Beach is the widest on the island. At high tide, especially in the center of the island, you'll see the impact of this erosion. At Palmetto Dunes, for instance, the beach is fairly wide at low tide, but at high tide, there's little if any beach in some places.

Which brings us to the other problem with Hilton Head beaches: access. The island has only four official public beach access points (see specific beaches, below). The rest of the entry points are off-limits to one degree or another. Local beach access may be completely prohibited to all but property owners or be available only to those staying at a particular hotel or residential development. The good news is that once on the beach, you may visit any part of it, because only the land above the high-water mark is private.

Does all this mean that the beaches of Hilton Head are not worth visiting? Not at all. For the most part, you won't notice the erosion problems. There are long strands of quality beaches all along the Atlantic. But if beach activities are important to you, before making reservations at any hotel or condo complex, be sure to ask what the current state of the beach is, what the beach is like at high tide, and where the access points are. (Note: Alcoholic beverages are prohibited on all Hilton Head beaches.)

Swimming: The swimming is pleasant on Hilton Head, although in areas such as Coligny Beach you'll be part of a large crowd in summer. Wave action is usually moderate. The ocean is quite shallow near Hilton Head, and even four miles out from the island the average depth is just ten feet. The four officially designated beach access points have swimming areas that are clearly marked. Lifeguard on duty May through September; some hotels have lifeguards in summer, but outside the hotel and official beach access points, miles of beach have no lifeguard.

Sand: Light gray to tan. It is finest and whitest at the south end of the island, and coarsest and a little darker at the north. Beach slopes, except where erosion is a factor, are gentle to moderate. Dunes, if any, are low.

Amenities: Rest rooms, changing areas, outdoor showers, and vending machines are at each designated beach access point.

Some beaches are also close to restaurants.

Sports: On Hilton Head, you can rent any water-sports equipment known to man: Jet Skis, pontoon boats, motorboats, sailboats, parasails, water bikes, you name it. Parasailing is prohibited directly off Hilton Head beaches, and from April to September, fishing, surfing, Boogie boarding, and team sports involving balls or Frisbees are not permitted from 10 to 6.

Parking: Availability is none too good during peak beach periods but adequate at other times. The best parking is at Coligny and Driessen beaches. Visitors staying in rental housing or at hotels near the beach usually bike or walk to the beach.

Folly Field Beach

Folly Field is the northernmost public beach access, close to the island's heel. It's just north of Driessen, to which it is similar, although Folly Field is wider and the parking is more limited. Like Driessen, it is in a residential area with no commercial development at the beach. *From William Hilton Pkwy. (U.S. Hwy. 278) turn toward the ocean on Folly Field Rd. Stay on Folly Field 3/10 mi. Bear right on Starfish Dr. and follow it a short distance to the beach. Park in one of 52 metered spaces (25 cents per 15 min.). The lot closes at 8 p.m.*

Driessen Beach Park

You enter Driessen (*DREE-sin*) Beach (formerly called Bradley Beach) near the island's heel, on a 200-yard boardwalk over low dunes and maritime shrubs. The beach here is attractive, with light-gray to tan sand, and has a gentle slope and moderate wave action, but it is very narrow at high tide because of erosion. In summer, Driessen is less crowded than Coligny, but the parking lot tends to fill early. In the spring and fall, you may find yourself one of only a few people on the beach. While it has rest rooms and vending machines, Driessen—unlike Coligny—is in a residential area with no nearby restaurants or bars. *From William Hilton Pkwy. (U.S. Hwy. 278) turn toward the ocean on Bradley Beach Rd. and follow it to the beach. Park in the large paved lot with 212 numbered spaces, and remember your number. You pay in advance (25 cents per 15 min.) at a metered box near the changing area. Parking lot closes at 8 p.m.*

Coligny Beach

In summer, Coligny (*Ko-LIG-nee*) Beach attracts an active group of young people, including college students. This is a beach at which to see and be seen, not one where you can commune with nature. You're close to a Holiday Inn and a number of beach condos and time-shares, with plenty of places to quench your thirst, get a sandwich, or to rent beach sports gear nearby.

The beach has a gentle slope. It is very wide at low tide and not skimpy even at high tide—erosion has not been a problem. There are no dunes or shade. If you trek north from here, toward the heel of the island, you'll come to North Forest Beach, where there has been beach erosion. Toward the toe, the beach is wider, with few erosion problems. *From the north on William Hilton Pkwy. (U.S. Hwy. 278), go around the traffic circle to Pope Ave. Follow Pope to the second traffic circle, at S. Forest Beach Dr. Coligny Beach is adjacent to the Holiday Inn. Park either in the 300-space lot on the right side of Pope Ave., across South Forest Beach Dr. from the beach, with the entrance on Pope Ave. ($4 per day; in and out allowed), or in one of 50 metered spaces (25 cents per 15 min.) on the beach side of the traffic circle.*

Alder Lane

This is a beach access point just south of Coligny Beach. It's in an area with numerous condo complexes and some motels, but it's not usually as crowded as Coligny. The beach is wide and pleasant here, and it is the closest public access point to the beaches in Sea Pines Plantation, including South Beach. As at most Hilton Head beaches, development, while altering the natural landscape, is not as intrusive as it would be if strict zoning and architectural controls were not in effect (condos, for example, are mostly low-rise). *From the north on William Hilton Pkwy. (U.S. Hwy. 278), go around the traffic circle to Pope Ave. Follow Pope to the second traffic circle. Bear right on South Forest Beach Dr. Alder Lane Beach is a short distance ahead on your left. Parking is very limited: just 22 metered spaces (25 cents per 15 min.).*

HOTELS/INNS/B&BS

Hilton Head has about 10,000 hotel rooms and rental condos. Most hotels here fall into one of two groups: the very expensive upscale chain hotels on the ocean, most of which cater to the corporate-meetings market ($200 to $300 per night and up, from early spring to early fall), and the surprisingly inexpensive chain motels, which are not on a beach but offer excellent value for thrifty tourists (under $50 a night in some cases). There are few independent motels and no B&Bs. Golf and tennis players or families coming for several days or a week are more likely to choose a rental condo (*see* "House Rentals"). In some cases, package plans including golf or tennis can save you as much as half the total cost of a hotel with golf and tennis.

◆ **Crowne Plaza Resort** (very expensive). This five-story hotel, until 1993 a Marriott, is on the ocean in Shipyard Plantation. Its strong points are service—it has been named the top-rated hotel for guest satisfaction among 1,800 Holiday Inn-affiliated properties worldwide—and well-appointed public rooms. The guest rooms, though attractive, are nothing special—certainly not for the rates charged here. Strangely, the resort was designed with only about 20 of the 340 rooms having ocean views. It is set on 11 landscaped acres, with a 27-acre golf course. It is close to Van der Meer Shipyard Racquet Club, with 20 tennis courts. The beach is nice, both at low and high tides. Health club, indoor and outdoor pools. *130 Shipyard Dr., Shipyard Plantation, Hilton Head, SC 29928; tel. 803-842-2400, 800-334-1881; fax 803-842-9975. In Shipyard Plantation gated area.*

◆ **Hilton Resort** (very expensive). The Hilton boasts that its 325 rooms are the largest of any hotel on the island. They are attractive and recently refurbished. All rooms are oceanside and have either a balcony or a patio. The beautifully landscaped grounds have a tropical feel and lead to a sandy beach. Two pools. Golf and tennis available nearby. *23 Ocean Lane, Palmetto Dunes, Hilton Head, SC 29938; tel. 803-842-8000, 800-221-2424; fax 803-842-4988. In Palmetto Dunes gated area.*

◆ **Westin Resort** (very expensive). This is the best hotel on Hilton Head. Very simply, it's stunning, both in its lushly land-scaped setting on the ocean in the Port Royal Plantation and in its 410 large guest rooms and luxurious public areas. Most rooms have ocean views. The Westin also has two- and three-bedroom villas—very luxe, with hot tubs. Guests have golf privileges at the three 18-hole courses of the adjacent Port Royal

Golf Club, plus access to 16 tennis courts. Health club, indoor and outdoor pools, and all the facilities of a five-star resort. The beach is attractive here, and just to the north of the hotel, it becomes very wide and expansive. The Westin's Barony restaurant is excellent (*see* "Restaurants"). *2 Grasslawn Ave., Port Royal Plantation, Hilton Head, SC 29928; tel. 803-681-4000, 800-228-3000; fax 803-681-1087. In Port Royal Plantation gated area.*

◆ **Holiday Inn Oceanfront Resort** (expensive). If you want to be at the heart of the action on Coligny Beach and right on the water, this 200-room, five-story motel could fill the bill. The beach is very wide and sandy but crowded in summer. The motel is nothing fancy—about what you'd expect from a beachside Holiday Inn. Many rooms have limited ocean views from small balconies. Outdoor pool. *1 S. Forest Beach Dr., Hilton Head, SC 29938; tel. 803-785-5126, 800-465-4329; fax 803-785-6678. Near Sea Pines Plantation at Coligny Circle but not in a gated area.*

◆ **Fairfield Inn by Marriott** (inexpensive). For one-fifth or less the cost of the big ocean-front hotels, you can stay here and play lots of golf and tennis, eat at fancy restaurants, and still come out ahead. Its 120 rooms are bright and in top condition. Continental breakfast included. Outdoor heated pool. It's a top choice if you don't need to be on the beach. *9 Marina Side Dr., U.S. Hwy. 278, Hilton Head, SC 29928; tel. 803-842-4800, 800-348-6000; fax 803-842-4800. Near Palmetto Dunes but not in a gated area.*

◆ **Hampton Inn** (inexpensive). Located near the Hilton Head airport but not close enough for airport noise to be a problem, this 125-room, two-story motel offers the typical good value for which the chain is known. Attractive rooms; continental breakfast included. *1 Airport Rd., Hilton Head, SC 29928; tel. 803-681-7900, 800-426-7866; fax 803-681-4330. Near Port Royal Plantation on U.S. Hwy. 278 but not in a gated area.*

HOUSE RENTALS

There are more than 6,000 rental houses and condos on Hilton Head. Most of the short-term rentals are in the south (toe) and center (sole) of the island. *Where* you rent makes more of a difference here than in most other areas, since much of Hilton Head consists of private gated communities. Before booking, always ask about beach and sports-facility access and about the current quality of the beach at both low and high tides.

High season for rentals on Hilton Head is April to Labor Day, with a shoulder season in spring and fall and low season from December through February. At prime times, expect to pay $3,000 to $5,000 or more per week for a large, luxurious home on the ocean, significantly less off the water. One- to three-bedroom condos go for $500 to $1,500 per week. Rates are up to 50 percent less off-season.

◆ **Hilton Head Realty.** Offers home and condo rentals in several areas of Hilton Head, including Sea Pines, Palmetto Dunes, and Shipyard plantations. *Box 5550, Hilton Head, SC 29938; tel. 803-842-2424, 800-845-5552. Open daily.*

◆ **Palmetto Dunes Resort.** Several hundred one- to four-bedroom condos in the 2,000-acre Palmetto Dunes gated community. Guests can play about 20 golf courses at "preferred rates." Tennis available on 25 clay and hard courts. The main beach area for resort guests is attractive, but high tide covers the sandy beach. *Box 5606, Hilton Head, SC 29938; tel. 803-785-1161, 800-845-6130; fax 803-686-2877. Open daily.*

◆ **Sea Pines Resorts.** Wide selection of luxury home and condo rentals. Golf at three courses at the Sea Pines Plantation. Tennis available on 28 courts at the Sea Pines Racquet Club, ranked the best tennis resort in the United States by *Tennis* magazine. Private access to wide, sandy beach. *Box 7000, Hilton Head, SC 29938; tel. 803-785-3333, 800-732-7463; fax 803-842-1475. Open daily.*

RESTAURANTS

Hilton Head has more than 200 dining choices, from fast-food and casual chain spots to *très cher* French restaurants. With only a few exceptions, island dining is casual—just wear a golf shirt and bring a credit card.

◆ **Barony** (expensive). The Westin's lead restaurant is traditional fine dining at its best: pricey, but with top-notch ingredients and excellent service. The atmosphere is sedately hunt club, with chandeliers and gilded mirrors. Good choices are the aged prime steaks, veal, and grilled seafood; try the filet mignon and grilled salmon combination. Desserts include the death-by-chocolate variety. *Westin Resort, 2 Grasslawn Ave., Port Royal Plantation, Hilton Head, SC 29928; tel. 803-681-4000. Open daily for dinner.*

◆ **Charlie's L'Etoile Verte** (moderate). The chef here, from Savannah, does wonderful things with local seafood and vegetables, marrying French cooking with Low Country ingredients. The menu changes often, but you can't go wrong with any fish entrée. Fresh baked bread. It's on busy U.S. Highway 278, but the restaurant itself is intimate and stylish. Reservations are a must. *1000 Plantation Center, U.S. Hwy. 278, Hilton Head, SC 29938; tel. 803-785-9277. Open Tue.-Sat. for lunch and dinner. Near Palmetto Dunes.*

◆ **Hudson's at the Docks** (moderate). Although the lines may not be quite as long as they once were, and although the branch at Coligny has closed, Hudson's remains a favorite seafood spot, especially among visitors. Certainly you can't get fresher seafood—the restaurant has its own fishing fleet. The fried seafood platter here is a way to sample everything. Start with the she-crab soup. If you're a shrimp lover, go for the local butterfly shrimp or the shrimp stuffed with crabmeat. To get the best table overlooking Skull Creek and the shrimp boats, go early, before the main restaurant opens, and have a drink or some boiled shrimp in the oyster bar. At opening time, those in the bar are seated first, before those waiting in line outside. *Squire Pope Rd., Hilton Head, SC 29928; tel. 803-681-2772. Open daily for lunch and dinner. At the north end of the island. Watch for signs on U.S. Hwy. 278. Don't be fooled by a similarly named restaurant on Squire Pope Rd. Hudson's is on the water, next to its sister restaurant, Carmine's.*

◆ **Le Bistro** (moderate). The tables are jammed close together, and the noise level makes it hard to talk, but locals flock here, especially for lunch. Le Bistro's cuisine is Mediterranean, with fish from the south of France, Greece, and Italy. The veal and pasta are inspired. *302 Pineland Mill Shops, U.S. Hwy. 278 at Mathews Dr., Hilton Head, SC 29928; tel. 803-681-8425. Open Mon.-Fri. for lunch and Mon.-Sat. for dinner.*

◆ **Truffles Cafe** (inexpensive). Lots of homemade soups, pastas, and chicken dishes, all served with breads baked fresh throughout the day. Many patrons come just for the light meals—the country French plate with Brie, pâté, fruit, and fresh-baked French bread or the fresh vegetable plate with new potatoes.

The chicken pot pie is delicious. Truffles also operates a take-out food market. *Sea Pines Center, Sea Pines Plantation, Hilton Head, SC 29938; tel. 803-671-6136. Open daily for lunch and dinner.*

NIGHTLIFE

◆ **Buffalo House Sports Cafe.** Sports bar with 50 TVs for viewing sports events. *37 New Orleans Rd., Hilton Head, SC 29938; tel. 803-785-2255. Open daily. South end of the island.*

◆ **Club Indigo.** Dancing and live music most nights. *Hyatt Regency Resort, 1 Hyatt Circle, Hilton Head, SC 29928; tel. 803-785-1234. Open daily. In Palmetto Dunes.*

◆ **Hurricane Hole, W. G. Shucker's Restaurant.** Live music on the deck in good weather. Crab races on Wednesday nights. *Palmetto Bay Marina, Hilton Head, SC 29938; tel. 803-785-8050. Open daily May-Sep. South end of the island.*

ATTRACTIONS

The attractions on Hilton Head are mostly of the golf, tennis, and beach variety.

◆ **Daufuskie Island.** Hurry and see this enchanting island before the developers turn Daufuskie into another Hilton Head. A tour of the island gives you a feel for the traditional side of Sea Island life. Some descendants of African slaves still living here speak Gullah, a mixture of African languages and English. The island is accessible only by private boat or a tour boat such as the *Vagabond*. A visit to Daufuskie is one of the highlights of a Hilton Head visit—don't miss it. And don't miss the Daufuskie crab cakes made fresh by local ladies and sold for $5 on the tour. *Harbour Town Marina, Sea Pines Plantation, Hilton Head, SC 29938; tel. 803-842-4155. The* Vagabond *tour boat leaves Harbour Town Marina at 11 and 2 Tue.-Sat.; other tour boats have varying hours. Admission.*

SHOPPING

Shopping is beginning to rival golf and tennis as a top sport on Hilton Head. Besides resort boutiques, gift shops, and the usual collection of mall stores, many factory outlets have opened here.

◆ **Low Country Factory Outlet Village.** About 45 outlet stores, including Brooks Brothers, Eddie Bauer, American Tourister,

Laura Ashley, Geoffrey Beene, London Fog, and Levi's. *1270 Fording Island Rd., Bluffton, SC 29910; tel. 803-837-4339. Open daily. North of the bridge to Hilton Head Island, on the mainland.*

◆ **Mall at Shelter Cove.** Large enclosed mall with 55 upscale shops and two department stores. *U.S. Hwy. 278, Hilton Head, SC 29938; tel. 803-686-3090. Open daily. About 1/2 mi. north of the entrance to Palmetto Dunes.*

◆ **Shops on the Parkway.** More than 35 factory-outlet stores, including Anne Klein, Dansk, Duck Head, and Jones New York. *U.S. Hwy. 278, Hilton Head, SC 29928; tel. 803-686-6233. Open daily. Between Palmetto Dunes and Shipyard plantations.*

BEST FOOD SHOPS

◆ **Harris Teeter.** *Main Street Village, U.S. Hwy. 278, Hilton Head, SC 29928; tel. 803-689-6255. Open daily. At the north end of the island, near Hilton Head Plantation.*

SANDWICHES: ◆ **P. J.'s Incredible Edibles.** *Shelter Cove, Hilton Head, SC 29938; tel. 803-842-5550. Open daily. Midisland, near Palmetto Dunes.*

BAKERY: ◆ **Signe's Heaven Bound Bakery.** *2 Bow Circle, Hilton Head, SC 29938; tel. 803-785-9118. Open Mon.-Sat. At the south end of the island, near Sea Pines Plantation.*

BEVERAGES AND WINE: ◆ **Reilley's Wines and Spirits.** Liquor and wine only. Reilley's party store, next door, sells beer and mixers. *2 New Orleans Rd., Hilton Head, SC 29938; tel. 803-785-3339. Open Mon.-Sat. At the south end of the island, near Sea Pines Plantation.*

SPORTS

Golf and tennis, tennis and golf: For many, that's Hilton Head sports. However, bicycling is popular on the island, and fishing, boating, and all water sports are available. Surfing (not very good on Hilton Head anyway) and surf fishing from beaches are prohibited from 10 to 6 April through September.

FISHING

It's not the main reason visitors come to Hilton Head, but you can get in some decent offshore or inshore fishing. Six man-made reefs offshore are Hilton Head's main fishing grounds. Crabbing is good at South Beach and Hilton Head marinas.

◆ **Palmetto Bay Marina.** A number of fishing charter boats are based here. *Palmetto Bay Rd., Hilton Head, SC 29938; tel. 803-785-7131. Operates daily. At the end of Palmetto Bay Rd. off Sea Pines Circle.*

◆ **Tammy Jane.** Try your hand at shrimping on a 40-foot shrimp trawler. Inshore fishing charters. *Hudson's Dock, Squire Pope Rd., Hilton Head, SC 29938; tel. 803-384-7833. Shrimping trips Tue.-Fri., fishing charters other days; weather permitting. From U.S. Hwy. 278, follow signs to Hudson's restaurant.*

BOATING

There are nine large marinas on Hilton Head. Sailboats, motorboats, Jet Skis, and other boating equipment are for rent. Parasailing directly from the beach is not permitted at any time; companies offering parasailing take you from the marina to the ocean or sound for this activity.

◆ **Harbour Town Yacht Basin.** Rents powerboats, sailboats, Jet Skis. Offers parasailing. *Sea Pines Plantation, Hilton Head, SC 29938; tel. 803-363-BOAT. Open daily.*

◆ **Shelter Cove Marina.** Rents powerboats, sailboats, Jet Skis. Offers parasailing. *Palmetto Dunes, Hilton Head, SC 29938; tel. 803-842-8181. Open daily mid-Feb.-Oct., depending on the weather.*

BICYCLING

Many people think a bicycle is the best way to get around Hilton Head. There are bike paths in most gated communities and along much of U.S. Highway 278.

◆ **Hilton Head Bicycle Company.** Rentals. *11B Archer Rd., Hilton Head, SC 29938; tel. 803-686-6888. Open daily. Off Sea Pines Circle.*

GOLF

Hilton Head is one of the leading golf centers on the East Coast, with 30 courses in and around the island. Of these, about 20 are public or semipublic and regularly available for play by visitors. The others either are for members only or are open just to guests staying within the gated community.

◆ **Harbour Town Golf Links.** Home of the MCI Classic each April, this Pete Dye course plays to 6,916 yards, par 71. The best-known course on Hilton Head, it has been rated as high as thirtieth among the best golf courses in the world by *Golf Digest*. Greens fees are very steep: up to $164 for 18 holes, including cart. Sea Pines has two other excellent courses, the 6,906-yard, par-72 Ocean Course, recently redesigned by Mark McCumber, and the 6,515-yard, par-72 Sea Marsh Course, designed by George Cobb and redesigned by Clyde Johnston. *Sea Pines, Box 7000, Hilton Head, SC 29938; tel. 803-842-8484, 800-845-6131. Open daily. Admission.*

◆ **Hilton Head National Golf Club.** Designed by Gary Player, Hilton Head National is known for its well-conditioned greens and fairways. *U.S. Hwy. 278, Bluffton, SC 29910; tel. 803-842-5900. Open daily. Admission. Just north of the bridge to Hilton Head.*

◆ **Palmetto Dunes Resort.** There are three challenging courses at Palmetto Dunes. At 6,918 yards, the par-72 Arthur Hills Course is the toughest. The 6,710-yard, par-72 Robert Trent Jones Course is links style and plays out toward the Atlantic. The George Fazio Course, par 70 and 6,873 yards, with only two par-5 holes, requires precision play. *1 Trent Jones Lane, Hilton Head, SC 29938; tel. 803-785-1138. Open daily. Admission.*

◆ **Port Royal Golf Club.** The port Royal Plantation has three excellent par-72, 18-hole courses: Barony, Robber's Row, and Planter's Row. The 6,530-yard Barony, designed by George Cobb with play along the Atlantic, and the 6,642-yard Robber's Row, newly redesigned by Pete Dye, are members-only courses on alternating months (open to the public the other months). The Willard Byrd-designed Planter's Row, which plays to 6,520 yards, is a narrow course with many water hazards. *10A Grasslawn Ave., Port Royal Plantation, Hilton Head, SC 29928; tel. 803-689-5600, 800-234-6318. Open daily. Admission.*

TENNIS

With more than 300 courts, Hilton Head is a major tennis resort. The following are among those permitting public play.

◆ **Palmetto Dunes Tennis Center.** A total of 25 courts: 19 clay, 2 hard, and 4 artificial grass; 6 are lighted. *Box 4798, 6 Trent Jones Lane, Palmetto Dunes, Hilton Head, SC 29938; tel. 803-785-1152. Open daily. Admission.*

◆ **Port Royal Plantation.** Ten clay, 4 hard, and 2 grass courts; 6 are lighted. *15 Wimbledon Court, Port Royal Plantation, Hilton Head, SC 29928; tel. 803-686-8803. Open daily. Admission.*

◆ **Sea Pines Plantation.** A total of 35 clay courts at two complexes; 7 courts are lighted. *Box 7000, Hilton Head, SC 29938; tel. 803-842-8484, 800-845-6131. Sea Pines Racquet Club (tel. 803-842-8484) is on Lighthouse Rd.; South Beach Racquet Club (tel. 803-671-2215) is at S. Beach Marina Village, both in Sea Pines Plantation. Both open daily. Admission.*

◆ **Van Der Meer Tennis Center.** A total of 27 courts, 10 clay and 17 hard, of which 11 are lighted. *19 DeAllyon Ave., Hilton Head, SC 29938; tel. 803-785-8388. Open daily. Admission.*

NATURE

◆ **Pinckney National Wildlife Refuge.** A 4,000-acre nature preserve with about 14 miles of hiking trails. *U.S. Hwy. 278, Hilton Head, SC 29926. Open daily 6:30 a.m.-7:30 p.m. Entrance is just north of the bridge to the island.*

◆ **Sea Pines Forest Preserve.** A 605-acre preserve on Sea Pines Plantation. Seven miles of trails and ponds as well as an Indian Shell Ring. No admission to preserve, but $3-per-car daily entry fee to Sea Pines Plantation for nonguests. *Greenwood Dr., Sea Pines Plantation, Hilton Head, SC 29938; tel. 803-785-3333. Open daily 8-7. Parking available at west entrance off Greenwood Dr. and at east entrance off Lawton Dr. (the east entrance is closer to the Indian Shell Ring).*

TOURIST INFORMATION

◆ **Hilton Head Chamber of Commerce Welcome Center and Museum.** Be sure to stop here just after you cross the bridge onto the island, not at the other visitors centers farther south on U.S. Highway 278 (such unofficial ones are set up mostly to sell real estate). A small museum upstairs has displays on Hilton Head history and nature. *100 U.S. Hwy. 278, Hilton Head, SC 29926; tel. 803-785-3673. Welcome center open daily 9:30-6:30; museum (tel. 803-689-6767) open Mon.-Sat. 10-5 and Sun. 12-5. On the right just after you cross the bridge onto Hilton Head Island.*

CHAPTER 17

Savannah & Tybee Island

Beauty	B-
Swimming	C
Sand	C
Hotels/Inns/B&Bs	B+
House rentals	B
Restaurants	A-
Nightlife	B+
Attractions	A-
Shopping	A-
Sports	B
Nature	C+

ou wouldn't come to Tybee Island just for the beach, which is relatively second-rate, its water often murky from marsh runoff and its sand constantly eroded by a hungry ocean. You wouldn't come to Tybee for the quaint seaside atmosphere, because Tybee's main beach area is vintage 1950s and 1960s, past due for a facelift. Nor would you be attracted by the lodging, for here most of what you'll find are functional motels and modest beach cottages.

But, you would come to Tybee, if you were a proper Savannahian, because it's what your parents and grandparents did before you, often staying the summer to enjoy the small-town beach life and the ocean breezes, which keep Tybee cooler than its steamy mainland neighbor. Summer at Tybee, which for a time was called Savannah Beach, is a longtime local tradition.

And if you aren't lucky enough to be from Savannah, you'd come for Savannah, with the beach as your base of operations. Tybee is only about 30 minutes from the historic areas of Savannah, with its oak-shaded squares draped in Spanish moss

HOW TO GET THERE

◆ Savannah anchors the extreme northeast corner of coastal Georgia, separated from South Carolina by the Savannah River. It is about 5 hr. by car southeast of Atlanta, 2 hr. south of Charleston, SC, and 2 1/2 hr. north of Jacksonville, FL. From the north or south, I-95 is the main route to Savannah. From Atlanta and points west, take I-75 to near Macon, then I-16 to Savannah. The historic district is about 10 mi. east of the intersection of I-16 and I-95.

◆ To get to Tybee Island from downtown Savannah (about 18 mi., roughly 1/2 hr., depending on traffic), take Bay St. (becomes President St. Extension) or Victory Dr. east to U.S. Hwy. 80, called Island Expwy. and also Tybee Rd. as it nears the island. On Tybee itself, Hwy. 80 is known as Butler Ave.

◆ Savannah's airport, which has jet and commuter service, is 16 mi. west of downtown.

◆ Savannah is also served by Amtrak.

and southern charm, its B&Bs, river-front hotels, active nightlife, and fine restaurants. This proximity is what brings Tybee Island into this book as an ideal "compromise" beach vacation, if you and your traveling companion(s) can't agree on whether to visit a beach or a city.

Savannah, always special to those who knew it, is suddenly a hot and popular vacation spot. In a 1995 poll, *Condé Nast Traveler* magazine's readers named Savannah one of the top ten destinations in the United States. Savannah may have already been ripe for a new wave of tourist interest, but the city, reluctant though its citizens are to admit it, also has to thank "the book," as it's referred to locally: *Midnight in the Garden of Good and Evil*, by John Berendt. *Midnight in the Garden*, prominent on the best-seller lists since its publication in 1994, is nonfiction, but it packs the elements of a good novel: sex, socialites, and sin, all revolving around a local murder and a series of murder trials. It's what the critics refer to as a page-turner. Until this book, Savannah had played third fiddle to its better-known southern port city sisters, New Orleans and Charleston, which had stolen most of the attention of writers and moviemakers in search of romance and decadence. But now, Savannah is famous in its own right, considered just as decadent and interesting as any place else, and tour guides routinely point out houses featured in *Midnight in the Garden*.

As a bonus for Tybee Island connoisseurs, though, Tybee is beginning its own renaissance of sorts. It is being rediscovered for its comfortable, unpretentious, affordable atmosphere. Old motels are being upgraded and new ones built. The beach benefited from a multimillion-dollar load of new sand. A $2.5 million beach pavilion and pier is set to open in mid-1996, replacing the famed Tybrisa pavilion, a magnet for big bands of the 1940s and beach bands of the '50s and '60s that burned down in 1967. The 1996 Olympic sailing events are set to be held in part at Tybee.

Some folks are even saying that Tybee is like the Key West of 20 or 30 years ago, before it was discovered by Jimmy Buffet's parrotheads and by real estate developers. And in 1995, it even got its own book: *Running with the Dolphins and Other Tybee Tales*, by Michael Elliott.

The prime beach season on Tybee is late May to early September, when the water is warm enough for pleasant swimming. Savannah is a year-round destination, with the fall and early spring bringing the most comfortable weather for sightseeing.

BEACHES
TYBEE BEACH

Tybee is part-Coney Island, part-old-style beach town, part-up-and-coming gentrified resort, and altogether as eccentric as Savannah itself. "Don't include us in your guide," said one motel operator. "We don't want any new people coming here who don't understand the kind of place we are." But he said it in a friendly way, and offered helpful pointers on beach life in Tybee. That's a typically atypical Tybee Island approach.

Beauty	C
Swimming	C
Sand	C+
Amenities	B+

A natural beauty Tybee Beach is not. But the beach front has an honest, old-shoe appeal, and the residential areas of Tybee, with many of the houses owned by summer people from Savannah, are pleasant.

Tybee's beaches, all open to the public, stretch along the Atlantic on the east side of the island. The beach is widest and in some ways most attractive in the middle of the island, around 10th Street. Parking is limited here, though, and most beachgoers congregate at the main beach area, around 14th to 16th streets. Beach shops and rickety beach bars are hopping in summer. There is also a marine-science center here. Very small and informal but a treat for kids, it's open 9 a.m. to 4 p.m., summer only.

Little Tybee Island, just south of Tybee itself, has a very nice stretch of undeveloped beach, but you can get to it only by private boat. *From Savannah, take U.S. Hwy. 80, also called Tybee Rd. as it nears the island and Butler Ave. on Tybee itself. As you enter the beach area, the road takes a sharp right along the Atlantic. Turn left at 16th St., or on other nearby streets, to get to the main beach parking area.*

Swimming: Fair. The water is usually discolored from river and marsh sediment. Lifeguard on duty at the main beach area from around Memorial Day to Labor Day.

Sand: The wide gray-white-sand beach has to be replenished frequently to compensate for erosion. Sand dollars can often be found on the beach, near the water's edge.

Amenities: With the completion of a new pavilion, 700-foot pier, concession stands, bait shop, and rest rooms at the main beach area at 16th Street—scheduled to be ready for the 1996 Olympic sailing events—Tybee Beach will have first-rate amenities.

Sports: Surfers and windsurfers sometimes practice their craft at Tybee, although conditions are often not perfect for either sport. Surf fishing and pier fishing are popular, as is kite flying on the windy beach.

Parking: The Tybee municipal lot (fee during the season) at 16th Street and metered street parking nearby are sufficient except on peak summer weekends, when it's best to arrive early.

HOTELS/INNS/B&BS

Lodging on Tybee Island is mostly in mediocre motels and vintage beach apartments. Their prime virtues are moderate cost and proximity to the water. All of the Tybee spots listed here are either on the Atlantic (though across the street from the beach) or a short stroll away. Savannah has accommodations to suit every taste and budget. Its B&Bs are concentrated in the historic district; convention hotels are on the river front and downtown; chain motels are all around town, with a cluster on Abercorn Street and Abercorn Extension in suburban Southside (southwest Savannah).

◆ **The Gastonian** (very expensive). Two 1860s mansions have been restored and turned into one of Savannah's top small inns. All 13 rooms have fireplaces and are furnished with antiques. Afternoon tea and breakfast included. Among the best room choices are the Carriage House and the gorgeous Emperor Caracalla room, which has a king-size canopy bed and a large hot tub. A favorite of honeymooners. Off-street parking is a plus. *220 E. Gaston St., Savannah, GA 31401; tel. 912-232-2869, 800-322-6603; fax 912-232-0710.*

◆ **Hyatt Regency Savannah** (expensive). This seven-story hotel looks out of place on Savannah's river front, but the rooms are attractive and the location, near clubs and shops on River Street, is unbeatable. From a river-view room you can watch the ships go by; if you have an atrium room, visit the hotel lounge for a good river view. *2 W. Bay St., Savannah, GA 31401; tel. 912-238-1234, 800-233-1234; fax 912-944-3678.*

◆ **Magnolia Place Inn** (expensive). Superb small inn in a Victorian mansion on Forsyth Park at the south end of the historic district. The best rooms are on the second floor, with floor-to-ceiling windows opening onto a screened porch. Most of the 13 rooms have hot tubs and fireplaces. *503 Whitaker St., Savannah, GA 31401; tel. 912-236-7674, 800-238-7674; fax 912-236-1145.*

◆ **Best Western Dunes Inn** (moderate). Unremarkable chain motel about one block from the beach, but among the best Tybee can offer. Clean, pleasant rooms. *1409 Butler Ave., Tybee Island, GA 31328; tel. 912-786-4591, 800-528-1234; fax 912-786-4593.*

◆ **Hunter House** (moderate). Small four-room inn in an old wood-frame house has a Key West ambience: casual, comfortable, semitropical, with a second-story front balcony for rocking and enjoying life. Suite 1, with a fireplace and kitchen, is the best choice. About a block from the water, it's often fully booked, and its intimate restaurant is popular too. *1701 Butler Blvd., Tybee Island, GA 31328; tel. 912-786-7515.*

◆ **Ocean Plaza Beach Resort** (moderate). This is Tybee's largest and second-newest hotel, a four-story, 250-room complex on the ocean. While the setting owes as much to asphalt and concrete as it does to palm trees, the water-front location makes it a popular choice in the summer. The best rooms and suites are upper-floor, on the Atlantic side. *15th St., Tybee Island, GA 31328; tel. 912-786-7664.*

HOUSE RENTALS

Most rentals on Tybee are modest beach cottages, typically older wood-frame houses a block or two from the beach. A few newer homes and condos are available. In season (mid-April to mid-September), expect to pay $800 to $1,400 per week for a three- or four-bedroom house. Off-season rates are 20 to 40 percent lower.

◆ **Tybee Island Rentals.** *U.S. Hwy. 80 and Second Ave., Tybee Island, GA 31328; tel. 912-786-4034, 800-476-0807. Open daily.*

RESTAURANTS

Savannah cooking, while less sophisticated than that of another southern port city, New Orleans—and, some would argue, of Charleston—does gracious justice to the region's plentiful supply of shrimp, crab, and other seafood. One of the area's best-known dishes is the Low Country Boil: shrimp, sausage, corn, and potatoes boiled in seasoned water. Restaurants on and near Tybee focus mostly on traditional fried and broiled seafood, but Savannah has several innovative restaurants of national standard.

◆ **Elizabeth's on 37th** (expensive). Savannah's most-famous non-touristy restaurant, it has made many national top-restaurant lists. In a large mansion in the Victorian district, Elizabeth's offers consistently creative cooking in a candlelit atmosphere. Seasonal specials change frequently, but expect good things from local seafood in distinctive sauces. *105 E. 37th St., Savannah, GA 31401; tel. 912-236-5547. Open Mon.-Sat. for dinner.*

◆ **Hunter House Restaurant** (moderate). Intimate inn dining in a restored 1910 house near the beach. Emphasis is on fresh fish and shrimp, but the varied and changing menu usually has old favorites, such as pot roast, and new combinations, like Praline Chicken. *1701 Butler Ave., Tybee Island, GA 31328; tel. 912-786-7515. Open daily for dinner; reservations a day in advance requested.*

◆ **Johnny Harris** (moderate). As Savannah as you can get. It opened in 1924 and has been a favorite of locals ever since. The unusual round dining room has a dome ceiling with faux stars. A classic meal here is barbecue with a dessert of trifle. Casual at most times, the restaurant features ballroom dancing on Saturday night. *1651 E. Victory Dr., Savannah, GA 31401; tel. 912-354-7810. Open Mon.-Sat. for lunch and dinner.*

◆ **Mrs. Wilkes' Boarding House** (inexpensive). Pass the biscuits! This is real southern boarding house food, served family-style: all those high-fat but delicious favorites southerners grew up on—fried chicken, collard greens with seasoning meat, mashed potatoes. Breakfasts are equally filling, with eggs, bacon, sausage, grits, and, of course, fresh-made biscuits. There's usually a line (the place is renowned even outside Savannah), but the wait is worth it and the food's an excellent value. *107 W.*

Jones St., Savannah, GA 31401; tel. 912-232-5997. Open daily for breakfast and lunch.

◆ **The Breakfast Club** (inexpensive). On Tybee, The Breakfast Club is almost a shrine. Locals, who make up the majority of the customers, show up in shifts, and visitors stand in line outside the little restaurant. Those who laugh in the face of cholesterol should enjoy the Grill-Cleaner: eggs, sausage, potatoes, two kinds of cheese, onions, and peppers, with grits on the side. *1500 Butler Ave., Tybee Island, GA 31328; tel. 912-786-5984. Open daily for breakfast and lunch.*

◆ **Williams Seafood Restaurant** (inexpensive). To say that a restaurant's fried seafood is "almost as good as Williams's" is high praise in Georgia. Although some claim Williams is not quite what it once was, the big, casual restaurant at the Bull River Bridge between Savannah and Tybee Island remains extremely popular for its heaping plates of shrimp, oysters, and fish. Williams, long a bastion of iced tea and fundamentalism, now serves beer and wine. *8010 Tybee Rd., Savannah, GA 31410; tel. 912-897-2219. Open daily for lunch and dinner.*

NIGHTLIFE

Cheap beer and loud music are staples here. A Beach Music Festival, featuring bands from the '50s and '60s, is held in late June. In Savannah, River Street is the main entertainment venue.

◆ **Shipwatch Lounge.** This is a classic beach bar, with shag dancing, live music most nights, and a popular amateur talent show on Sunday nights in summer. *Desoto Beach Motel, 212 Butler Ave., Tybee Beach, GA 31328; tel. 912-786-6658. Open daily.*

ATTRACTIONS

The area's main sights are in the historic district and on the river front in Savannah.

◆ **Fort Pulaski National Monument.** It took less than two days for Union forces to capture this fort in a fierce bombardment in 1862. You can take a self-guided tour of the fort and museum; demonstrations and realistic reenactments of military life are scheduled periodically. *U.S. Hwy. 80, Tybee Island, GA 31328 (mailing address: Box 30757, Savannah, GA 31410); tel. 912-786-*

5787. *Open daily 8:30-6:45 Memorial Day-Labor Day and 8:30-5:15 the rest of year. Because of continued cutbacks in National Park Service budgets, hours could be reduced. Admission. From Savannah on U.S. Hwy. 80, turn left on Fort Pulaski Rd. Watch for signs.*

◆ **Savannah Historic District.** Savannah developed in the 18th century, based on a series of public squares that had green space and human scale. Today, 21 of the original 24 squares remain. Thanks to the Historic Savannah Foundation and individual preservationists, Savannah has kept and restored many of its fine old buildings. The 2 1/2-square-mile historic district, with more than 1,200 restored structures, is ideal for walking. The Savannah Visitors Center (*see* "Tourist Information") has maps and information. There are too many important buildings and sites to name, but among those of special note are the Owens-Thomas House & Museum, Davenport House, Scarbrough House, the birthplace of Juliette Gordon Low (founder of the U.S. Girl Scouts), Green-Meldrim House, and Telfair Mansion. *Open daily. Savannah's historic district is bounded roughly by Bay St. on the north, Gaston on the south, E. Broad on the east, and Martin Luther King Blvd. on the west. Most of the Victorian district, south of Gaston, is not yet gentrified.*

◆ **Savannah History Museum.** Adjacent to the Savannah Visitors Center in a restored train station, the museum provides a quick overview of Savannah history. Displays include a cotton gin, an 1890 train engine, and the bench made famous in the movie *Forrest Gump*. A number of tour companies offer bus, van, and trolley tours, with a bewildering variety of itineraries, lengths, departure times, and prices, all leaving from the parking lot of the Visitors Center (where you'll find information about them). *303 Martin Luther King Blvd., Savannah, GA 31401; tel. 912-238-1779. Open daily 8:30-5. Admission.*

◆ **Savannah Riverfront.** At water level, River Street is a boisterous blend of boutiques, bars, and cafés in renovated cotton warehouses. On nice days and on weekend nights, the plaza by the river is packed with people. Up on the bluff above the river, Factor's Walk on Bay Street is more sedate, with stately oaks and statues of local heroes. The top and bottom of the bluff are connected by cobblestone streets. Like the historic district, this is an area made for walking, against a backdrop of ocean-going ships gliding toward sea. *At the north end of the historic district.*

◆ **Tybee Lighthouse and Museum.** If your lungs are up to it, you can climb to the top of this 1773 lighthouse for a terrific view of the island. Across the street, included in the admission price, is a small and eccentric museum with a little bit of everything on local life, including sheet music by Savannah native Johnny Mercer, who wrote "Moon River" in honor of a Savannah waterway. *30 Meddin Dr., Tybee Island, GA 31328; tel. 912-786-5801. Open Wed.-Mon. 10-6 Apr.-Sep.; Mon. and Wed.-Fri. 12-4, Sat.-Sun. 10-4 off-season (subject to change). Admission. At the northern tip of Tybee Island. From Butler Ave., turn right on Van Horn St. and follow to Fort Screven and the lighthouse.*

SHOPPING

Shopping on Tybee, other than for basic beach gear, is limited. Savannah shopping, on the other hand, is almost unlimited, from antiques shops in the historic district, to the boutiques of River Street and the art galleries of City Market, to the malls and strip centers on the Southside. Savannah's two regional malls are both located on the same street in the same area: Oglethorpe Mall is at 7804 Abercorn and the newer Savannah Mall is at 14045 Abercorn.

◆ **City Market.** A two-block area of shops, restaurants, and art galleries in restored 19th-century buildings. *Jefferson St. at W. St. Julian St., Savannah, GA 31401; tel. 912-232-4903. Open daily.*

◆ **E. Shaver's.** One of the Southeast's best independent book-stores, with a strong selection of regional books. *326 Bull St., Savannah, GA 31401; tel. 912-234-7257. Open Mon.-Sat.*

◆ **T. S. Chu & Co.** Chu's is an institution on Tybee, and its motto, "If it's something you use . . . you'll find it at Chu's," says it all. The emphasis now is on inexpensive beachwear and gear, but the back shelves still have general-store variety. *16th St. and Strand, Tybee Island, GA 31328; tel. 912-786-4561. Open daily.*

BEST FOOD SHOPS

◆ **Tybee Market IGA.** Small supermarket sells grocery basics, plus beer and wine. (For a wider selection, visit one of the Publix or

Piggly Wiggly stores in Savannah). *1111 Butler Ave., U.S. Hwy. 80, Tybee Beach, GA 31328; tel. 912-786-4601. Open daily.*

SEAFOOD: ◆ Wilmington Island Seafood. *120 Johnny Mercer Blvd., Savannah, GA 31410; tel. 912-897-5151. Open daily.*

ICE CREAM: ◆ Tybee Island Ice Cream. *16 15th St., Tybee Island, GA 31328. Open daily in season.*

BEVERAGES: ◆ Tybee Beverage Center Liquors. Liquor, beer, soft drinks, mixers. *1504 Butler Ave., U.S. Hwy. 80, Tybee Island, GA 31328; tel. 912-786-5233. Open Mon.-Sat.*

WINE: ◆ Sandfly Fine Wines. *7359 Skidaway Rd., Savannah, GA 31406; tel. 912-354-1426. Open Mon.-Sat.*

SPORTS

Savannah is known more for its sightseeing than for its high-energy sports, but Tybee has the usual water activities, and boating is extremely popular. Bicycling, while easy on Savannah's flat terrain, suffers from a lack of designated bike paths. Surfing is poor to nonexistent, except after storms, when larger waves roll in. Diving is difficult in the murky waters around Savannah's rivers and marsh.

FISHING

Sport fishing is good in the nutrient-rich coastal waters and offshore in the Atlantic.

◆ **Lazaretto Creek Marina.** Charters. *Box 787, Tybee Island, GA 31328; tel. 912-786-5848, 800-242-0166. Open daily. From Hwy. 70, turn south on the first road to the east of Lazaretto Creek bridge.*

◆ **Miss Judy.** Charters. *124 Palmetto Dr., Savannah, GA 31410; tel. 912-897-4921. Open daily in season.*

BOATING

With its coastal waters and hundreds of miles of rivers, the Savannah area is an Eden for sailors and pleasure-boaters. There are more than a dozen marinas in the Savannah/Tybee area.

◆ **Bull River Marina.** Jet Ski rentals, fishing charters, bait-and-tackle sales, and standard marine services. *8005 Old Tybee Rd., Savannah, GA 31410; tel. 912-897-7300. Open daily. Off U.S. Hwy. 80, just across from Williams Seafood.*

GOLF

◆ **Savannah Resort.** Although the hotel at this resort is closed, the 18-hole, par-72 golf course remains open. It is the nearest public course to Tybee Island. Designed by Donald Ross and opened in 1927, it plays up to 7,000 yards around four lakes and several small streams. *612 Wilmington Rd., Savannah, GA 31410; tel. 912-897-1612. Open daily. Admission.*

NATURE

◆ **University of Georgia, Marine Extension Service and Aquarium.** This small aquarium, operated by the University of Georgia, focuses on Georgia marine animals and fish. Nature trail, Native American displays, picnic area. *30 Ocean Science Circle, Savannah, GA 31411; tel. 912-598-2496. Open Mon.-Fri. 9-4 and Sat. 12-5. Admission. From U.S. Hwy. 80, turn south on Skidaway Rd., then right on Ferguson Ave., and then left (east) on Diamond Pkwy. Turn left on McWhorter Rd. and watch for signs.*

◆ **Skidaway Island State Park.** A 530-acre park with picnic tables, boat rentals, nature trails, it's set in marshland and maritime forest. The park also has an 88-site campground. *52 Diamond Causeway, Savannah, GA 31411; tel. 912-598-2300. Open daily 7-10. Admission. From U.S. Hwy. 80, turn south on Skidaway Rd., then right on Ferguson Ave., and then east on Diamond Pkwy. Skidaway State Park is off Diamond Pkwy. at McWhorter Rd. (watch for signs).*

◆ **Wassaw Island.** This beautiful barrier island just south of Tybee Island is reachable only by boat. Once on the island, you have access to seven miles of beach and about 20 miles of trails and old roads. *Open daily for day-use only. For a private tour, contact Sea Kayak Georgia, Box 2747, Tybee Island, GA 31328; tel. 912-786-8732.*

TOURIST INFORMATION

◆ **Tybee Island Visitors Center.** *U.S. Hwy. 80, Tybee Island, GA 31328; tel. 912-786-5444. Open daily 10-4 Apr.-Oct. and Sat.-Sun. 10-4 Nov.-Mar.*

◆ **Savannah Visitors Center.** Tons of brochures and plenty of staff to answer your questions. A variety of tours depart from the parking lot. *301 Martin Luther King Blvd., Savannah, GA 31401; tel. 912-944-0455. Open Mon.-Fri. 8:30-5 and Sat.-Sun. 9-5.*

St. Simons & Sea Islands

Beauty	**B+**
Swimming	**B**
Sand	**B**
Hotels/Inns/B&Bs	**B+**
House rentals	**B**
Restaurants	**B+**
Nightlife	**B-**
Attractions	**B**
Shopping	**B**
Sports	**B+**
Nature	**B+**

St. Simons, Sea Island, and Little St. Simons are three of the four "Golden Isles" of Georgia. (The other is Jekyll Island—*see* Chapter 19.) North of the Golden Isles is Sapelo Island, a barrier island owned mostly by the state of Georgia.

St. Simons Island is one of the largest barrier islands in the region, about the same size as the island of Manhattan. It is connected to the mainland at Brunswick by bridge and by the St. Simons Causeway. St. Simons is a year-round residential and resort area with a population of about 12,000. Connected to St. Simons by bridge is Sea Island, one of the country's most exclusive resort communities, established in 1927 by Hudson Motor Car magnate Howard Coffin. The island is overseen by the Sea Island Company, which limits access to the beaches to residents and renters, and to guests of The Cloister resort. Little St. Simons is a 10,000-acre privately

HOW TO GET THERE

◆ St. Simons is about about midway between Savannah (75 mi. north) and Jacksonville, FL (65 mi. south). Heading south on I-95, the major north-south route in the region, take Exit 8 and follow the Golden Isles Pkwy. east. Turn right on U.S. Hwy. 17 south (also called Glynne Ave.), then left on St. Simons Causeway (also known as the F. J. Torras Causeway; 35 cents toll) and across the Marshes of Glynn to the island (35 cents toll). Heading north on I-95, take Exit 6 and follow the Golden Isles Pkwy. (U.S. Hwy. 17 north) to the St. Simons Island Causeway, a right turn.

◆ Sea Island is accessible by bridge from St. Simons, via Sea Island Rd. across the Black Banks River. Little St. Simons Island is accessible only by private boat. Sapelo Island is accessible only by ferry or private boat. For details, *see* "Beaches."

◆ By air, there is very limited commuter service to Brunswick-Glynco airport. The nearest airports with jet service are Savannah and Jacksonville. Amtrak has service to Jacksonville and Savannah.

owned island seaward of St. Simons.

The Golden Isles have a long and colorful history. Spanish Franciscan priests first established a mission on St. Simons in 1568. The British built a fortified town here, Fort Frederica, in 1736, and in 1742, aided by Creek Indians and Scottish Highlanders, they defeated the Spanish at the battle of Bloody Marsh. Aaron Burr, after shooting Alexander Hamilton in a duel, sought refuge on St. Simons in 1804.

St. Simons and its environs offer something for just about everyone, in every price range. If you want luxury in a social-register setting, it's here at The Cloister (heavens, no—you can't pay the $500-a-day tab with a credit card, but they'll be glad to bill you). If you dream of a private island with your own seven-mile beach (perhaps for a little discreet skinny-dipping), that's here too, at Little St. Simons. Just want a good plate of seafood and an inexpensive place to lay your head? You got it, at any number of spots on St. Simons. Shopping, sports, simple motels and old hotels, beach-front rentals, live oaks, alligators, and Spanish moss—it's all here. And if you really want to get away—to an island that's almost in another world—just pop over to Sapelo, one of the uniquely wonderful places in the region.

Sapelo is one of several intriguing barrier islands that are part of a delightfully untouristed area along the coast north of—and quite different in character from—the Golden Isles. About 20 miles north of St. Simons, Sapelo Island is perhaps as exotic a place as you'll find in eastern America, and it has one of Georgia's best and most pristine beaches, to boot. Unfortunately—or fortunately, depending on your perspective—access to Sapelo is limited, and it's not really set up for tourism. Most of the 10,000-acre island is state-owned and overseen by the Georgia Department of Natural Resources, which operates a marine institute (not open to the public) there. The island has fewer than 75 permanent residents, most in the small Gullah community of Hog Hammock. Gullah, probably derived from the African country of Angola, is the name of the indigenous culture, as well as the Creole language, of the emancipated slaves who lived in near isolation along the coast and on barrier islands such as Sapelo. There are no restaurants on the island and no stores to speak of. Roads are narrow dirt-and-shell paths. Accommodations are basic: in a single small guesthouse and seven mobile homes rented to visitors by island residents. Sapelo is a no-frills destination but an interesting one.

Separated from Sapelo by a narrow creek is Blackbeard Island, named for the pirate (Edward Teach) who is said to have buried some of his treasure here.

As retirement and residential communities, St. Simons and Sea Island are pretty much year-round destinations. Spring and fall offer the best weather for outdoor sports and sightseeing, with daytime temperatures in the 60s to the low 80s. Summer, with highs in the upper 80s, is for those who don't mind humidity, or who want to spend most of their time on the beach or in the water. Water temperatures reach the mid-70s by May and stay there, or go higher, until late September or early October. High season on Little St. Simons is fall to spring, not summer, since the one lodge is not fully air-conditioned. With so little tourism on Sapelo Island, there really is no high or low season.

BEACHES
ST. SIMONS ISLAND BEACHES

On St. Simons, you have a choice of beaches on the southeastern end of the island. None of them will knock your swim trunks off, but each is pleasant, and one, East Beach, is unusual for its exceptional width at low tide.

Beauty	B
Swimming	B-
Sand	B-
Amenities	B

Swimming: Fair to good at most beaches. The exception is East Beach, where currents make it dangerous to swim. You may be disappointed by the water quality: The nutrient-rich salt marshes and rivers in the area dump considerable sediment in the water, leaving it less than clear. There are lifeguards on duty at most area beaches from early June to early September.

Sand: Gently sloping beaches (except where erosion has impacted the beach) have light-gray to tan sand, mostly firmly packed.

Sports: Swimming, surf fishing.

Amenities: Several of the beaches have rest rooms, picnic areas, and other amenities.

Parking: Parking at the beach access points is free (and adequate, except in summer when demand exceeds supply).

East Beach

A massive shoal drifting down from a spit off Sea Island now extends more than 2,000 feet out at low tide. You can walk way, way out on the somewhat muddy, exposed bottom: This makes for a dramatic and different beach experience. No amenities. No lifeguard. *Park at Coast Guard Beach and walk north a few hundred feet to East Beach.*

Coast Guard Beach

This is probably the best-known beach on St. Simons, located next to a former Coast Guard Station building. A lifeguard is on duty June to August. You'll find rest rooms and a sailboat launch area, and there's free parking for more than 100 cars in an unpaved lot. *From St. Simons Causeway, bear right on Kings Way, which becomes Ocean Blvd. past the village. Turn right on E. Beach St. to the Coast Guard Beach parking lot.*

Massengale Park Beach

This is a sandy beach, hard-packed and gray. Narrow at high tide, it is expansive at low. The shoreline here, not far from the King and Prince Hotel, has had much less accretion than the beaches farther north. There are picnic tables and rest rooms, and a lifeguard is on duty 10 to 4 early June to early September. There's free parking for more than 100 cars in a lot at the beach. *From St. Simons Causeway, bear right on Kings Way, which becomes Ocean Blvd. past the village. Turn right at Massengale Park.*

SEA ISLAND BEACH

Understated is the word for the beach on Sea Island. The elaborate homes and estates, most discreetly situated among the trees beside the beach rather than directly on it, give Sea Island's beach front a distinctly upper-crust atmosphere. The beach itself, inviting and pleasant rather than spec-

Beauty	B
Swimming	B
Sand	B
Amenities	C

tacular, is a bit nicer than those on St. Simons.

Part of the island's exclusivity, however, is that its beach has no public access, unless you're renting on Sea Island or staying at The Cloister. There is no means for day visitors to get to the beach (except by private boat, since—as with all beaches in the region—it is public up to the high-water mark). *From St. Simons Causeway, turn left on Sea Island Rd., which becomes Sea Island Causeway. Follow to Sea Island. The Cloister Beach Club is on the right. Access to the rest of the beach is private and restricted.*
Swimming: Good.
Sand: Nice, light tan, with low dunes.
Sports: Swimming, surf fishing.
Amenities: No public amenities, but if you're staying at The Cloister, you have access to the Beach Club.
Parking: Park at the hotel lots.

LITTLE ST. SIMONS ISLAND BEACH

The seven-mile beach at Little St. Simons is more beautiful than all the St. Simons and Sea Island beaches combined. It's a marvel! It's all one long beach, with the area at the main access point called, not surprisingly, Main

Beauty	A
Swimming	B
Sand	B+
Amenities	NA

Beach, and a section to the south known as Rainbow Beach. The strand here is usually so deserted that if you slip off your bathing suit and frolic naked in the water, nobody will know.

Since Little St. Simons Island is privately owned, access to the beach is primarily available to guests of The Lodge (*see* "Hotels/Inns/B&Bs"). However, the beach (to the high-water mark) is open to those arriving by boat, and sometimes permission to visit the island is granted to those who request it in advance (tel. 912-638-7472). *Access is by private boat only. The hotel water taxi leaves from the Hampton River Club Marina at the north end of St. Simons Island. From the ferry landing and The Lodge on Little St. Simons, it's about 1 mi. across the island on Beach Rd. to Main Beach.*
Swimming: Very good, especially at Main Beach. No lifeguard.
Sand: Light-tan sand and low dunes. The beach is wide at low tide. Your heart will skip a beat or two at the beauty of it.

Sports: Swimming, surf fishing. Good shelling.
Amenities: A beach gazebo provides sun shelter at Main Beach.
Parking: You can't bring your car to Little St. Simons. Park bikes anywhere.

SAPELO ISLAND BEACHES

Sapelo Island has among the best beaches in Georgia. In fact, its beaches were rated No. 1 in the state by Dr. Stephen Leatherman, director of the University of Maryland's Laboratory for Coastal Research and a consultant to this book

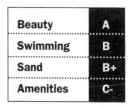

Beauty	A
Swimming	B
Sand	B+
Amenities	C-

series. Sapelo is a showplace of nature, not man, a place to escape all the cares of civilization. Crowds are unheard of here, and you can explore the pristine beach to your heart's content, often walking for long distances without seeing anyone.

The rub is access. There are very few places for individuals (as opposed to organized groups of, say, an educational or scientific nature) to stay overnight on the island. And unless you're staying there, about the only way to visit the island is by ferry tour. On the tour, you must stay with the group and are given only about 10 or 15 minutes to explore the beach—not enough time to swim. However, the tour does expose you to many of the interesting historical and natural sights the island has to offer.

The two main beach areas on the island, totaling some five miles, are Nanny Goat Beach and Cabretta Beach. Most visitors on the organized tour will be brought to Nanny Goat, just north of the remains of the old lighthouse. *Access to Sapelo Island is limited. You can get there only by private boat or on a ferry tour, which has just 2 to 4 public trips a week (additional trips are available for local residents and for visitors staying overnight). To reach Darien, the jumping-off point, take U.S. Hwy. 17 north from St. Simons. The state-run ferry to Sapelo departs from the Meridian docks northeast of Darien. To get to the docks from Darien, follow GA Hwy. 99 north about 8 mi. Turn right on Sapelo Dock Rd. and follow to its end, at the ferry dock. The trip across Doboy Sound takes about 30 min. Those staying overnight can ride the residents' ferry (3 or 4 round-trips daily). To book the ferry and bus tour of Sapelo ($10 per person),* *contact the Sapelo Island National Estuarine Research Reserve office at the Sapelo docks (tel. 912-437-3224). Reservations are essential. There are 3 small roads (all island roads are unpaved) leading to the beaches: Beach Rd., Old Beach Rd., and Cabretta Rd. All lead off E. Perimeter Rd. Roads are not marked—ask locally for directions— although it's hard to get lost on the island.*

Swimming: You can swim here if you're staying overnight. The wave energy is usually low, with gentle surf. Typical of much of the Georgia coastal waters, there may be may be discoloration from marsh and river runoff. No lifeguard.

Sand: Light gray to tan, with low dunes.

Sports: Swimming, surf fishing, crabbing. Bring your own fishing gear—none is available for rent or sale on the island.

Amenities: A boardwalk across the dunes, a small sun shelter, and rest rooms are located at the end of Beach Road.

Parking: You cannot bring a private car to Sapelo Island. A few old cars are rented by local residents, and there's adequate parking at beach access points.

HOTELS/INNS/B&BS

◆ **The Cloister at Sea Island** (very expensive). The Cloister is like a bumblebee—logic tells you it shouldn't fly, but it does. In a casual world, The Cloister is formal: The tradition is for guests to dress for dinner, and men need to have their arms covered at any meal in the dining rooms. In a world of travel bargains, The Cloister charges more per night than the average per-capita income in many Third World countries: up to $552 plus tax and a 15 percent service charge for a beach-front room (not even a suite) in season, with meals included. In a world of plastic, The Cloister doesn't take credit cards. The Cloister opened in 1928 as a 46-room hotel, and its original Spanish Mediterranean style has been preserved (with Caribbean influences) in its expansion to 262 rooms. Among the best are the deluxe ocean-front rooms and the ocean-front parlor suites ($580). While attractive, the rooms are not luxurious—what you pay for here is the sheltered ambience and exclusivity. The Cloister's guest roster has included a number of U.S. presidents. Golf, tennis, trap and skeet range, and swimming pools are available—as well as access to the beach, of course. *100 First St., Sea Island, GA 31561; tel. 912-638-3611, 800-732-4752.*

◆ **The Lodge at Little St. Simons Island** (very expensive). You and no more than 23 other guests enjoy the use of Little St. Simons, a 10,000-acre privately owned barrier island. Accommodations are in rustic hunting lodge-style rooms and cabins, including the main lodge (built in 1917), a house built in the 1930s, and two lodge buildings added in the 1980s. Everything is included here: meals, horseback riding, bikes, transportation to the island, even booze at the self-service bar. Paradise doesn't come cheap, though. Nightly rates in high season are $375 to $515 per double. High season is October to March—not the summer, since The Lodge has limited air-conditioning (more is slated to be added). Two dozen close friends can book the entire island for $3,150 to $4,550. The fishing is excellent here, and the seven-mile-long beach is incredibly beautiful. *Box 21078, St. Simons Island, GA 31522; tel. 912-638-7472; fax 912-634-1811. Open year-round except for variable periods in Nov.-Jan. Access by boat only. The hotel water shuttle leaves from the Hampton River Club Marina at the north end of St. Simons Island at 10:30 and 4:30 daily.*

◆ **King and Prince Hotel** (expensive). Although this grand old charmer, one of the best-known hotels in Georgia, could stand some refurbishing, the 175 rooms are large and comfortable, and many have ocean views. The grounds and public areas are lovely. The beach here is fair. For more luxe accommodations, spring for the two- and three-bedroom condos (very expensive but very nice) adjoining the hotel and managed by it. Golf packages. Tennis on four courts. Three pools. *201 Arnold Rd., St. Simons Island, GA 31522; tel. 912-638-3631, 800-342-0212.*

◆ **St. Simons Inn by the Lighthouse** (moderate). Despite the name, this is a motel—but a good one. The location is perfect for those who want to walk around the village, an area of shops, restaurants, and public buildings near the pier and a small water-front park. It's not on a beach, though. The rooms are clean, bright, and perky, all with microwave and fridge. *609 Beachview Dr., Box 20225, St. Simons Island, GA 31522; tel. 912-638-1101. In the village.*

◆ **Epworth by the Sea** (inexpensive). This conference center, operated by the South Georgia Conference of the United Methodist

Church, also offers accommodations to the general public. It's one of the area's best values for unpretentious but clean rooms— in ten motel buildings, condo apartments, and cabins. Lighted tennis courts, sports field, swimming pools, fishing piers. No alcohol permitted on grounds. *Box 20407, St. Simons Island, GA 31522; tel. 912-638-8688; fax 912-634-0642. From St. Simons Causeway, bear left onto Demere Rd., then left at the traffic light on Sea Island Rd. Watch for the entrance on your left.*

◆ **Open Gates B&B** (inexpensive). For day-trips to Sapelo Island, this B&B in an 1876 home in Darien's historic district makes a great home base. Owner Carolyn Hodges, a world traveler, is knowledgeable about the area and its history. The high-ceilinged rooms are decorated with family quilts, antiques, original art, and unusual heirlooms such as a Victorian hair wreath. A well-stocked library, a small pool, air-conditioning, and gourmet breakfast are among the comforts. Hodges also offers tours to Sapelo and other barrier islands on her small boat. *Vernon Sq., Box 1526, Darien, GA 31305; tel. 912-437-6985.*

◆ **Weekender** (inexpensive). This small guesthouse on Sapelo Island is owned and operated by a local resident who did the tabby construction of the modern building according to traditional methods. It's one of the very few accommodations available on the island (the others are mobile home rentals). Although not fancy, the rooms are clean and offer a double bed, TV, air-conditioning, and private bath. Guests have use of a small common kitchen for preparing their own meals. There's also a three-bedroom apartment with a kitchen (moderate). *General Delivery, Hog Hammock Community, Sapelo Island, GA 31327; tel. 912-485-2277. Weekender's van will meet you at the ferry landing on Sapelo and take you to the guesthouse.*

HOUSE RENTALS

St. Simons and Sea islands are more year-round residential areas than seasonal beach resorts, so there are fewer house rentals here than at some other destinations. Expect to pay about $1,000 to $1,500 a week May to September for a typical two- or three-bedroom rental. Rates drop about 20 percent the rest of the year.

Some of the most luxurious homes are on Sea Island. About a third of the 500 homes and four condos on Sea Island are available for rent (at $1,250 to $3,000 per week). In addition, there is a required temporary membership in the Cottage Club ($40 to $100 a week, depending on the size of the house rented). This permits use of the Sea Island Beach Club, with access to the beach and pools, and The Cloister facilities.

◆ **Sea Island Cottage Rentals.** Rents houses on Sea Island. *600 Shops at Sea Island, St. Simons, GA 31522; tel. 912-638-5112. Open Mon.-Fri.; open Sat. until noon Mar.-mid-Aug. only.*

◆ **Trupp Hodnett Enterprises.** Rents houses and condos on St. Simons and operates the Island Inn motel. *520 Ocean Blvd., St. Simons Island, GA 31522; tel. 912-638-5450, 800-627-5450; fax 912-638-2983. Open Mon.-Sat. Jun.-Aug. and Mon.-Fri. the rest of the year.*

RESTAURANTS

◆ **Chelsea** (moderate). A very popular dinner restaurant, it's casual but not too casual, serving a little bit of everything in a comfortable setting—grilled seafood, prime steaks, rack of lamb, loads of pasta dishes. Many items have an Italian touch. You're sure to have an enjoyable meal here. *1226 Ocean Blvd., St. Simons Island, GA 31522; tel. 912-638-2047. Open daily for dinner. From St. Simons Causeway, bear right on Kings Way, which becomes Ocean Blvd.*

◆ **Crab Trap** (moderate). It's jam-packed year-round, and it's easy to see why: fresh seafood, well-prepared (fried, broiled, blackened, or grilled), at moderate prices, in a casual, anything-goes atmosphere. Specialties include you-crack-'em boiled crabs in season (about $10 for six) or you-peel-'em boiled shrimp (about $12). Just throw the shells down the hole in the center of the table. No reservations—wait in line. *1209 Ocean Blvd., St. Simons Island, GA 31522; tel. 912-638-3552. Open daily for dinner. From St. Simons Causeway, bear right on Kings Way, which becomes Ocean Blvd.*

◆ **Dressner's Village Cafe** (inexpensive). Extremely popular, with seating hard to get at lunch, even off-season, this café serves good soups, sandwiches, and scratch biscuits. Breakfast served all day. *223 Mallery St., St. Simons Island, GA 31522; tel. 912-634-1217. Open daily for breakfast and lunch.*

◆ **The Fourth of May Cafe & Deli** (inexpensive). Always busy, the

Fourth of May (also known as the Village Deli) offers more than just deli items. Every day there's a pot-luck special, such as baked chicken with cream gravy, cornbread, and veggies. And good fried seafood, great deli sandwiches, and delicious desserts are offered by these longtime St. Simons restaurateurs who know how to serve tasty food at modest prices. *444 Ocean Blvd., St. Simons Island, GA 31522; tel. 912-638-5444. Open daily for lunch and dinner. In the village.*

NIGHTLIFE

Since St. Simons has many retirees, much of the nightlife is geared to the older set.

◆ **Ziggy Mahoney's.** Live music from the '50s and '60s, beach music, and country, featuring two local musicians. *5514 Frederica Rd., St. Simons Island, GA 31522; tel. 912-634-0999. Open Wed.-Sat. Next to Bennie's Red Barn.*

ATTRACTIONS

◆ **Fort Frederica National Monument.** Explore the archaeological site of a British colonial fort and town dating to 1736. *Rte. 9, Box 286-C, St. Simons Island, GA 31522; tel. 912-638-3639. Open daily 8-5. Visitors center opens daily at 9. Admission. From St. Simons Causeway, turn left at the first light onto Sea Island Causeway and follow this 2 mi. to the next light. Turn left on Frederica Rd. and follow it to the entrance gate.*

◆ **St. Simons Lighthouse and Museum of Coastal History.** Climb the 129 steps to the top of this 1872 lighthouse for a panoramic view of St. Simons and nearby islands. *101 12th St., St. Simons Island, GA 31522; tel. 912-638-4666. Open Tue.-Sat. 10-5 and Sun. 1:30-5. Admission. Near the village.*

SHOPPING

The village, at the southern end of St. Simons, is one of the island's main shopping areas. Shopping on Sapelo Island is, to put it mildly, extremely limited: Bring all needed items with you.

◆ **G. J. Ford Bookshop.** Good selection of local and regional books. *Shops at Sea Island, St. Simons Island, GA 31522; tel. 912-634-6168. Open daily. Next to Harris Teeter.*

BEST FOOD SHOPS

◆ **Harris Teeter.** Groceries, baked goods, seafood, produce, wine, beer, and soft drinks. *Shops at Sea Island, 600 Sea Island Rd., St. Simons Island, GA 31522; tel. 912-638-8100. Open daily.*

SANDWICHES: ◆ **The Fourth of May Cafe & Deli.** *444 Ocean Blvd., St. Simons Island, GA 31522; tel. 912-638-5444. Open daily.*

ICE CREAM: ◆ **Clifton's.** *214 Mallery St., St. Simons Island, GA 31522; tel. 912-638-1862. Open daily.*

BEVERAGES: ◆ **Village Package Store.** *508 Ocean Blvd., St. Simons Island, GA 31522; tel. 912-638-9738. Open Mon.-Sat.*

SPORTS

In addition to the usual mix of outdoor and water sports available in the St. Simons area, you can enjoy horseback riding on Sea Island.

◆ **Sea Island Stables.** *Box 30281, Sea Island, GA 31561; tel. 912-638-1032. Open daily. Admission.*

FISHING

The St. Simons area offers river, surf, and offshore fishing.

◆ **Capt. Fendig's Golden Isle Charters.** *Golden Isle Marina, No. 209, St. Simons Island, GA 31522; tel. 912-638-5678. Operates daily in season, weather permitting.*

BOATING

◆ **Barry's Beach Service.** Rents sailboats, Boogie boards, bicycles, beach equipment. Offers kayak tours. *420 Arnold Rd., St. Simons Island, GA 31522; tel. 912-638-8053. Open daily Mar.-Sep. Above is office address; operation is on the beach in front of the Beach Club.*

◆ **Golden Isle Water Sports.** Jet Ski and power boat rentals. Parasailing. *Marina Dr., St. Simons Island, GA 31522; tel. 912-638-7245. Open daily in season. At the Golden Isle Marina.*

DIVING

Offshore, about 18 miles east of Sapelo Island, is Gray's Reef, America's northernmost coral reef, home to many fish and thus a popular dive spot.

◆ **Island Dive Center.** Dive charters. *101 Marina Dr., Golden Isles*

Marina, St. Simons Island, GA 31522; tel. 912-638-6590, 800-940-3480. Open daily.

BICYCLING

◆ **Benjy's Bike Shop.** Rentals. *130 Retreat Plaza, St. Simons Island, GA 31522; tel. 912-638-6766. Open Mon.-Sat.*

GOLF

There are seven clubs on St. Simons Island and at nearby Brunswick.. Value-conscious golfers may decide to head over to neighboring Jekyll Island (*see* Chapter 19), which offers four public courses with some of the lowest greens fees in Georgia.

◆ **Sea Island Golf Club.** Four 9-hole courses are rotated weekly to make two outstanding 18-hole courses. They're open for public play: Marshside/Plantation Course (par 72, 6,740 yards, designed by Joe Lee, and built in 1973), Retreat/Marshside Course (par 72, 6,550 yards, designed by Dick Wilson, and built in 1959), Plantation/Seaside Course (par 72, 6,935 yards, designed by Walter Travis, and built in 1927), and Seaside/Retreat Course (par 72, 6,745 yards, designed by Colt & Alison, and built in 1928). The last two classic courses were redesigned by Robert Trent Jones and later by Rees Jones. The courses are part of The Cloister at Sea Island resort but are located on St. Simons Island. The immortal Bobby Jones long held the course record here. *100 Retreat Ave., St. Simons Island, GA 31522; tel. 912-638-5118. Open daily. Admission.*

◆ **Sea Palms Golf & Tennis Resort.** Three 9-hole courses, with designs by George Cobb and Tom Jackson, are played as three 18-hole combinations. All are open for public play. Great Oaks/West is a par-72, 6,658-yard course. Tall Pines/Great Oaks is a par-72, 6,658-yard course. Tall Pines/West is a par-72, 6198-yard course. *5445 Frederica Rd., St. Simons Island, GA 31522; tel. 912-638-3351. Open daily. Admission.*

TENNIS

In addition to the resort facilities listed below, which offer non-guest play when court time is available, there are four public courts on St. Simons: two at Epworth Park and two at Mallery Park.

◆ **Sea Palms Golf & Tennis Resort.** Twelve courts, three lighted. *5445 Frederica Rd., St. Simons Island, GA 31522; tel. 912-638-3351. Open daily. Admission. From St. Simons Causeway, turn left on Frederica Rd. and follow it to the Sea Palms entrance, on the right.*
◆ **St. Simons Island Club.** Ten courts, two lighted. *100 Kings Way, St. Simons Island, GA 31522; tel. 912-638-5133. Open daily. Admission. From St. Simons Causeway, bear right on Kings Way. The entrance is the second road to the left.*

NATURE
◆ **Okefenokee Swamp Park.** Made famous by Hollywood in many swamp movies and by the late Walt Kelly's wonderful Pogo comic strip, the Okefenokee National Wildlife Refuge is a vast area (nearly half a million acres) of primeval swamp and slow-moving, tea-colored waters. The Okefenokee Swamp Park, eight miles south of Waycross, Georgia, at the northern entrance to the refuge, provides an accessible introduction to the refuge and guided boat trips into the park. *5700 Swamp Park Rd., Waycross, GA 31501; tel. 912-283-0583. Open daily 9-6:30 Jun.-Aug. and 9-5:30 the rest of the year. Admission (includes boat trip). About 50 mi. west of St. Simons.*

TOURIST INFORMATION
◆ **Brunswick-Golden Isles Visitors Bureau.** Tourist information for all the Golden Isles. *4 Glynn Ave., Brunswick, GA 31520; tel. 912-264-5337, 800-933-2627. Open daily 9-5.*
◆ **St. Simons Island Visitors Center.** *530B Beachview Dr., St. Simons Island, GA 31522; tel. 912-638-9014; fax 912-638-2172. Open daily 9-5.*
◆ **McIntosh County Chamber of Commerce.** Provides information on Darien and Sapelo Island. *Box 1497, Darien, GA 31305; tel. 912-437-4192. Open Mon.-Fri. 9-5 and Sat. 9-12. Also operates a visitors center at the Meridian docks Mon.-Sat. 7:30-4:30.*
◆ **Sapelo Island National Estuarine Research Reserve.** *Box 15, Sapelo Island, GA 31327; tel. 912-485-2251; fax 912-485-2141. For ferry and tour information and reservations, contact the visitors center (tel. 912-437-3224).*

CHAPTER 19

Jekyll Island

Beauty	B+
Swimming	C+
Sand	B
Hotels/Inns/B&Bs	B
House rentals	B°
Restaurants	C
Nightlife	D
Attractions	B
Shopping	C
Sports	B
Nature	B+

I n the good old days before federal income tax, America's capitalist elite— the Rockefellers, Goodyears, Morgans, Vanderbilts, Pulitzers, and Astors—could afford to live and vacation anywhere in the world. For half a century, many of them chose to winter on Jekyll Island.

Beginning in 1887, they came to this small barrier island, the southernmost of Georgia's Golden Isles, by yacht and private railcar. Soon, attracted initially by the natural beauty, sandy beaches, and good hunting and later by the golf, tennis, and bicycling, members of the Jekyll Island Club began constructing vacation cottages on the island. Eventually, several dozen cottages and outbuildings stood among the live oaks and overlooking the marshes. The Jekyll Island Club's stockholders' roll was limited to 100 of the wealthiest and best-connected families in New York, Boston, Philadelphia, Chicago, and elsewhere. At its height, Jekyll Island was said to be home to one-sixth of the entire wealth of the world. In fact, the U.S. Federal Reserve banking system had its origins in a secret meeting on Jekyll in 1910.

Before it became a playground for the wealthy, Jekyll Island was owned by one family for nearly a century. The DuBignons of France bought the island in the 1790s, using slave labor to grow Sea Island cotton profitably on much of the island's 11,000 arable acres until the Civil War. Jekyll Island occupies a notorious place in the history of slavery in America. In 1858 the slave ship *Wanderer* landed its cargo of slaves on Jekyll—illegally, since importing slaves was by then against the law in the United States.

HOW TO GET THERE

◆ Jekyll Island is located midway between Savannah and Jacksonville, FL, about 1 1/4 hr. from both. I-95 is the major north-south route to Jekyll. Take I-95 to Exit 6; from there, take U.S. Hwy. 17 east 4 1/3 mi. to the Jekyll Island Causeway (GA Hwy. 520), then 6 mi. to the island entrance. The $2 daily parking fee is paid on entering the island.

◆ A 3,700-foot air strip on Jekyll handles private planes, but there is no scheduled air service. The small airport at Brunswick (12 mi.) has limited commuter service. Savannah and Jacksonville airports have jet and commuter service, and both cities have Amtrak.

This was the last known occasion when slaves were brought directly from Africa to the United States. The DuBignon family retained possession of the island until 1886, when they sold it for $125,000 to the millionaires of the Jekyll Island Club.

Income taxes, the Great Depression, the development of new enclaves for the rich in south Florida, and, most critically, World War II combined to put the Jekyll Island Club out of business. It closed in early 1942. Ironically, this historic bastion of American free enterprise is today owned by the state of Georgia. In 1947, the state used its power of eminent domain to confiscate the island, settling with the remaining club owners for $675,000. Development has been strictly limited and controlled by the charter of the Jekyll Island Authority, a state agency. Jekyll's pace of development has been decidedly low-key—in contrast to many of the other islands and beaches of the region, where high-rise hotels vie with luxury retirement homes and trendy seafood restaurants for precious beach-front footage. Thanks to controls that limit development to about 35 percent of land area, not one new house has been built on the island since 1974, and hotel construction mostly came to a halt in the late 1960s and early '70s. You won't find a mall or a McDonald's here.

For many visitors, the island's slower pace and family-style offerings, harking back to a safer, quieter time in American history, are the allure. Jekyll remains an accessible island with a permanent population of fewer than 1,000, where little changes from year to year. In that respect, it differs markedly from its busier neighbor, St. Simons, and the aggressively upmarket resort communities of Hilton Head, Sea Island, Seabrook, and Kiawah to the north.

BEACHES

Jekyll Island has almost 11 miles of beach. Although there is access to the water on the mainland side of Jekyll at many points—along St. Simons Sound, Jekyll Creek (including the Intracoastal Waterway), and St. Andrew Sound—the

Beauty	B
Swimming	C+
Sand	B
Amenities	B

best beaches and swimming are on the Atlantic side. The main public beach areas on the Atlantic are along Beachview Drive. Most of the island's hotels and motels also have their own beach areas here, although all beaches are public up to the high-water mark. Water temperatures average at least 74 degrees from May to September; the highest temperature, in August, is 82 degrees.

Swimming: First-time visitors to Jekyll may be disappointed. While the salt marshes are a bonanza for wildlife and a critical link in the food chain that supports marine life, backwash from the marsh and run-off from the rivers often leave the water looking murky. This can vary from day to day, with the water sometimes being clear and at other times tea-colored from the suspended sediment. The difference between high and low tides in this area is about seven feet, and at low tide swimmers will find the water in most areas shallow for a long way out. There are few rocks or underwater dangers, though, so Jekyll is a good place for kids to swim. In 1995, lifeguards were eliminated at the main public beaches on the island, although hotels may have lifeguards in season. Check locally.

Sand: Sand on Jekyll's wide Atlantic beaches ranges from light gold to dark gray, with most of the Atlantic-side beaches having lighter colored sand than the beaches on the sound and mainland sides. Even the finest sand may be temporarily discolored by river and marsh sediment deposited on the beach at high tide and exposed at low tide.

Amenities: Some of the beaches have rest rooms; all have picnic tables nearby.

Sports: Surf fishing (no permit required) is sometimes good.

Parking: Even in the busy summer, parking at the main public lots along Beachview Drive is usually adequate. Parking is free—your entrance fee to the island covers it.

Central Dunes Beach

The most popular swimming beach on the island is this unnamed, now-duneless main public beach on Beachview Drive. For the most part, it lacks the shade available at the picnic areas and at the beach-front hotels along Beachview Drive, where there are dunes. The beach has a small pavilion just north of Blackbeard's Restaurant, as well as rest rooms and changing areas. The Central Dunes Picnic Area, immediately north of the Convention Center, has picnic tables. *From Ben Fortson Pkwy., turn left on Beachview Dr. Park in the public lots near Blackbeard's Restaurant and the beach pavilion.*

St. Andrew Beach/South Dunes Picnic Area

This is one of the nicest picnic and recreation areas on the Golden Isles, with frontage on the Atlantic and on St. Andrew Sound. A long and winding boardwalk goes over the dunes to a pleasant beach. Signs reading "Danger: Alligators in Pond" are posted, but don't worry, this doesn't apply to the Atlantic. The kids will enjoy the swimming here, but the water is often the color of tea. The best shelling on the island is found in winter on the beach. There are plenty of picnic tables (including large enclosed cabanas for groups) and grills at the picnic area. Parking is free and plentiful. *From Ben Fortson Pkwy., turn right on Beachview Dr. Park in the shaded public lots just beyond the Holiday Inn.*

Driftwood Beach/Clam Creek Picnic Area

Bicycle trails, a fishing and crabbing pier, attractive picnic areas, and proximity to historic sights make this a popular recreational and picnic spot on the north end of the island, with views of St. Simons Sound. The swimming is not as good as at the main public beach, however, and the sand may be discolored with sediment. Amenities include rest rooms and plenty of picnic tables. Some of the best surf fishing and crabbing can be found here. There's plenty of free, shaded parking. *From Ben Fortson Pkwy., turn left on Beachview Dr. Go past the hotels and residential areas to the northern tip of the island. The parking area is on the right, across from the campground. Or, from the Historic District, take Riverview Dr. north. The parking area will be on your left, just past the DuBignon Cemetery.*

HOTELS/INNS/B&Bs

Most of the island's 1,350 rooms are in chain motels or condo-style units. Eight of the ten motels are on the water on Beachview Drive (the Jekyll Island Club Hotel and the Seafarer Inn are not directly on the water).

◆ **Jekyll Island Club Hotel, A Radisson Resort** (expensive). Certainly the most interesting place to stay on the island, with 134 rooms in the original Millionaires Club buildings, attractively restored, in the heart of the Historic District. It's not on a beach, but the hotel runs a free shuttle to its own "beach club" on Beachview Drive. The 24 large rooms in the former Sans Souci apartments, most with working fireplaces and some with whirlpool tubs, are top choices, but the three-story building has no elevators. The Presidential Suite, perched on the circular tower of the Club House, is popular with newlyweds and is often booked months in advance. Heated pool, croquet, beautiful grounds with ancient live oaks, lending library, putting green, nine tennis courts, extensive children's program in season. *371 Riverview Dr., Jekyll Island, GA 31527; tel. 912-635-2600 or call Radisson reservations at 800-333-3333; fax 912-635-2818.*

◆ **Clarion Resort Buccaneer** (expensive). The Clarion's 206 rooms are standard-issue motel, but more than half have ocean views from a small private patio or balcony. Ask for an oceanside room in the 300, 500, or 600 building. Of the units, 102 are efficiencies with small kitchens. Pool, one tennis court, children's program in season. *85 S. Beachview Dr., Jekyll Island, GA 31527; tel. 912-635-2261 or call Clarion reservations at 800-253-5955; fax 912-635-3230.*

◆ **Villas by the Sea Condominiums** (expensive). It has 76 privately owned condos in 17 buildings. Managed as a hotel, it includes minisuites, efficiencies, and one-, two-, and three-bedroom villas, many with ocean views on the 1,800 feet of beach front. Pool, playground, sports facilities, children's program in season, limited maid service. *1175 N. Beachview Dr., Jekyll Island, GA 31527; tel. 912-635-2521 or 800-841-6262; fax 912-635-2569.*

◆ **Holiday Inn Beach Resort** (expensive). This hotel has attractive, newly renovated rooms. Although the hotel is close to the ocean, rooms do not have beach views because of the high dunes in this area. A scenic, winding boardwalk provides beach access. Pool, tennis, very attractive grounds. *200 S. Beachview Dr., Jekyll Island, GA 31527; tel. 912-635-3311 or call Holiday Inn reservations at 800-753-5955; fax 912-635-2901.*

◆ **Jekyll Estates Inn** (inexpensive). Clean but basic rooms and efficiencies with cinderblock walls and inexpensive furnishings. Most units have beach views. Pool; lower rates for weekly and monthly stays. *721 N. Beachview Dr., Jekyll Island, GA 31527; tel. 912-635-2256.*

HOUSE RENTALS

Renting a house is one of the best ways to enjoy Jekyll. Off-season, many of the island's 200 rental homes are let on a monthly basis by retirees, although weekly and some daily rentals are available. From late February to late August, rentals are on a weekly basis, with rates ranging from $300 to $2,500, the majority going for $500 to $1,000. The typical rental is a ranch-style house built in the 1950s or 1960s. Few homes have ocean views, but most are within a few blocks of the ocean.

◆ **Jekyll Realty.** *Jekyll Island Shopping Center, Box 13096, Jekyll Island, GA 31527; tel. 912-635-3301. Open Mon.-Sat.*

◆ **Parker-Kaufman.** *Jekyll Island Shopping Center, Box 13126, Jekyll Island, GA 31527; tel. 912-635-2512. Open Mon.-Sat.*

RESTAURANTS

Jekyll does not have the resident population to support many restaurants, and a large number of island visitors stay in efficiencies, condos, and rental houses, choosing to prepare most of their own meals. For a wider selection of restaurants, you may want to drive to St. Simons Island (about 15 miles; *see* Chapter 18) or to the town of Brunswick (about 9 miles).

◆ **Grand Dining Room at Radisson Jekyll Island Club Hotel** (expensive). This is the fanciest and best restaurant on the island, with an elegant, romantic, slightly dressy atmosphere for dinner. Its eclectic menu includes basic seafood and meat, with some innovative dishes. *371 Riverview Dr., Jekyll Island, GA 31527; tel. 912-635-2600. Open daily for lunch and dinner (off-season hours vary).*

◆ **Blackbeard's Seafood Restaurant & Lounge** (moderate). This is your basic fried-, broiled-, and baked-seafood restaurant. Blackbeard's dramatic setting right on the Atlantic is the best of any on the island. Food and service are inconsistent, however. The restaurant is owned and managed by a government agency, the Jekyll Island Authority. *200 N. Beachview Dr., Jekyll Island, GA*

31527; tel. 912-635-3522. Open daily for lunch and dinner. Closed Dec.

◆ **Zachry's Seafood** (inexpensive). This is where the locals eat. Good fried seafood and blue-plate specials, served up by David and Barbara Zachry since 1987. *Jekyll Island Shopping Center, 44 Beachview Dr., Jekyll Island, GA 31527; tel. 912-635-3128. Open daily for lunch and dinner.*

NIGHTLIFE

Jekyll has little nightlife, outside the hotel/motel lounges and the restaurant bars. If you want more than a cocktail, a TV, and perhaps a budget crooner, you'll have to drive to St. Simons Island (*see* Chapter 18).

◆ **Blackbeard's Seafood Restaurant & Lounge.** *200 N. Beachview Dr., Jekyll Island, GA 31527; tel. 912-635-3522. Open daily. Closed Dec.*

ATTRACTIONS

Jekyll and the surrounding areas offer many family attractions and historic sites (for others nearby, *see* Chapter 18, St. Simons Island, and Chapter 20, Cumberland Island).

◆ **Jekyll Island Historic District.** The historical biggie on Jekyll is the 240-acre Millionaires Village National Historic Landmark District, under continuing restoration. The beauty of the area is enhanced by the many graceful live oaks. You can tour the Historic District on a free, self-guided walking tour (a small walking-tour booklet is sold in local shops) or a guided tour with the Jekyll Island Authority Museum, a small museum that is also worth a quick visit. Entrance to several historic buildings is possible only on the official guided tour. Private horse-and-carriage tours are also available. Among the highlights are the Millionaires Club House (now a part of the Radisson), DuBignon House, Indian Mound (the site of the first transatlantic telephone call, in 1915), and Mistletoe Cottage, which houses a gallery of works by the late, nationally known sculptor and Jekyll resident Rosario Fiore. *Jekyll Island Museum, Stable Rd., Historic District, Jekyll Island, GA 31527; tel. 912-635-4036. Daily guided tours, in jitneys or vans, depart on the hour 10-3. Unguided walking tours are possible anytime. Admission to guided tour.*

◆ **Summer Waves Water Park.** This small water park touts itself as "a million gallons of splashing water fun." It has a wave pool, speed flumes and inner tube flumes, and a Pee Wee Puddle section for youngsters. *210 S. Riverview Dr., Jekyll Island, GA 31527; tel. 912-635-2074. Open Sun.-Fri. 10-6 and Sat. 10-8 Memorial Day-Labor Day; open some weekends in May and Sep. Admission.*

SHOPPING

Jekyll has two small shopping areas: the Jekyll Island Shopping Center, a 1960s-vintage strip center at the northwest corner of Ben Fortson Parkway and Beachview Drive, and a group of gift shops and specialty boutiques in renovated buildings in the Historic District. During the off-season, business hours may be reduced. For full-scale shopping, you'll need to drive about eight miles to Brunswick.

◆ **Art Gallery.** Exhibits the work of regional artists, including members of the Jekyll Island Arts Association. *Goodyear Cottage, Riverview Dr., Historic District, Jekyll Island, GA 31527; tel. 912-635-3920. Open daily; hours vary.*

◆ **Nature's Cottage.** Attractive selection of gifts, art, and books, all with a nature theme. *21 Pier Rd., Historic District, Jekyll Island, GA 31527; tel. 912-635-3933. Open daily.*

BEST FOOD SHOPS

In a small place like this, you won't find a huge selection of specialty food stores.

◆ **IGA Supermarket.** Groceries, wine, beer. *Jekyll Island Shopping Center, Jekyll Island, GA 31527; tel. 912-635-2253. Open daily.*

◆ **The Commissary.** Gourmet coffee and specialty foods. *24 Pier Rd., Historic District, Jekyll Island, GA 31527; tel. 912-635-2878. Open daily.*

BEVERAGES: ◆ **Jekyll Beverage Center.** Liquor, wine, beer, soda. *Jekyll Island Shopping Center, Jekyll Island, GA 31527; tel. 912-635-2080. Open Mon.-Sat.*

SPORTS
FISHING

Surf fishing (no license required) is sometimes good along the Atlantic beaches and is best at the St. Andrew picnic area at the southern tip of the island. Trout and flounder can be caught from the fishing pier at the Clam Creek Picnic Area, also a good spot to try crabbing for blue crab. Freshwater fishing (Georgia license required) is permitted at the small lake behind the Amphitheater on the west side of the Oleander golf course and at the small lake across Beachview Drive from the Villas by the Sea.

◆ **Sea Wolf Charters.** Half- and full-day charters, in the sounds or offshore. *Jekyll Island Marina, Jekyll Island, GA 31527; tel. 912-635-2865. Open daily, weather permitting.*

◆ **Maxwell's Variety and True Value Hardware.** The place for fishing gear and advice. *Jekyll Island Shopping Center, Jekyll Island, GA 31527; tel. 912-635-2205. Open daily.*

BOATING

◆ **Jekyll Island Marina.** Boat rentals, transient dockage, charters. *1 Pier Rd., Jekyll Island, GA 31527; tel. 912-635-2891. Open daily.*

BICYCLING

During the days of Millionaires Village, bicycling was hugely popular here. Today, the island has 20 miles of bike trails, flat and well-maintained, making for an easy ride. Bicycles can be rented at most hotels as well as at the airport and the campground.

GOLF

Thank the millionaires of the Jekyll Island Club for bringing golf to the island. Ironically, rates at these state-owned courses are among the lowest in the region. Today, Jekyll offers 63 holes on one 9-hole and three 18-hole courses, making it Georgia's largest public golf resort. All of the courses are open to day visitors and to guests of any of the hotels and motels on the island. They offer entertaining play and plenty of water hazards, including alligators.

◆ **Oceanside Nine.** Built in 1917 by Scotsman Walter Davis and remodeled in the 1920s by Walter J. Travis, it plays 3,289 yards and has a par 36. *Jekyll Island, GA 31527; tel. 912-635-2170. Open daily. Admission.*

◆ **Oleander.** Designed by Dick Wilson, Oleander plays 6,679 yards off the blue and has a par 72. It is considered one of the state's best courses. *322 Capt. Wylly Rd., Jekyll Island, GA 31527;*

tel. 912-635-2368. Open daily. Admission.

◆ **Pine Lakes.** Another Dick Wilson design, Pine Lakes is Jekyll's longest course, at 6,802 yards, par 72. *322 Capt. Wylly Rd., Jekyll Island, GA 31527; tel. 912-635-2368. Open daily. Admission.*

◆ **Indian Mound.** Designed by Joe Lee, this is the most scenic of the island's courses. It plays 6,596 yards off the blue, par 72. *322 Capt. Wylly Rd., Jekyll Island, GA 31527; tel. 912-635-2368. Open daily. Admission.*

TENNIS

In addition to the tennis center below, the Radisson and other hotels also have tennis courts.

◆ **Jekyll Island Tennis Center.** Thirteen clay courts. *Capt. Wylly Rd., Jekyll Island, GA 31527; tel. 912-635-3154. Open daily. Admission.*

NATURE

Because much of Jekyll Island remains undeveloped, visitors may see a variety of wildlife, including many shore and wading birds such as pelicans, terns, herons, egrets, and oystercatchers. A favorite path for bird-watchers runs between Ben Fortson Parkway and Shell Road, with an entrance just east of the gas station. Bottle-nosed dolphins and, rarely, manatees, can be seen in the sounds. Nature walks, conducted by trained naturalists, are available year-round. A special treat are the turtle walks during the loggerhead turtle nesting season, mid-June to mid-August. *For information, contact Jekyll Island Museum, Stable Rd., Historic District, Jekyll Island, GA 31527; tel. 912-635-2119.*

◆ **Jekyll Island Campground** (inexpensive). It has 200 campsites on 18 wooded acres. *1197 Riverview Dr., Jekyll Island, GA 31527; tel. 912-635-3021. On the northern end of the island, across from the Clam Creek picnic area.*

TOURIST INFORMATION

◆ **Jekyll Island Welcome Center.** *901 Jekyll Island Causeway (Box 13186), Jekyll Island, GA 31527; tel. 912-635-3636, 800-841-6586. Open daily 9-5. On the Jekyll Island Causeway, before you get to the island. It's on the left, next to the Georgia Highway Patrol station.*

CHAPTER 20

Cumberland Island

Beauty	A+
Swimming	B+
Sand	A
Hotels/Inns/B&Bs	B
House rentals	C
Restaurants	C+
Nightlife	D+
Attractions	B
Shopping	C-
Sports	B
Nature	A

Cumberland Island is the most beautiful place on the Georgia coast. It has the longest stretch of undeveloped beach—more than 17 pristine, windswept miles—anywhere in the state. The island's dunes, some 40 or more feet high, are a world of shifting, scenic white. Tall pines, cedars, and moss-draped live oaks in its maritime forest provide a canopy of haunting beauty inland. Because a maximum of just 300

HOW TO GET THERE

◆ St. Marys is about 45 min. north of Jacksonville, FL, and about 2 hr. south of Savannah. From I-95, the main north-south artery along the coast, take Exit 2 and follow GA Hwy. 40 east to the St. Marys historic district and the ferry to Cumberland Island. GA Hwy. 40 is also known as Osborne St. as it nears St. Marys.

◆ To get to Cumberland Island for day-trips or camping, take the pedestrian ferry, operated by a Park Service concessionaire. The ferry departs from docks at the foot of Osborne St. in the historic district. Mid-Mar. to Sep. the ferry leaves St. Marys at 9 and 11:45 daily, with additional 2:45 departures Wed.-Sat., and returns at 10:15 and 4:45. From Oct.-mid-Mar., the ferry departs St. Marys at 9 and 11:45 Thu.-Mon., returning at 10:15 and 4:45. Round-trip fares are $9.50 for adults, $7.50 for senior citizens, and $5.65 for children 12 and under. The Greyfield Inn boat (*see* "Hotels/Inns/B&Bs") departs from Fernadina Beach, FL ($8 one way if you're not staying at the inn).

◆ Only 300 people are allowed to visit Cumberland Island each day. Call for reservations up to 11 months in advance (tel. 912-882-4335 Mon.-Fri 10-4). Private boats can also be hired in St. Marys for trips to Cumberland. Call David Lang for information and reservations (tel. 912-882-4452).

◆ By air, the closest major airport is Jacksonville, FL, about a 35-min. drive (the airport is on the north side of town). Jacksonville also has Amtrak service.

people per day are permitted to visit the 40-square-mile island, and because the island has only about 30 permanent residents, you can spend hours on Cumberland without seeing or hearing another person.

The island, 85 percent of which is protected as a national seashore, is first and foremost a place of nature. More than 300 kinds of birds have been spotted here. In winter, right whales calve in the Atlantic just a few miles off Cumberland's beaches. Manatees poke around the docks on Cumberland Sound, and bottle-nosed dolphins play around the island. The waters of the saltwater marshes are full of fish. In late spring and early summer, huge loggerhead turtles pull themselves across the beach to lay their eggs. Tramping the miles of nature trails and wilderness, you're almost sure to see white-tailed deer and wild turkey. You may hear the booming of a bull alligator or see a big diamondback rattler. Armadillos—exotics that came to the island on their own in the early 1970s—and that southern pest, the fire ant, are also here. Mosquitoes and several varieties of flies make things interesting in the spring and summer.

Humans have left their mark too, of course. Human occupation of the island dates back several thousand years, according to Indian shell middens found on Cumberland. Spanish soldiers arrived in the 1500s. A herd of more than 250 wild horses that roam the island are descendants of horses left here by visitors, perhaps starting with the Spanish conquistadores and later the English settlers. Wild pigs, whose forebears were also let loose by islanders, run through the underbrush.

Cumberland was once home to thriving antebellum plantations, although little besides irrigation dikes remains as evidence of that period of its economy. The most prominent monuments of people are a handful of remaining homes on the island. Thomas Carnegie, brother of steel magnate Andrew Carnegie, acquired much of the island in the late 19th century. He and his wife, Lucy, erected a fabulous mansion on the ruins of Dungeness, a four-story tabby home built in the late 1700s by the widow of Revolutionary War hero General Nathanael Greene. The newer Dungeness is itself now a ruin, the victim of a 1959 fire, but visitors can tour the site. Plum Orchard, the most elaborate of the remaining island houses, was built by the Carnegies for one of their children. Greyfield, another house built for a Carnegie offspring, is now an inn (*see* "Hotels/Inns/B&Bs"). There are also about 15 other homes on the island, sitting on the one-sixth of the land that is still privately owned.

Cumberland is accessible only by boat. You cannot bring a car onto the island, and once you're on the island there is no transportation. The jumping-off point is St. Marys, the southernmost town in southeast Georgia. St. Marys is a peculiar blend. It is part quaint village (the mostly 19th-century historic district is on the National Register of Historic Places), part high-tech military center (the Naval Submarine Base at Kings Bay is the only base in the Navy that supports the advanced Trident II nuclear submarines, employing 10,000 military and civilian personnel in St. Marys), and part industrial town (featuring a pungent paper plant tolerated and even championed by locals for its good-paying jobs).

The National Park Service concessionaire ferry leaves from the St. Marys docks and arrives about 45 minutes later at the Dungeness dock on Cumberland Island. It then stops at Sea Camp, which has a small visitors center staffed by Park Service rangers.

High season on Cumberland is spring and fall. April, with its pleasant spring weather and good birding, is the busiest month. Summer, while good for swimming—with water temperatures in the high 70s to low 80s through September—is so hot and buggy that the island's one inn, Greyfield, closes for the month of August. Winter is the off-season, but Cumberland aficionados know that it's one of the best times to see the island, when there are few bugs and fewer people, with mild weather that in most cases would bring out shirtsleeves in Connecticut.

BEACHES
CUMBERLAND ISLAND

Cumberland Island has more than 17 miles of ocean beach: one long stretch of sand along the Atlantic. You can walk for hours along the beach, collecting sand dollars, taking a quick, refreshing dip from time to time, watching the lit-

Beauty	A+
Swimming	B+
Sand	A
Amenities	C-

tle sanderlings skitter by the waves. You can stroll for hours and see nobody. Imagine it: You have miles of beach almost entirely to yourself. The farther north you go, the fewer people you are likely to see, since the ferries land at the southern end of the island, where the inn and the main campground—and most of the houses—are. The northern end is a designated wilderness area.

What gives the Cumberland beach its character, besides the lack of people, is the wide expanse of dunes behind the wide, sandy beach. The highest dunes are toward the northern end of the island.

On a map, you may see the names Sea Camp Beach and Stafford Beach, but these are just names. The Atlantic side of Cumberland, for all intents and purposes, is one long beach. Dunes may be higher or lower in one area or another (a characteristic that changes depending on the impact of storms and wind), and simple amenities near the beach vary (*see* below), but to the casual visitor Cumberland's beach is a long and constant ribbon of sand stretching far into the distance.

Stakes, painted in bands of black and white, mark access paths to the beach. There are beach crossings from Main Road, which runs north-south along most of the island, to nine points along the beach, with the most commonly used ones being (from south to north) Dungeness Ruins, Sea Camp, Greyfield Inn, and Stafford Beach. You should not cross the dunes except at designated beach crossings, where there are boardwalks or marked trails. *From St. Marys, take the Park Service ferry (see "How to Get There"), which drops visitors at either Sea Camp or Dungeness. The Greyfield Inn ferry from Fernandina Beach drops visitors at the Greyfield dock, where guests are met by a van for the short ride to the inn. Day visitors are likely to enter the beach at marked paths through the maritime forest and across the dunes either at Sea Camp or near Dungeness. When hiking along the beach, watch carefully for the black-and-white stakes that mark beach crossings; do not walk on the dunes or disturb the sea oats. Be sure to carry the "Cumberland Island Official Map and Guide," available free from the Park Service office in St. Marys. This will orient you and help you avoid getting lost.*
Swimming: Swimming is very good here. The water off the beach is shallow, and the wave action is usually gentle to mod-

erate. Some sediment from marsh runoff may be present, but typically not to the degree it is on other Georgia beaches (the state has a third of all the marshland on the East Coast; a boon for wildlife, it sometimes makes the water less appealing for swimming). Jellyfish are sometimes present. No lifeguard.

Sand: The sand is white to light gray, some of the most appealing beach sand in the region. The beaches of Cumberland have a gentle slope. They are wide at low tide, but because of the large difference between low and high tides in this area, they can be fairly narrow at high tide. Shelling is often excellent here, especially following fall or winter storms.

Sports: Besides swimming, there's bodysurfing.

Amenities: You must bring everything you need to the island, since there are no stores (except a small hotel shop at Greyfield Inn, primarily for guests). There are rest rooms and drinking water at Sea Camp and at Dungeness. Well water is available at the four primitive campsites on the island, but it has to be treated before drinking. Greyfield Inn has a small beach cabana, with beach chairs and umbrellas for hotel guests, near the beach, about ten minutes from the hotel.

Parking: Visitors cannot bring vehicles onto the island, and those coming on the Park Service ferry cannot bring bicycles. Greyfield Inn guests have access to bikes, but they are not for use on the beach.

HOTELS/INNS/B&BS

There is just one hotel on Cumberland Island. In the historic district of St. Marys you can choose among three small "personality" inns and B&Bs. Along I-95 at Exit 2, about nine miles west of the St. Mary's historic district, there are several chain motels, including a Hampton Inn, a Comfort Inn, and a Best Western, and about halfway between I-95 and the historic district, near the submarine base, there are a couple of small independent motels.

◆ **Greyfield Inn** (very expensive). This 1901 inn on 1,300 acres offers gracious hospitality and an unparalleled setting of natural beauty on the marsh side of the island. It comes at a price, however: The daily rate for two is $245 to $350 (plus a 17 percent service charge and 6 percent tax). The room rate includes all meals, evening canapes, a private ferry between Cumberland and Fernandina Beach, the use of bicycles, beach chairs, and other equipment, and a guided tour by the inn's naturalist. Wine, beer, and liquor are extra. Greyfield is operated by descendants of the Carnegie family, who in the late 19th century owned most of the island, and it is decorated with family heirlooms and treasures. One of the most charming parts of the inn is its main living room, where guests gather to talk, read a book from the inn's library, or, in winter, enjoy the fireplace. The main inn has ceiling fans but no air-conditioning. The rooms are pleasant and tastefully decorated but not luxurious, and several are tiny. One of the best choices is the Master Suite, a bright corner room with a mahogany king-size bed (but shared bath). There are also two simple cottages near the main inn, both with air-conditioning. Breakfast and dinner are served family-style; lunch is in a picnic basket. Guests are expected to dress for dinner. The food is prepared from the highest-quality ingredients and is attractively presented, although it falls short of gourmet standards. The beach is about a ten-minute walk away. *Box 900, Fernandina Beach, FL 32035; tel. 904-261-6408. (The inn is on Cumberland Island, but its mail is delivered to a Florida address.) Closed Aug. When you make reservations, the hotel will explain how, when, and where to catch the private boat to the inn's dock. It departs 3 or more times daily from Fernandina Beach.*

◆ **Spencer House Inn Bed & Breakfast** (moderate). This is your best choice in St. Marys: It's friendly, inviting, and a good value. With 14 rooms in a large, three-story 1872 building, Spencer House is large enough to offer guests the privacy of an inn, but owners Mike and Mary Neff provide the personal touches of a good B&B. The guest rooms are comfortable without being stuffy, and all have private baths, cable TV, and telephones. The best room is the third-floor suite (expensive). Breakfast is served buffet style. The inn has an elevator. *101 E. Bryant St. (200 Osborne at Bryant), St. Marys, GA 31558; tel. 912-882-1872. In the St. Marys historic district, within a short walk of the Park Service ferry to Cumberland Island.*

◆ **Goodbread House Bed and Breakfast** (inexpensive). A homey, small B&B with four rooms, each with private bath. This

Victorian 1870 home, attractively restored, is for those who want a true B&B atmosphere, rather than that of an inn. Full breakfast. Rooms have nonworking fireplaces. *209 Osborne St., St. Marys, GA 31558; tel. 912-882-7490. In the St. Marys historic district, within a short walk of the Park Service ferry to Cumberland Island.*

◆ **Riverview Hotel** (inexpensive). Atmospheric small hotel with a good restaurant and a lively bar. Although the 1916 structure has been remodeled, the rooms are far from fancy and they are small: With their high ceilings, they are nearly as tall as they are wide. No phones in rooms. Continental breakfast. *105 Osborne St., St. Marys, GA 31558; tel. 912-882-3242. In the St. Mary's historic district, directly across from the Park Service ferry to Cumberland Island.*

HOUSE RENTALS

Beach house rentals are not available on Cumberland. Your best bet in the area is one of the cottages at Crooked River State Park, near St. Marys.

◆ **Crooked River State Park.** The park has 11 attractive two- and three-bedroom cottages on or near the Crooked River. Rates range from $55 to $75 per night. The only problem is that odors from the nearby paper mill may mar your enjoyment of the natural setting. Reservations for spring, summer, and fall should be made at least two months in advance. *3092 Spur 40, St. Marys, GA 31558; tel. 912-882-5256. Open daily. Call the Dept. of Natural Resources for reservations (tel. 800-864-7275) and for information and brochures (tel. 404-656-3530). 10 mi. north of St. Marys. From the historic district, take Hwy. 40. Turn right on Spur 40 and follow it past the submarine base to the end of the road.*

RESTAURANTS

St. Marys has several inexpensive spots where you can get a good, though not a sophisticated, meal. The local specialty is rock shrimp, which are small shrimp with a taste somewhere between shrimp and lobster. Each October there is a rock shrimp festival. The only place to dine on Cumberland is the Greyfield Inn (*see* "Hotels/Inns/B&Bs"), whose restaurant is open to nonguests by advance arrangement. Alcohol cannot be served in St. Marys or on Cumberland Island on Sundays.

◆ **Borrell Creek Landing** (moderate). This is St. Marys's honest attempt at fine dining. Fish, steaks, surf-and-turf, and other middle-of-the-road entrées. Very good service and nice views over the marsh. *Borrell Creek, St. Marys, GA 31558; tel. 912-673-6300. Open Mon.-Sat. for dinner. Off Hwy. 40, about midway between St. Marys historic district and I-95, across from a Food Lion.*

◆ **Seagle's** (moderate). It has the best fried shrimp and rock shrimp in St. Marys, but other dishes, and the service, get mixed reviews. The restaurant also packs picnic lunches for day-trips to Cumberland Island ($10 for two, including a sandwich, cheese and crackers, fruit, chips, and lemonade). *Riverview Hotel, 105 Osborne St., St. Marys, GA 31558; tel. 912-882-4187. Open daily for dinner. In the St. Marys historic district, directly across from the Park Service ferry to Cumberland Island.*

◆ **St. Marys Seafood & Steak House** (inexpensive). This is where the locals go. The fried seafood and other basic American fare is as simple as it can be but consistently good. The prices, like the decor, are a throwback to the 1970s. Friendly, down-home service. *1837 Osborne St. (Hwy. 40), St. Marys, GA 31558; tel. 912-882-6875. Open daily for lunch and dinner.*

NIGHTLIFE

Nightlife on Cumberland Island is watching the stars and swatting mosquitoes. Most of what little nightlife there is in St. Marys is oriented to the Navy folks at the submarine base. One or two spots in the historic district offer good drinks and conversation.

◆ **Seagle's Saloon.** Friendly watering hole for gregarious locals and visitors. *Riverview Hotel, 105 Osborne St., St. Marys, GA 31558; tel. 912-832-3242. Open Mon.-Sat.*

ATTRACTIONS

◆ **Kings Bay Naval Submarine Base.** Parts of the 16,000-acre nuclear submarine base, home to ten giant Trident subs, began opening to the public in late 1995. Visit the information center at the base entrance and request a pass and a self-guided tour booklet. Those seriously interested in Naval or submarine matters may call the base's Public Affairs Office (tel. 912-673-4714) and request a guided tour. *Stimson Gate, Spur 40, St. Marys, GA*

31558; tel. 912-673-2000. Open daily. Closed to visitors occasionally for reasons of military security.

◆ **Orange Hall.** This beautiful example of Greek Revival architecture is now a house museum open for self-guided tours. The St. Marys visitors center is in the basement. *315 Osborne St., Box 1291, St. Marys, GA 31558; tel. 912-882-4000, 800-868-8687. Open Mon.-Sat. 9-5 and Sun. 1-5. Admission.*

◆ **St. Marys Historic District.** The historic district is small but charming, and an easy walk. The highlights can all be toured within a couple of hours. In addition to Orange Hall, these include: St. Mary's Presbyterian Church, dating from the 1820s and the oldest Presbyterian church in Georgia; the Oak Grove Cemetery, established 1780; and the original Toonerville Trolley, the rail car made famous in the 1930s comic strip "Wash Tubbs," by Roy Crane. *St. Marys Visitors Center, 315 Osborne St., Box 1291, St. Marys, GA 31558; tel. 912-882-4000, 800-868-8687. Open Mon.-Sat. 9-5 and Sun. 1-5.*

SHOPPING

The historic district of St. Marys has a few small boutiques catering to visitors. Other than a few items available at Greyfield Inn, there is no shopping on Cumberland Island. For more choices, head to St. Simons Island, about half an hour away (*see* Chapter 18), or to Jacksonville, about 45 minutes away.

◆ **Blue Goose.** Gifts and collectibles. *126 Osborne St., St. Marys, GA 31558; tel. 912-673-6828. Open Mon.-Sat.*

◆ **Once Upon a Bookseller.** Small bookshop with intelligent selection. *110 Osborne St., St. Marys, GA 31558; tel. 912-882-7350. Open Mon.-Sat. and Sun. "when the mood strikes."*

BEST FOOD SHOPS

St. Marys has a Publix, a Winn-Dixie, and a Food Lion. All are full-size grocery stores, but the Food Lion is closest to the ferry docks.

◆ **Food Lion.** Besides groceries, baked goods, and produce, it sells wine and beer (except on Sundays). *2714 Osborne St., Hwy. 40, St. Marys, GA 31558; tel. 912-882-6714. Open daily.*

SANDWICHES: ◆ **Seagle's.** This shop packs picnic lunches with sandwiches. *Riverview Hotel, 105 Osborne St., St. Marys, GA*

31558; tel. 912-882-3242. Open daily.

SEAFOOD: ◆ **Lang's Seafood Retail Market.** *2202 Osborne Rd., St. Marys, GA 31558; tel. 912-882-1056. Open Mon.-Sat.*

BEVERAGES: ◆ **Borrell Creek Package Store.** *1270 Hwy. 40, St. Marys, GA 31558; tel. 912-882-6498. Open Mon.-Sat.*

SPORTS
FISHING

Fishing is good around the Greyfield Inn dock and elsewhere on the sound side. Fishing is also productive in spring and fall in the surf on the Atlantic side. Georgia state law applies to catch limits and sizes. No license is needed for saltwater fishing. You should bring your own poles and tackle, since none is available on the island.

◆ **David Lang.** Fishing charters onshore and offshore. *100 E. St. Marys St., St. Marys, GA 31558; tel. 912-882-4452. Operates daily, weather permitting.*

◆ **Toby Morman.** Fishing charters on 28-foot sports fishing boat. *St. Marys, GA 31558; tel. 912-882-6248. Operates daily, weather permitting.*

BICYCLING

Bicycles are the preferred form of transportation on Cumberland Island, but they are not permitted on the Park Service concession ferry. Bikes may be brought over on the Greyfield Inn ferry from Fernandina Beach or on other private boats. Greyfield Inn provides bikes to guests at no extra charge, but they cannot be used on the beach. Biking is also good around St. Marys historic district. As of this writing there is no source of rentals.

GOLF

◆ **Osprey Cove.** This 6,800-yard, par-72 public course designed by Mark McCumber plays through coastal woods and by salt marshes. *123 Osprey Dr., St. Marys, GA 31558; tel. 912-882-5575, 800-352-5575. Open Tue.-Sun. and on Mon. holidays. Admission. Take I-95 Exit 1 and go east 2 mi.*

NATURE

Also nearby is the Okefenokee Swamp (*see* Chapter 18).

◆ **Crooked River State Park.** A 500-acre park on the banks of the

Crooked River, it has 11 rental cottages, 60 tent and trailer sites, a pool, picnic shelters, hiking trails, fishing, and boat ramps. The beauty of the area is marred only by the strong smell from the nearby paper mill. *3092 Spur 40, St. Marys, GA 31558; tel. 912-882-5256. Open daily 7-10. Admission. 10 mi. north of St. Marys. From the historic district, take Hwy. 40. Turn right on the Spur 40 and follow it past the submarine base to the end of the road.*

◆ **Cumberland Island National Seashore.** Cumberland Island has one of the last remaining undeveloped seashores on the East Coast. The island's complex ecological system includes saltwater marshes and maritime forest as well as beach, all home to many species of wildlife. Camping is available at one developed and four primitive campsites. Reservations for all sites must be made in advance. *Box 806, St. Marys, GA 31558; tel. 912-882-4335. Open daily. Accessible only by boat; for information and ferry schedules, see "How to Get There."*

Tourist Information

◆ **Cumberland Island National Seashore.** *Box 806, St. Marys, GA 31558; tel. 912-882-4336. Open Mon.-Fri. 7-4:30.*

◆ **St. Marys Welcome Center.** The visitors center is housed in the basement of Orange Hall, which is a house museum open for tours (*see* "Attractions"). *Orange Hall, 315 Orange St., St. Marys, GA 31558; tel. 912-882-4000, 800-868-8687. Open Mon.-Sat. 9-5 and Sun. 1-5.*